Re-Cognizing W. E. B. Du Bois in the Twenty-First Century

Ruth,
I think you will
enjoy these essays.

Elaine
April 29, 2011

MERCER
UNIVERSITY PRESS

Endowed by
TOM WATSON BROWN
and
THE WATSON-BROWN FOUNDATION, INC.

Re-Cognizing W. E. B. Du Bois in the Twenty-First Century

Essays on W. E. B. Du Bois

Edited by Mary Keller and Chester J. Fontenot, Jr.

Mercer University Press
Macon, Georgia

MUP/H737//P335
ISBN 978-0-88146-077-3 (HB)
978-0-88146-059-9 (PB)

First Edition.

Library of Congress Cataloging-in-Publication Data

Re-cognizing W.E.B. Du Bois in the twenty-first century : essays on W.E.B. Du
Bois / edited by Mary
Keller and Chester J. Fontenot, Jr. -- 1st ed.
p. cm.
Includes bibliographical references and index.
ISBN-13: 978-0-88146-077-3 (hardback : alk. paper)
ISBN-10: 0-88146-077-X (hardback : alk. paper)
1. Du Bois, W. E. B. (William Edward Burghardt), 1868-1963—Political and social
views. 2. Du Bois, W. E. B. (William Edward Burghardt), 1868-1963—Influence. 3. Du
Bois, W. E. B. (William Edward Burghardt), 1868-1963—Criticism and interpretation.
4. Genius—United States—Case studies. 5. Religion and sociology—United States.
6. Religion and politics—United States. 7. African Americans—Religion. 8. African
Americans—Intellectual life. 9. African Americans—Historiography. 10. African
Americans--Study and teaching. I. Keller, Mary, 1964- II. Fontenot, Chester J.
E185.97.D73R43 2007
305.896'0730092—dc22
2007012029

Contents

Series Foreword
Mary L. Keller, On Re-Cognizing
    W. E. B. Du Bois and Frantz Fanon in Two Volumes   1
Robin Law, Du Bois as Pioneer of African History:
    A Reassessment of the Negro (1915)   14
David Chidester, Religious Animals, Refuge of the Gods,
    and the Spirit of Revolt: W. E. B. Du Bois's
    Representations of Indigenous African Religion   34
Jemima Pierre and Jesse Weaver Shipley, The Intellectual
    and Pragmatic Legacy of Du Bois's Pan-Africanism in
    Contemporary Ghana   61
Rodney Roberts, Rectificatory Justice and the Philosophy
    of W. E. B. Du Bois   88
Carole Lynn Stewart, Challenging Liberal Justice: The Talented
    Tenth Revisited   112
Stephen Andrews, Toward a Synaesthetics of Soul:
    W. E. B. Du Bois and the Teleology of Race   142
Marta Brunner, "The Most Hopeless of Deaths…Is the
    Death of Faith": Messianic Faith in the Racial Politics
    of W. E. B. Du Bois   186
Charles Long, Rapporteur's Commentary
Contributors   245
Index   249

Acknowledgments

We would like to thank the University of Stirling, Scotland, who housed and provided financial support for the conference, *W. E. B. Du Bois and Frantz Fanon: Post-colonial Linkages and Trans-Atlantic Receptions* in Spring, 2001 from which the majority of these papers were drawn. Especially we thank the Religious Studies Department and their staff, and the Centre for Commonwealth Studies at Stirling who provided intellectual and ground support for the conference. We also want to thank the team at Mercer University Press, especially Marsha Luttrell, for their hard work and care in editing and publishing this collection. We owe a special debt of gratitude to the contributors for their faith over time.

Foreword

When we first launched the publication of this book series, "Voices of the African Diaspora," we had in mind to publish solid scholarship in the field of African American Studies that would contribute to the development of the interdisciplinary methodologies that have characterized this hybrid area of intellectual inquiry since its inception. Since that time, we have offered a number of books that have worked within this scope by providing sustained analysis of various aspects of life within the African diaspora utilizing the methodologies of a number of academic disciplines.

In Spring 2001, Mary Keller, who was then a faculty member at the University of Stirling in Scotland, organized and directed an international conference, "W. E. B. Du Bois and Frantz Fanon: Postcolonial Linkages and Trans-Atlantic Receptions". Anchored by a number of international scholars, and energized by a number of up-and-coming intellectuals, this gathering attempted to both contribute its voices to the upcoming celebration of the 100th year anniversary of the publication of Du Bois's seminal work, *The Souls of Black Folk*, and mark the upcoming 50th year anniversary of the war in Algeria that led to its independence, and the development of the revolutionary theories of Frantz Fanon. The presentations at this conference were so significant that we felt compelled to bring them together in this publication.

Because of the number and quality of the presentations offered at this conference, we have devoted this volume to W.E.B. Du Bois, and have reserved the essays on Frantz Fanon for a second volume to be published at a later date. We hope that after reading the essays contained herein, you will agree that this collection makes a significant contribution to the reassessments of W.E.B. Du Bois.

Chester J. Fontenot, Jr.
Series editor, Voices of the African Diaspora
Macon, Georgia
23 February 2007

On Re-Cognizing W. E. B. Du Bois and Frantz Fanon in Two Volumes

Mary Keller

Reading W. E. B. Du Bois and Frantz Fanon in their respective contexts and in relation to each other is perhaps the single most important step one can take in order to grapple with the world as it is and as it promises to be in the coming century. It was this conviction that led to a conference at the University of Stirling, Scotland, in March 2001 to discuss their work jointly. "W. E. B. Du Bois and Frantz Fanon: Postcolonial Linkages and Trans-Atlantic Receptions" drew an interdisciplinary core of major theorists and young scholars to discuss the work of these two pivotal twentieth-century writers and to reflect upon the importance of their respective works for the twenty-first century. We have gathered selected texts from that conference into two volumes: *Re-Cognizing W. E. B. Du Bois in the 21ˢᵗ Century* and *Re-Cognizing Frantz Fanon in the 21ˢᵗ Century*, published by Mercer University Press under the guidance of Chester Fontenot, editor of their series *Voices of the African Diaspora*. It is significant that while the goal of the organizers was to think about the relationship of these two thinkers for postcolonial and transatlantic theories, by and large the presenters addressed Du Bois of Fanon individually. This is due, I will speculate, to the complexity of each writer's thought and legacy. By producing two volumes that begin and end with inference and then reflection on their singular and related importance, we can provide a foundation for reflection on the bold claim that begins this introduction.

Facilitating the coherence of these two volumes is the contribution of Charles Long as *rapporteur* to each volume. He is an eminent United States historian of the Atlantic and he is based in the field of the history of religions, a field that might not be familiar to the interdisciplinary audience we assume will be interested in this collection. It is his location in the history of religions that gives him a unique leverage on conceptual issues involved in the Atlantic. His Atlantic is an Atlantic of contact, exchange, and the dynamics produced by the particular geographies, technologies, chances, and rhetorics that have marked what might be called the track record of the Atlantic. Working with the conceptual frames of contact and exchange, which I will discuss below in relation to the larger conceptual frame of "orientation," he has altered the way that knowledge, history, and religion are conceptualized in the North American academic scene, though British academics were not well aware of his work from what I could tell during my five years in Scotland. Thus, the contribution that these two volumes make to Du Bois and Fanon research is that we not only bring significant essays from scholars working in South Africa, the United Kingdom, and the United States that highlight particular elements of each man's work as it relates to the twenty-first century, but also we bring the major theoretical reflections of Dr. Long's conceptual frames to bear on how force and meaning are evaluated in the academic interpretation of Du Bois and Fanon.

One of the problems that faced Du Bois and Fanon, and continues to face contemporary scholars of the Atlantic, is that of religion and diaspora religion. This problem was a point of analysis for both Du Bois and Fanon—what to make of religiousness and the roots of African Traditional Religion in relation to the lives of postcolonial African subjectivity. And in the contemporary scene, one of the central academic quagmires has been how religion and religiousness is represented and evaluated by academics. Central to the dilemma of discussing postcolonial subjectivity is the problem of identifying and evaluating the relationship of religion and culture, and these volumes will contribute a very different perspective to this question by bringing discipline-specific research into conversation with Dr. Long's take on the Atlantic.

Du Bois and Fanon analyzed the problem of raced subjectivity in relation to social systems of power as they saw that problem at work in the lives of men and women struggling to overcome the legacy of the transatlantic slave trade, European colonialism, and the burgeoning power of global capitalism that each man recognized as a force of neocolonialism. From their respective territories, Du Bois, located in the United States but a traveler to Europe, China, Japan, and Africa, especially Ghana, and Fanon, located in the triangulation between Martinique, France, and Algeria, their texts probe the human condition as they saw it, which meant using interdisciplinary academic tools for social analysis as well as the interrogation of their own experiences in the world. As brilliant rhetoricians they gave voice to the souls and psyches of the people who underwent the historical trauma of the slave trade, colonialism, and imperialism. They each wrote with such poetry and passion that their texts have inspired major libratory political movements. Their texts have influenced the way many who struggle for global and local forms of economic justice see and engage in their struggles. The role of material and psychological violence in the racist oppression of people is made obvious in each man's relation of their individual experiences to the larger social structures in which they lived. Du Bois, *cum laude* graduate of Harvard, described his experience of the two-ness required of the African American living in the States: "two warring ideals in one dark body held together only by its dogged determination."(Du Bois, Souls, 1994 [1903], 2) And Fanon, veteran of the French resistance in World War II and brilliant young doctor of the French medical schools, described the nausea and fragmentation he underwent with the repeated assaults on his identity that occurred in his everyday movement among Parisians and in his various roles as soldier and doctor for the French government. Their texts recognize the momentous work that lay ahead for all who strove for racial justice by identifying the subjective struggles of individuals in relation to the socioeconomic systems in which those individual lives were constrained. Nevertheless, their texts never doubt that the wretched of the earth would come to be recognized in society as fully human through their own sheer will and determination. Reading the predictions they each made that the powerful would be unseated by the powerless makes for uncanny resonance in the contemporary world. I will return to this point below with reference to the relationship of religious subjectivity and struggles for power and meaning.

Both writers opened up new kinds of scholarship in their creative demand for a picture of the world that was adequate to the task of making sense of the material and human costs of the history into which they were born and which they both altered. Both men were so forceful in their writings that they experienced times of censure and restriction from the authorities of their respective nations and this perhaps helps to explain why their works have been more largely taken up by readers of resistance movements than by readers more firmly situated in comfortable or privileged positions. Because of the power and disparate appropriations of their writings, this collection was selected to present an overview of their most significant texts, providing reassessments of those texts in some cases with an eye towards the question "What is at stake in re-cognizing their work in the contemporary world?" Part of the answer to this question lies in understanding the role of religious lives from a postcolonial perspective. Not all of the essays included in these volumes address issues of religion or religiosity, but it is my location in the history of religions that crystallized for me the importance of bringing these two authors together *now*. Du Bois predicted in his 1901 text *The Souls of Black Folk* that the color line would be *the problem* of the twentieth century for the United States, and it is safe, so to speak, to assume that religion, intimately interrelated with color lines, will be the major problem of the twenty-first century. If Du Bois and Fanon were still writing, they would be addressing the question of religion. Hence to re-cognize these two thinkers for the twenty-first century is in large part to re-cognize how their work relates to religiousness.

We assume that for many people residing in the concepts and contexts of the Western tradition, religion occupies an anachronistic space. For many people in what has been called the secular West, religion is perceived to be an experience grounded in belief and faith, both terms that have little authority for persons who regard evidence, reason, and science to be the firm ground upon which modern democracies stand and upon which the social sciences can build coherent argument. Thus for many concerned people religion appears to be an anachronistic throwback to less enlightened times, a throwback that is responsible for many of the most violent conflicts on the globe today. Indeed, one might argue that in the texts of Du Bois and Fanon religion occupied just such a space, for their ultimate faith was always placed in the human, not the divine. But religion and religiousness occupies a much more complicated place in their texts and indeed in order to understand how either of them approached the topic of religion it is important to approach religion from a postcolonial perspective, which means to look at the limitations of the modern Western understanding of religion and reorient the concept of religion away from its Eurocentric trappings. To leave religion in the anachronistic space in which the modern Western tradition confines it leaves one unable to assess the vital role of religiousness in the world today, so we propose to introduce the collection by way of reorienting how "the religious" is understood. With an adequate hermeneutic for thinking about the enduring power of religiousness for many people, one can then provide analysis of religious bodies in the world today. By framing the two volumes with an approach for thinking about religion and religiousness in the twenty-first century, we can better apply the insights of Du Bois and Fanon to the current world scene. To do so requires the transformation of the concept of religion, breaking apart the habit of thought that associates religion with belief and ideology.

Following the pioneering work of Charles H. Long, we propose the following redefinition of religion and religiousness that provides a radical shift in how one perceives religion and religiousness at work in the world. If religion is more broadly understood as the practice of determining the significance of one's *location* in the world, then religiousness is understood to be the disciplinary practices and strategies by which one locates the meaning of one's existence when confronted by borders or boundaries against which one can establish a sense of location.[1] For example, a Christian baptism is not understood to be an exercise of sheep-like people herded together because they all believe in the Christian God. From the perspective of religion as orientation, a baptism is seen to be the embodied negotiation of a community that finds the temporal border of birth to be compelling enough to participate in marking a child, which simultaneously reinforces the sense of significance of all who participate: older children, adolescents, people with and people without their own children, and older people in the congregation. A baptism is an orienteering strategy and gives meaning to the congregants who share in marking the child as Christ's own. With this approach, one can assume that a wide array of participants are engaged in the ritualization of the child's emergence into the community. While no two people may have the same relationship to the actual baptism as a sacrament, the power of the ritual is that it allows for disparate people to gather and

---

[1] See Charles H. Long, *Significations* (Aurora CO: Davies Group, 1995). He writes: "As a historian of religions I have not defined religion in conventional terms. To be sure, the church is one place one looks for religion. Given the situation of Americans of African descent, their churches were always somewhat different from the other churches of the United States. But even more than this, the church was not the only context for the meaning of religion. For my purposes, religion will mean orientation—orientation in the ultimate sense, that is, how one comes to terms with the ultimate significance of one's place in the world. The Christian faith provided a language for the meaning of religion, but not all the religious meanings of the black communities were encompassed by the Christian forms of religion. I have been as interested in other forms of religion in the history of black communities—as those forms are contained in their folklore, music, style of life, and so on. Some tensions have existed between these forms of orientation and those of the Christian churches, but some of these extra-church orientations had had great critical and creative power. They have often touched deeper religious issues regarding the true situation of black communities than those of the church leaders of their time" (7).

mark an event together, perhaps agreeing to disagree on sectarian or other distinctions, such as not being a churchgoer, in order to agree that welcoming the child into the congregation is a good practice in which to participate. Each and every person there is a negotiator determining their significance vis-à-vis the child's emergence into the congregation.

This very broad and very embodied approach to religion suggests that many cultural phenomena that otherwise might not be perceived to be religious can be argued to carry a significance that is religious. The crossing of new territory, for instance, is understood to be highly charged activity imbued with cosmological significance for those explorers who set out to map and territorialize the globe. The experience of having strangers arrive, occupy, and/or remove one from one's land also can be seen to have had a huge impact on the sense one might hold of the significance of one's locatedness in the world. A highly charged religiousness can be seen to have accompanied travel, discovery, contact, exchange, occupation, and the slave trade for people on all sides of those events.

Two of the major themes Long has developed as central for interpreting the Atlantic are contact and exchange. Contact with a person or community that was different and new is seen from this perspective as creating moments requiring orientation. The track record of the Atlantic suggests that this encounter is fraught with an all-too-human propensity to establish a sense of meaning with a Manichean frame based on the most visceral and phenomenal responses of humans, producing hierarchically organized binarisms. To propose a theory of contact is to propose epistemological as well as ontological claims regarding the overdetermined process of coming into contact with an other. Exchange is the driving motor of any contact situation. Long develops his theory of exchange influenced by Marcel Mauss's *The Gift*, arguing that exchange is always a matter of a surplus economy.[2] Trade and the materiality of cultural contact are imbued with surplus significations, effects of which include mimesis, appropriation, rejection, and critical evaluations that are imbued with religious significance because the very act of encountering a stranger requires one to accomplish the work of giving meaning to one's location vis-à-vis human similarities and differences.

---

[2] Marcel Mauss, *The Gift: The Form and Reason for Exchange in Archaic Socities*, trans. W. D. Halls, foreword by Mary Douglas (New York/London: W. W. Norton, 1990).

From this reoriented approach to religion, one can employ the tools of critical theory because it is essential to this definition of religion that embodied power negotiations related to territory and material existence are central to the practices by which communities mark, remember, forget, and experience the significance of their locations in the world. From this perspective, belief is not the determining characteristic of a religious person. Rather, events that create border crossings are considered to be religious because they create the cosmological experience of providing a sense of location, a sense that demands reflection because it has the power to disorient or reorient.

From this perspective there are many borders and boundaries that are essential to the religious life. As described by Catherine Albanese, key boundaries include: geographical boundaries (mountains, the entrance to a temple, foreign territory, diaspora experiences that force one to cross boundaries), temporal boundaries (birth, puberty, adulthood, menopause, death), the boundaries of our bodies (hence contact between bodies that are differently aged, gendered, raced, and classed; especially contact that crosses bodily boundaries such as intercourse, eating, and defecating produce heightened experiences of one's location, thus raising the potential for reflecting on the meaning of one's locatedness), social boundaries (such as the Veil in Du Bois's terms), and the boundaries by which one establishes a sense of identity.[3] The encounter with and negotiation of these boundaries are understood to be the central characteristics of the religious life because boundaries serve to orient persons in their worlds, much like the orienteer uses the peak, the ridgeline, or the river to determine their location.

Cosmology as the horizon by which people locate and navigate their sense and their actions is central to human existence from this perspective: people may not have gods but their responses to boundaries take on comparable forms (marriage, burials, and creative elements of folk culture such as regional music, theater, and arts) that can be fruitfully regarded as religious in their ability to provide meaning and significance to one's embodied and located experiences.

With this alternative approach to religion, we can revisit the texts of Du Bois and Fanon. Both men largely employed the word religion in the traditional sense, as though it referred to a set of beliefs, and both were

---

[3] Catherine Albanese, *America: Religions and Religion*, 2d ed. (Belmont CA: Wadsworth Publishing Co., Inc., 1992) 5.

suitably critical of the potential for religion (as ideology) to enslave humans or justify enslavement. Nevertheless, both wrote texts that are richly laced with the tropes of orienteering and orientation, the language of mapping one's locatedness in relation to things with power. Approaching religion as orientation, one can make sense of why Du Bois the agnostic was so concerned with souls and messianic tropes and why Fanon prayed that he would always ask questions and talked of language as the "God gone astray in the flesh."[4] Their texts are deeply concerned with the borders and boundaries by which people orient themselves, epistemologically, ontologically, and socioeconomically. Both employ narratives of their own experience in order to facilitate an identification on the part of the reader with the process of identifying where one stands in relation to others, be it Du Bois's notions of double-consciousness and the veil or Fanon's depiction of black skin, white masks and the wretched of the earth. The impact of race is not merely philosophical or psychological in their texts. The impact of poverty and economic exploitation is not merely materialist. What was at stake as Du Bois mapped not only black consciousness but also black housing in Philadelphia, and first mapped out an African history, was a social imaginary that recognized, studied and validated the significance of racialized locatedness in the world. We can approach the messianism of Du Bois and Fanon understanding that it was meant to lead people to a new significance and new locatedness in the world.

The essays that follow do not refer to or employ this definition of religion. I suggest it as a lever that helps to relate the significance of the many facets of Du Bois that are examined in these chapters to the question of his intellectual significance in the twenty-first century. I will pick up a few conceptual threads as I introduce the essays, but leave to Dr. Long's concluding *rapport* the work of re-cognizing Du Bois in the twenty-first century.

---

[4] Chester Fontenot, *Frantz Fanon: Language as the God Gone Astray in the Flesh*, new ser. no. 60 (Lincoln: University of Nebraska, 1979).

Volume I: Re-Cognizing W. E. B. Du Bois in the Twenty-first Century

Robin Law's chapter reevaluating Du Bois's role as a historian of Africa begins the collection of essays on W.E.B. Du Bois. Law's chapter raises the question of Du Bois's absence in the accepted pantheon of important African historians. Law's argument firmly places Du Bois as an important founder of the field whose work not only challenged Eurocentric assertions that Africa was a place of no real history but also raised key theoretical revaluations and posed exciting new possibilities for the parameters of African history. Law focuses on a text that African historians have neglected, *The Negro* (1915), and presents a new critical evaluation of that text that also allows Law to reconsider the contributions to African history made by the English journalist Winwood Reade and the German ethnologist Leo Frobenius, who have largely been denounced in contemporary evaluations of the racist roots of European scholarship in Africa. Law's clear presentation of the interpretive issues points toward the richness we can expect as African history moves into the twenty-first century, for there are no Manichean lines of evaluation in which good guys and bad guys are placed and/or dismissed. A richer, frank, and more ambivalent picture of what African history means constitutes the groundbreaking work of Du Bois. Law's essay marks a significant contribution towards how Du Bois figures in the larger context of African history and also toward the evaluative schemes employed in contemporary constructions of African history.

Let me now argue the importance of relating Law's essay to the concept of orientation. Because the identifying of boundaries is itself understood to be central to the work of human religiousness, not only do I read Law's text as an argument that alters the horizon of the academic pantheon by addressing an absence and asserting a place in that horizon for Du Bois as an African historian, but also Law's argument highlights the theological significance of Du Bois's efforts to discern and map Africa as a place of significance. Du Bois contributed significantly to the production of a backdrop against which Africa and Africans gain new significance in their specific *locatedness*.

David Chidester's essay effectively picks up the work of recontextualizing *The Negro* in his larger project of tracking how Du Bois represented African indigenous religion. This is a very important argument not only for thinking about how religion functioned categorically for Du

Bois—Chidester tracks how that changed over time—but also in that it raises the larger issue of how African religion functions in the academic imagination of Africa then and today. Chidester identifies three problems or thematics at work in Du Bois's texts, and at the meta-level one could apply Chidester's three themes to the larger question of how African religiousness has been and is constructed in discourse. The three problems are humanity, divinity, and continuity and Chidester elegantly relates these problems to the transformations Du Bois's construction of African religion underwent. Chidester argues that the problem of humanity, that is, of depicting the humanity of religious Africans, was intimately related to the overdetermined significance of fetishism as a European concept. Not only was African religion called fetishism and evaluated as simplistic and superstitious, a problem Du Bois challenged by offering a revaluation of fetishism, but also Africans were imagined as objects, fetishes, throughout the slave trade and under the rubrics of European colonialism. With regard to divinity as a problem of representation, Du Bois revalued African theology, recasting how African divinity was described and asserting the superiority of African divinity to European divinities in his later reflections on the Yoruba god Shango. With regard to continuity as a problem of the representation of African religion, over time Du Bois altered his valuation of the continuity of African religious culture as it impacted African Americans. Tracking that alteration allows Chidester to see the changing significance Du Bois gave to diaspora cosmology, a difference we see mirrored in Marta Brunner's analysis of messianic tropes in Du Bois's literary work.

We pick up on the problem of continuity and diaspora in the third chapter as Jemima Pierre and Jesse Weaver Shipley examine the intellectual and pragmatic legacy of Du Bois's Pan-Africanism. Moving from the richness of Chidester's thematic argument to a study of Du Bois's pragmatic and dramatic Pan-African theorizations and participation signals the awesome breadth of Du Bois's intellect and vision. The question of Pan-Africanism for the twentieth and twenty-first centuries is given shape in the chapter, marking critical historical junctures and posing interpretive perspectives on the politics of Pan-African discourses. Noting the problems of race and geography for Pan-African politics, Pierre and Shipley focus their study on the particular role that Ghana played for Du Bois. They also study contemporary efforts in Ghana to revitalize the historical link to Du Bois in political discourse and the development of a lively artistic/touristic culture aimed at diaspora travel.

Again, what might at first seem to be a political argument can be productively related to the conceptual frame of orientation. Shipley and Pierre argue that two purposes are served in Ghana's contemporary remembrances and revitalization of Du Bois's legacy. First, remembrance of Du Bois recalls "Ghana's position as the symbolic center of Pan-African politics and practice." Secondly it allows for "practical relations between (African) continental and diaspora peoples." From the perspective of orientation, symbolic centers function to orient people and give significance to one's relationship to the center. When relationships are strengthened, Pan-Africanism takes on greater force and meaning in people's lives, blurring any comfortable distinction between the way Pan-Africanism functions politically and religiously.

The final four chapters relate more specifically to Du Bois in a North American context. We begin with Rodney Roberts and contemporary philosophical arguments regarding rectificatory justice. Roberts notes that Du Bois turned "back from the field of philosophy," which he found to be sterile, but Roberts speculates that the contemporary arguments of American philosophy pose fruitful questions that Du Bois would surely have found effective for his pragmatic drive for social justice. Roberts specifically analyses what Du Bois's texts offer to current debates and political movements regarding reparations for slave-trade injustices as those debates are carried on in the field of rectificatory justice. And while Roberts couches his discussion in North American philosophy we are reminded of the Pan-African context because Du Bois linked the need for reparations to the African continent. Roberts begins by explaining his previously articulated theory of rectificatory action and amends that theory in this article, taking heed from Du Bois's concerns and relating them to moral psychology. Roberts contrasts the reparations made to Japanese Americans with the stalled effort to deliver a United States policy on reparations to the descendants of the slave trade. Noting Du Bois's blind spots with respect to indigenous North Americans as well as his commitment to social justice for the displaced, Roberts elucidates the contribution that a historicized reading of Du Bois brings to contemporary ethics.

Carol Stewart's reevaluation of the question of elitism in Du Bois's early texts is the best and most comprehensive interpretation I have read. Her argument is both thorough and subtle, attending to context and nuance as she places Du Bois's words in their sociohistorical context, depicting a focused, coherent, and radically democratic drive throughout his work. She addresses the question of elitism as it has been raised by Joy James, Cornel West, and Wilson Moses and argues against the veritable tradition they support that suggests Du Bois began writing as an elitist and later became democratic in his vision. Her paper will mark a turning point in terms of this question and provides readers with a firm foundation in the history of ideas regarding talent and race as they have figured in the American imagination with its unique conflation of religious ideology and political spaces. Her article also sets the stage beautifully for the next two papers as she calls for further examination of the spiritual as it figured in Du Bois's *Souls*, which Stephen Andrews's paper provides, and her discussion of despair and hope in Du Bois's work sets the critical foundation for Marta Brunner's study of messianic tropes in Du Bois's later novels.

With Andrews's study of synaesthetics in Du Bois's *Souls of Black Folk*, I am once again awed by the breadth of Du Bois's creative and intellectual scope. Andrews's chapter provides a focused study of *Souls*, arguably one of the most elegant, complex and important of twentieth-century texts. Andrews provides an exciting, new perspective on the genius with which Du Bois constructed *Souls* by taking seriously Du Bois's use of musical annotations in the text as well as identifying the affective power of Du Bois's weaving together themes of transitivity (motion, liquidity, vagueness) with the music of the spirituals. Not only does Andrews provide a rich and historicized context for appreciating synaesthetics in Du Bois but also he contributes a web page that includes performances of the spirituals found in *Souls*, thus contributing to pedagogical as well as interpretive agendas with regard to the study of this text.

From *Souls* we move to a study of three later texts in Marta Brunner's discussion of messianism in *Darkwater*, *Dark Princess*, and *Dusk of Dawn*. In Brunner's study of messianism and messianic tropes she points to some of the problems that arise from applying conventional ideas about religion, a dualistic perception of transcendence and divinity (which a postcolonial perspective does not perpetuate in my reading of orientation) to Du Bois's use of messianic tropes. Whereas in their received senses the terms transcendent and divine refer to "that which operates outside of the realm of human control," Brunner argues that the implication of Du Bois's use of the messianic requires reconceiving notions of immanence and transcendence. Echoes of shared interest are heard between Brunner's concern with the role faith has in translating ideas into plans of action—that is, why Du Bois would create characters inspired by faith—and Robert's ethical concern with the compulsion to act for social justice. Recalling Chidester's article that traced the changing significance of African religion for Du Bois, we see parallels with Brunner's argument that a transformation is marked in Du Bois's use of messianism, but nevertheless at the literary level, faith, in a reconceived version of divinity as a human potential, was a significant element of Du Bois's vision for transforming raced relationships in American and Pan-African contexts. Chidester's argument dovetails with the need to reorient how religiousness, belief, divinity, and transcendence are approached by academics and provides a focused literary exploration of the need to reconceive these categories in order to understand why an intellectual powerhouse like Du Bois took seriously the force of messianism in the lives of raced, diasporic people in the North American context. From the perspective of religion as orientation, messianism does not reflect a belief in God but rather messianism is the power to lead the way, through the valley of the shadow of death, or negotiating with the veil. Messiahs are orienteers, and their paradigmatic lives lead people to a new sense of the significance of their locatedness.

From here I will allow the individual essays to speak for themselves and hope only that this foregrounding might contribute to the work of developing a hermeneutic adequate to the task of relating the work of Du Bois, and later of Fanon, to the world as it is where understanding the problem of the twenty-first century will mean reconceptualizing how bodies that are raced and religious engage with each other.

Works Cited

Albanese, Catherine. *America: Religions and Religion.* Second edition. Belmont CA: Wadsworth Publishing Co., Inc., 1992.

Du Bois, W.E.B. *The Souls of Black Folk* (New York: Dover Publications, 1994 [1903]).

Fontenot, Chester. *Frantz Fanon: Language as the God Gone Astray in the Flesh.* New series number 60. Lincoln: University of Nebraska, 1979.

Long, Charles H. *Significations.* Second edition. Aurora CO: Davies Group, Publishers, 1995.

Mauss, Marcel. *The Gift: The Form and Reason for Exchange in Archaic Societies.* Translated by W. D. Halls. Foreword by Mary Douglas. New York/London: W. W. Norton, 1990.

Du Bois as a Pioneer of African history:
A Reassessment of *The Negro* (1915)

Robin Law
University of Stirling

This paper essays a reassessment of the contribution of W. E. B. Du Bois to the development of African historiography. Its specific focus is one particular book among the many which he wrote, *The Negro*, published in 1915.[1] This is probably one of the lesser-known and less-regarded of his works. Much of the material and argument of this book were also reused, and to some extent elaborated and revised, by Du Bois in subsequent publications which may be better-known, especially *The World and Africa*, published in 1947.[2] But the original 1915 publication remains the most coherent and effective, as well as the original, presentation of the argument. It is argued here that it represents a very significant pioneering work in the early development of African historiography.

This judgment will be surprising to many historians of Africa. Although Du Bois is of course acknowledged as an important figure in African history, he is known mainly for his central role in the Pan-African movement and his influence through the latter on the early development of anticolonial nationalism in Africa. He is not generally recognized as having made any significant contribution to writing about African history.[3] For

---

[1] W. E. B. Du Bois, *The Negro* (New York & London: Home University Library of Modern Knowledge, 1915).

[2] W. E. B Du Bois, *The World and Africa: An inquiry into the part which Africa has played in world history*, enl. ed. (New York International Publishers 1965, repr. 1992). See also *Black Folk Then and Now: An essay on the history and sociology of the Negro Race* (1939; repr. New York: Monthly Review Press 1975).

[3] An exception is the tribute by William Leo Hansberry, "W. E. B. Du Bois's influence on African history," *Freedomways* 5 (1965): 73–87, which acknowledges

example, at a conference on "The emergence of African history at British universities," held at Oxford in 1992, when a number of the pioneers of the study and teaching of African history in the United Kingdom offered their autobiographical reminiscences of the beginnings of the discipline in the 1940s and 1950s, none of them mentioned Du Bois as an influence or acknowledged him as a predecessor.[4] The lack of reference to Du Bois in this particular context may partly reflect the fact that in general the participants in the Oxford conference had little at all to say about questions of intellectual ancestry, as opposed to the institutional and political context, of the emergence of the discipline of African history. But, in fact, one of those who spoke at the conference, the late John Fage, also published essays on the early development of African history-writing prior to the emergence of the academic historiography of the 1950s, what he called the 'prehistory of African history,' and in these too he found no occasion to mention Du Bois.[5] As another illustrative example, at an early conference of African historians in 1965, the only paper that mentioned Du Bois's writings on African history, by George Shepperson, dealt with the African diaspora in America rather than with Africa itself.[6]

If historians of Africa cite any of the works of Du Bois, these are likely to be not the overview of African history in *The Negro* but his research on the Atlantic slave trade, especially his Harvard PhD thesis, published in 1896 as *The Suppression of the African Slave-Trade to the USA.*[7] He is in fact

---

personal inspiration from reading *The Negro* soon after its publication. But although Hansberry at the time of writing was a visiting professor at the University of Nigeria, Nsukka, he was outside the mainstream of historical studies on sub-Saharan Africa; his own work related to Nubia/Ethiopia, mainly in classical antiquity.

[4] A. H. M. Kirk-Greene, ed., *The Emergence of African History at British Universities: An autobiographical approach* (Oxford: Worldview Publications, 1995).

[5] J. D. Fage, "Continuity and change in the writing of West African history," *African Affairs* 70/282 (July 1971): 236–51; "The prehistory of African history," *Paideuma* 19/20 (1973/4): 46–61.

[6] George Shepperson, "The African abroad or the African Diaspora," in T. O. Ranger, ed., *Emerging Themes of African History: Proceedings of the International Conference of African Historians held at University College, Dar es Salaam, October 1965* (London: Heinemann Educational Books, 1968) 158–60. Shepperson here referred to the later *World and Africa* rather than to *The Negro*.

[7] This is, e.g., the only work by Du Bois cited in *Historiography*, vol. 5 of *The Oxford History of the British Empire*, ed. Robin W. Winks (Oxford: Oxford University Press, 1999); the reference occurs in the chapter by Toyin Falola, "West Africa," 487.

probably best known to historians of Africa as the intermediate source (in a paper of 1911) of the conventional estimate of the number of slaves exported from Africa to the Americas, at around 15 million, which attracted critical demolition at the hands of Philip Curtin.[8] This was, of course, as Curtin pointed out, not based on Du Bois's own research but quoted from an earlier writer, Edward Dunbar (1861). Ironically, it may be noted that in repeating the citation of Dunbar in *The Negro*, Du Bois expressed implicit caution about his figures, offering his own opinion of the volume of the transatlantic slave trade as 'at least 10,000,000,' which is in fact within the parameters of Curtin's revisionist estimate.[9]

I have also to confess that, although I can claim credit for one of the few citations of Du Bois as a pioneer of African historiography, in a paper co-written with Paul Lovejoy in 1996, we referred to his work in an unfortunately dismissive way. In the course of explaining why the first generation of academic historians of Africa, John Fage et al., adopted a definition of "African" history that restricted its boundaries to the African continent, effectively excluding the African diaspora in the Americas, we acknowledged the compulsion they felt to establish African history as a subject of interest in its own right rather than merely as part of the background to the history of the Americas; and we cited Du Bois's *The Negro* to illustrate this earlier perspective.[10] This is not inaccurate, since the book is, as its title implies, a racial rather than a continental history, and its framework does indeed begin with Africa only to proceed via 'the Trade in Men' to end up with 'the Negro in the United States.' But in fact, the bulk of the book (8 of 12 chapters) comprises a sketch of specifically African history before its focus shifts to the Atlantic slave trade and the African-

---

[8] Philip D. Curtin, *The Atlantic Slave Trade: A Census* (Madison: University of Wisconsin Press, 1969) 6–7.

[9] Du Bois, *Negro*, 155. It should be noted that Du Bois's often-repeated claim of the demographic cost of the slave trade to Africa as 100 million persons is, in fact, based on this estimate of the volume of the transatlantic trade at 10 million, combined with the belief that the slave trade to the Muslim world accounted for "nearly as many more" and the assumption that "every slave imported represented on average five corpses in Africa or on the high seas."

[10] Robin Law and Paul E. Lovejoy, "The changing dimensions of African history: reappropriating the Diaspora," in Charles Jedrej, Kenneth King, and Jack Thompson, eds., *Rethinking African History* (Edinburgh: Centre of African Studies, University of Edinburgh, 1997) 184.

American diaspora. From another perspective, and more fairly, as Kristin Mann has more recently suggested, one might commend Du Bois for his anticipation of recent approaches to the study of the diaspora, conceiving it in "global" terms and giving a central place to the African homeland.[11] And certainly, at the time and in the context in which it was written, it represented a remarkable pioneering venture in what was a largely undeveloped field, whose neglect in considerations of the history of the writing of African history seems altogether unwarranted.

It is less clear that *The Negro* is similarly neglected or undervalued by scholars in the field of Du Bois studies. The text certainly has not been wholly forgotten. It was reprinted in 1970 (with an introduction by George Shepperson) and again no less than three times during the two years 2001 to 2002.[12] But, for example, the recent intellectual biography of Du Bois by David Levering Lewis does not make much of the book, to which it devotes a mere two paragraphs.[13] While acknowledging its status as "a pioneering synthesis of the latest scholarship brilliantly beamed through a revisionist lens," otherwise Lewis's observations are mainly critical, in particular referring to its reproduction of European racist stereotypes of Africans, "broad characterizations of African peoples that would have been seen as invidious if propounded by a European scholar." This is not an unjust criticism, since Du Bois's text is indeed peppered with language which implies negative stereotypes of African societies—in his perception, Africa is populated in part by "wild and unruly...tribes" and even sometimes "fearful cannibals"[14]; the word "primitive" is liberally applied to both its human population and its institutions; and its religion characterized as "fetishism," which is arguably meaningless as well as pejorative. As a representative example: "The religion of Africa is the universal animism or fetishism of

---

[11] Kristin Mann, "Shifting paradigms in the study of the African Diaspora and of Atlantic history and culture," in Kristin Mann and Edna G. Bay, eds., *Rethinking the African Diaspora: The making of a Black Atlantic world in the Bight of Benin and Brazil* (London: Frank Cass, 2001) 4.

[12] The reprints of which I am aware are London: Oxford University Press, 1970 (with an introduction by George Shepperson); Philadelphia: University of Pennsylvania Press, 2001 (with an afterword by Robert Gregg); New York: Dover Books,, 2001; and New York: Humanity Books, 2002 (with an introduction by Kenneth W. Goings).

[13] David Levering Lewis, *W. E. B. Du Bois: Biography of a Race, 1868–1919* (New York: Henry Holt, 1993) 461–62.

[14] Du Bois, *Negro*, 34, 72.

primitive peoples, rising to polytheism and approaching monotheism chiefly, but not wholly, as a result of Christian and Islamic missions"[15]—a statement which may be judged to be more informative about Du Bois's preconceptions than about the nature of African religion. To be fair, this terminology (positing an explicitly evolutionist hierarchy of religions) is basically simply old-fashioned, which perhaps sounds more pejorative now than it did at the time. Essentially it reflects the age and context in which Du Bois wrote; his failure to liberate himself entirely from its prejudices is unsurprising and indeed arguably inevitable.

When I first read *The Negro* in the early 1980s, what mainly struck me about it was the framework within which Du Bois presented African history. The sequence of chapters is at first sight purely geographical: after an initial chapter on the peopling of Africa ("The coming of the Black man"); successive chapters deal with the civilizations of the Nile valley ("Ethiopia and Egypt"); inner West Africa, including the spread of Islam there ("The Niger and Islam"); Atlantic Africa, including European maritime enterprise, especially the impact of the slave trade ("Guinea and Congo"); East and East-Central Africa ("The Great Lakes and Zimbabwe"); and finally South Africa, including European settlement and its impact on the indigenous African population ("The War of Races at the World's End"). This shifting geographical focus, however, also incorporates a chronological progression: the Nile valley civilizations are discussed mainly with reference to antiquity; inner West Africa mainly with reference to the medieval period; and Atlantic Africa with reference to the slave trade in the early modern era. The progression is somewhat interrupted by the chapter on East Africa, whose chronological focus is blurred, partly because of its fragmented focus (divided between the civilization of Great Zimbabwe, the Swahili city-states of the East Coast, and the states of the Great Lakes area) but also reflecting uncertainty about the antiquity of Zimbabwe. However, this basically replicates the western African chapters in focusing on the medieval and early modern periods. The final chapter on South Africa focuses on the modern era, mainly the nineteenth century.

The sense of chronological progression is reinforced by the fact that the chapters are linked by a series of posited migrations: from Ethiopia to inner West Africa; from inner West Africa to the coast; from West Africa, the migrations of the Bantu to the Congo and East-Central Africa and

---

[15] Ibid., 124.

thence into South Africa. Du Bois's conception of African history is indeed built upon a series of migrations, "endless movement and migration." These migrations were seen as often disruptive and destructive in their impact, and as a factor that thereby contributed to inhibiting African state formation: "we continually have whirlwinds of invading hosts rushing now southward, now northward, from the interior to the coast, and from the coast inland, and hurling their force against states, kingdoms, and cities."[16] Robert Gregg, in an afterword to one of the recent reprints of *The Negro*, regards this focus on migration as an element that looks forward intellectually, anticipating emphases in modern studies of ethnicity,[17] but Du Bois is talking about *Völkerwanderungen*, migrations of whole peoples, rather than of diasporas. From an African-history perspective, the emphasis on migration actually looks rather old-fashioned—what was stigmatized in the 1960s as the "Clapham Junction Theory of African history."[18]

It should be noted that Du Bois himself later expressed dissatisfaction with the framework of *The Negro*, characterizing it as "a condensed and not altogether logical narrative," and he rearranged the ordering of the material in later presentations.[19] But the self-criticism seems over-severe; certainly, from an Africanist perspective, the later reconstruction of the narrative in *The World and Africa*, which begins with European colonialism and the Atlantic slave trade and engages with specifically African history only from chapter 4, seems something of a regression.[20]

What struck me about the narrative framework of *The Negro* was its familiarity, since it very much resembled the structure of the undergraduate course on precolonial African history taught by John Fage at Birmingham, which I as a postgraduate teaching assistant was enlisted to teach from 1969. The overall conception, with its combination of shifting geographical focus

---

[16] Du Bois, *Negro*, 80, 106–107.

[17] Gregg, "Afterword" to the 2001 reprint of *The Negro*, 260–62.

[18] The phrase is credited to David Dalby by P. E. H. Hair, "Ethnolinguistic continuity on the Guinea Coast," *Journal of African History* 8/2 (1967): 266.

[19] Du Bois, *World and Africa*, vii–viii.

[20] The later version also modifies the sequence in which regions of Africa are treated, beginning again with Egypt and Ethiopia but now dealing with coastal western Africa ("Atlantis") and Central/Southern Africa before moving to the Arab/Islamic impact ("Asia in Africa") and interior West Africa (the "Black Sudan"). It is not clear why Du Bois regarded this as "a more logical arrangement," but probably the point is to de-emphasize the role of external influences in the history of sub-Saharan Africa.

and chronological progression, and the specific topics chosen for attention, correspond quite precisely. Even the emphasis on migration in the formation of states and peoples, which now seems old-fashioned, was central to the conception of John Fage and his contemporaries of the pioneering generation into the 1970s.

What remains unclear to me is whether this resemblance is due to the direct influence of Du Bois on Fage and his contemporaries; but if so, as noted earlier, the borrowing is unacknowledged. Maybe there was some influence of Du Bois, if not directly on the academic pioneers, through their amateur contemporaries. Du Bois does, for example, figure in the bibliography of the 1959 pioneering work of the most distinguished early popularizer of African history, Basil Davidson, although it was the later work, *The World and Africa*, rather than the earlier text *The Negro*, which was cited.[21] Alternatively, however, the similarities may reflect merely parallel responses to the same historiographical issues on the basis of much the same range of available published source material. Either way, in its conceptualization as much as its detailed content, Du Bois's presentation seemed to me, in its historiographical context (or, one might equally say, given effective the lack of any historiographical context), quite a remarkable achievement.

Du Bois's achievement seems all the more remarkable when compared with the work of the outstanding Afro-American intellectual of the previous generation, Edward Wilmot Blyden (1832–1912). Blyden in his life was much more closely linked to Africa than Du Bois, having emigrated there in 1851 to settle in the African-American colony of Liberia. His experience also extended beyond Liberia and other similar colonial coastal enclaves; he traveled in the interior to states still under independent African sovereignty in 1862 and 1872 (an experience that played a critical role in his "discovery" of Islam as an African religion). But despite this greater familiarity with Africa, Blyden never seriously sought to engage with the continent's history.[22] Although he regularly drew upon history to combat allegations of

---

[21] Basil Davidson, *Old Africa Rediscovered* (London: Gollanaz, 1959). Du Bois is also cited once (on the scale of the Atlantic slave trade), although oddly not included in the bibliography, in the work of an early Ghanaian non-academic writer on history: J. C. deGraft-Johnson, *African Glory: The story of the vanished Negro civilizations* (London: Watts, 1954) 164.

[22] See further Robin Law, "Constructing 'a real national history': a comparison of Edward Blyden and Samuel Johnson," in P. F. de Moraes Farias and Karin Barber, eds.,

black racial inferiority, the dominant tendency in his work was to cite examples of individual persons of African origin or descent who had achieved intellectual or political distinction in the diaspora, in Europe or America rather than the history of societies in Africa itself. When he sought to establish the contribution of Africa (as opposed to individual Africans) to world civilization, as in his essay "The Negro in Ancient History" (1869),[23] he did so primarily through emphasis on the role of Egypt as the cradle of civilization and by insistence on the Negro contribution to Egyptian culture; the history of sub-Saharan Africa still did not figure largely in his conception. When he did finally attempt a substantial study of Tropical Africa, towards the end of his life in 1908, he did so not through a study of its history but in a generalized, timeless, and essentialist (and highly idealized) description of supposedly traditional "African life and customs."[24]

Du Bois's achievement was not of course created altogether *ex nihilo*. His account was not based on any detailed research of his own, nor indeed on any firsthand familiarity with Africa, which he did not visit for the first time until several years later in 1923. According to his own later account, he originally knew little of Africa and had assumed it "had no past"; his interest in African history was originally inspired when he heard a visiting lecture by the anthropologist Franz Boas at Atlanta University in 1906 which dealt with the "Black Sudan" (i.e., the Islamic empires of medieval West Africa)—by which, he says, "I was utterly amazed, and began to study Africa myself."[25]

For *The Negro*, Du Bois basically synthesized material he collected from available published sources. The range of his reading was impressive. It included a fair number of primary sources, in the form mainly of accounts by European explorers, traders, and missionaries (including such figures as Mungo Park and David Livingstone). This project of using European (and,

---

Self-Assertion and Brokerage: Early cultural nationalism in West Africa (Birmingham: Centre of West African Studies, University of Birmingham, 1990) 78–100.

[23] Reprinted in Hollis R. Lynch, *Black Spokesman: Selected Published Writings of Edward Wilmot Blyden* (London: Frank Cass, 1971) 141–57.

[24] Edward Wilmot Blyden, *African Life and Customs, Reprinted from "The Sierra Leone Weekly News"* (1908; repr., London: African Publication Society, 1969).

[25] Du Bois "The Future of Africa: Address to the All-African People's Conference, Accra [1958]," in *World and Africa*, 305–6. The lecture by Boas is presumably that listed in the bibliography of *Negro* as "Commencement Address (Atlanta University Leaflet, No. 19)."

in almost all cases, essentially Eurocentric) sources to reconstruct an Afrocentric African history of course raises problematic issues of methodology; but this approach is both unavoidable, given the general paucity of other categories of source material, and one that remains the basis of much work in precolonial history. Du Bois also incorporated, as far as he was able through available translations into European languages, Muslim Arabic sources such as the memoirs of the Andalusian traveler Ibn Battuta. These even included some material of internal African provenance, notably the seventeenth-century chronicle of Timbuktu by Abd al-Rahman al-Sadi, which had been published in a French translation in 1900.[26] On the other hand, Du Bois missed the histories based on local oral traditions that were beginning to be published by scholars in West Africa, such as the Reverend C. C. Reindorf in the Gold Coast (1895) and John O. George in Lagos (1897);[27] the only West African publication he cites, James Caseley Hayford's *Gold Coast Native Institutions* (1903), is not historical. In his defense, one can only assume that maybe this material did not circulate in the United States.

For the overall conceptualization, as opposed to the detailed empirical content, of his history of Africa, Du Bois had few earlier models to draw upon. As he himself observed in a note of "suggestions for further reading," there was no previous "general history of the Negro race." He observed that the man who "perhaps...has come as near covering the subject as any one writer" was the British colonial administrator Sir Harry Johnston in his various works on Africa, which he described as "valuable" although containing "puzzling inconstancies and inaccuracies."[28] Johnston, however, had adopted an imperial rather than an Africanist perspective, focusing on European activities in Africa, as explicitly expressed in the titles of two of his works which Du Bois explicitly cites: *A History of the Colonization of Africa by Alien Races* (1899) and *The Opening Up of Africa* (1911). His framework was therefore provided by successive waves of foreign colonizers/traders—Phoenicians, Greeks, Romans, Arabs, Portuguese, Dutch, English, French.

[26] However, the actual quotations of this work in *Negro* (54–55, 59, 62) are cited at secondhand, mainly from Lady Lugard's *A Tropical Dependency* (1906).

[27] See Paul Jenkins, ed., *The Recovery of the African Past: African pastors and African history in the nineteenth century* (Basel: Basler Afrika Bibliographien, 1998); Robin Law, "Early Yoruba historiography," *History in Africa* 3 (1976) 69–90.

[28] Du Bois, *Negro*, 244.

This did not, evidently, offer a suitable framework for the periodization of the history of Africans themselves.

There were, however, some earlier studies of particular regions within Africa that had established a local narrative framework. Most importantly, some European writers of the mid-nineteenth century had drawn upon Arabic sources to reconstruct the history of Islamic West Africa, including the generally undervalued work of W. D. Cooley, *The Negroland of the Arabs Examined* (1841), as well as the better-known writings of the German explorer Heinrich Barth, *Travels and Discoveries in Central Africa* (1857–1858).[29] It was presumably upon such works that Franz Boas drew in the 1906 lecture on the "Black Sudan" that so inspired Du Bois, and both are listed in the bibliography of *The Negro*. Some early colonial writers had also begun to use local Arabic sources to construct regional histories, notably, in the case of northern Nigeria, the British journalist and travel-writer Flora Shaw (later Lady Lugard) in *A Tropical Dependency* (1905), which Du Bois also cites in *The Negro*.

However, for the synthesis of such regional studies into a continental history, earlier literature is generally assumed to have provided little guidance. The received earlier view had been, in fact, that there was no African history to synthesize; for example, in 1767 the Scottish philosopher Adam Ferguson had observed that "the torrid zone," including Africa, "has furnished few materials for history."[30] More notoriously, the German philosopher G. W. F. Hegel, in his lectures on "The Philosophy of History," had offered the explicit declaration that "Africa...is no historical part of the world; it has no movement or development to exhibit...[it] is the Unhistorical, Undeveloped Spirit, still involved in the conditions of mere nature," which could be considered only as resting "on the threshold of the World's History."[31] Hegel sustained this view of the lack of history in Africa only by treating those African societies that did figure within his master narrative of world history, in northern or Mediterranean Africa—Carthage and ancient Egypt—as being not "really" African; the former (perhaps

---

[29] See the recent assessment emphasizing Cooley's contribution: Pekka Masonen, *The Negroland Revisited: Discovery and Invention of the Sudanese Middle Ages* (Helsinki: Finnish Academy of Science and Letters, 2000).

[30] Adam Ferguson, *An Essay on the History of Civil Society, 1767*, with intro. by Duncan Forbes (Edinburgh: Edinburgh University Press, 1966) pt. 3, sec. 1, 110.

[31] Georg Wilhelm Friedrich Hegel, *The Philosophy of History*, trans. J. Sibree, with intro. by C. J. Friedrich (New York: Dover Publications, 1956) 99.

reasonably) on the grounds of its being an alien colony, the latter (less clearly defensibly) as being also basically Asian. It should be stressed that Hegel's view (unlike Ferguson's) was not that Africa did not have a recoverable past. The first serious European attempt to reconstruct the history of a Tropical African society had in fact already been published before Hegel: *The History of Dahomy*, by the Scotsman Archibald Dalzel, appeared in 1793. Hegel was not only aware of this work but actually quoted it (though perhaps indirectly, through a summary or quotation in some intermediate source).[32] His argument was rather that, although there were "historical" events in Africa, there was not historical "development" in the sense of progressive change and such events had no connection with the mainstream of world history.

However, Du Bois was not in fact the first person to challenge this perspective and to insist that Africa did form part of the "historical world." The remainder of this essay, in fact, draws attention to two writers who anticipated Du Bois and whose work was clearly (from Du Bois's own evidence) known to him and indeed an inspiration and source of his own thinking: the English journalist and travel-writer Winwood Reade and the German ethnologist Leo Frobenius. Citing these writers in this context may appear controversial since they are not highly regarded by historians of Africa; indeed, it is likely that the generality of the latter would not only not accept these writers as intellectual ancestors but would indignantly repudiate them. Indeed, part of the purpose of this paper is, in addition to claiming for Du Bois the credit he deserves as a pioneer of African history, to use the cover of his authority to vindicate these earlier writers.

First, William Winwood Reade (1838–1875), is certainly familiar to at least some historians of Africa because he visited Western Africa on three occasions and wrote extensively about his experiences on the continent.[33] The writings best known are his *Savage Africa* (1863) and *African Sketchbook* (1873); he was also the *London Times* correspondent covering the Ashanti War of 1873–1874, an assignment that prompted a third book, *The Story of*

---

[32] See ibid., 97–98, for material derived from Dalzel; the imprecision of the reference (confusing the kingdoms of Dahomey and Oyo) suggests that it may have been accessed secondhand.

[33] See J. D. Hargreaves, "Winwood Reade and the discovery of Africa," *African Affairs* 56/225 (October, 1957): 306–16; George Shepperson, "Winwood Reade and Africa," in Roy Bridges, ed., *An African Miscellany for John Hargreaves* (Aberdeen: University of Aberdeen African Studies Group, 1983) 83–86.

the Ashanti Campaign (1874). These books are of course sometimes drawn upon as sources for detailed information; a brief extract from *Savage Africa* describing trading conditions in Bonny, for example, was included in a pioneering anthology of texts on African history by Basil Davidson.[34] But they are more likely to be cited as illustrations of European attitudes toward and perceptions of African societies and more particularly of the increasingly negative representation of African societies, informed by an increasingly virulent racialism, that characterized British writing during the second half of the nineteenth century; Reade is cited for his negative evaluation of African peoples and of their potential for future development.[35] Citation of Reade in this context seems to carry the implicit assumption that he was an apologist for European imperialism on the grounds that the progress of Africa would depend upon its being subjected to European colonial rule. But, in fact, Reade's attitude was rather more ambivalent than this; he was skeptical of the viability of European colonies in Tropical Africa and predicted its partition between "the British [i.e., Western-educated] Negroes" from the coast, the Muslim Africans from inner West Africa, and the white settlers from South Africa.[36]

Reade is therefore commonly cited as a proponent of racialism and an apologist for European imperialism, not as a pioneer of African, far less of Afrocentric, history. The case for the latter view rests not upon his travel writings about Africa, but on another of his books, *The Martyrdom of Man*, published in 1872.[37] This work is certainly read much less nowadays than in his own time, when it achieved at least a certain *succès de scandale*. It is seldom

---

[34] Basil Davidson, *The African Past: Chronicles from Antiquity to Modern Times* (Boston: Little Brown and Co., 1964) 350–51, describes Reade, benignly but inadequately, as "a radical-minded English landowner who traveled much in Africa and wrote books which were widely read."

[35] See, e.g., citations of Reade in V. G. Kiernan, *The Lords of Human Kind: European attitudes to the outside world in the imperial age* (1969; repr., Harmondsworth: Penguin Books 1972); Christine Bolt, *Victorian Attitudes to Race* (London: Routledge and Keegan Paul, 1971).

[36] See Winwood Reade, *The Martydom of Man*, with an introduction by F. Legge (London: The Rationalist Press, 1924) 317–18. It should be noted that Reade was writing (in 1872) in a context where it was still presumed that the existing British colonies in coastal West Africa might soon be granted self-government, as had been recommended by a parliamentary select committee in 1865.

[37] Frequently reprinted; cited here from the 1924 edition.

mentioned in relation to the development of African historiography—although (here again) a noted exception is George Shepperson.[38] Even now, after many years of my own missionary zeal, I still come across historians of Africa who have never heard of the work, far less read it.

The Martyrdom of Man is a text on world history, in Reade's own words "an outline of Universal history," a selective history of humanity from ancient Egypt to the present; the title expresses the idea that the historical progress of humanity has been achieved through human suffering. The work is divided into three thematic sections, which are also at least vaguely arranged in a chronological sequence: "War" (ancient Egypt to the Arab conquests), "Religion" (actually Judaism, Christianity, and Islam), and "Liberty" (from feudal Europe to the abolition of the slave trade and slavery, ending in 1865 with the conclusion of the American Civil War). A fourth section entitled "Intellect" comprises a rather abstract "brief summary of the whole" plus Reade's projection for the future, culminating in advocacy of the destruction of Christianity as an obstacle to man's future progress. At first sight, the text appears to be just another of the essays in "philosophical history" (in the original sense of that term) in the tradition of Hegel. At the time of its publication, what attracted attention was mainly its virulent hostility to Christianity, which led to charges of atheism at a time when this was still a shocking allegation to make (although technically Reade was not an atheist, he had an abstract rather than a personal conception of the Deity). From today's perspective, however, what is striking about the book—especially by comparison with earlier ventures in philosophical history—is the prominence of Africa within its conception of world history.

The account Reade gives of the origin of this book is that he had originally intended to write a history of Africa, but the work outgrew its originally projected parameters: "With respect to the present work, I commenced it intending to prove that Negroland or Inner Africa is not cut off from the main-stream of events as writers of philosophical history have always maintained."[39] Basically, his argument was that Egypt and Carthage

---

[38] In addition to his short 1983 essay "Winwood Reade and Africa," see earlier references in "African abroad," 158, and the introduction to the 1970 reprint of *Negro*, xvi-xvii. Shepperson, however gives the misleading impression that Reade's case for the contribution of Africa to "world history" related only to its role as a supplier of slaves to the Americas.

[39] Reade, *Martyrdon*, xlix.

"contributed much to human progress,"[40] the former by educating Greece (an idea that evidently survived later than Martin Bernal's recent work implies),[41] the latter by its role in the beginnings of Roman imperial expansion. Further, much of "Central" (i.e., Tropical) Africa was linked to Asiatic civilization through Islam; and coastal West Africa contributed, via the Atlantic slave trade, to the material progress of Europe and the Americas and also (through the campaign for its abolition) to their moral progress. Reade says, however, that he found that "In writing a history of Africa, I am compelled to write the history of the world, in order that Africa's true position may be defined."[42] More specifically:

> I could not describe the Negroland of ancient times without describing Egypt and Carthage. From Egypt I was drawn to Asia and to Greece, from Carthage I was drawn to Rome. That is the first chapter...Next, having to relate the progress of the Mahometans in Central Africa, it was necessary for me to explain the nature and origin of Islam; but that religion cannot be understood without a previous study of Christianity and Judaism, and those religions cannot be understood without a study of religion among savages. That is the second chapter...Thirdly, I sketched the history of the slave-trade, which took me back to the discoveries of the Portuguese, the glories of Venetian commerce, the Revival of the Arts, the Dark Ages, and the Invasion of the Germans....[43]

The result is a world history in which Africa bulks large and from which a sketch of specifically African history can be readily extracted.

Admittedly this is at base an externally focused perspective on African history. Although Egypt and Ethiopia are claimed for Africa, it is assumed that they had little impact on Tropical Africa; furthermore, the latter was

---

[40] Ibid., 130.

[41] Martin Bernal, *The Fabrication of Ancient Greece, 1785–1985*, vol. 1 of *Black Athena: The Afroasiatic roots of Classical civilization* (New Brunswick NJ: Rutgers University Press, 1987). Note also the later argument of the explorer and pioneer anthropologist (and friend of Winwood Reade) Richard Burton, although commonly accounted a racialist and Negrophobe, that not only did "civilisation" originate from Egypt but also that "the ancient Egyptians were Africans, and pure Africans [i.e., Negroes]," *The Book of the Sword* (1884; repr., New York:Dover Publications, 1987) 143–44.

[42] Reade, *Martyrdom*, 132–33.

[43] Ibid., xlix–l.

linked to the mainstream of history essentially passively, as the recipient of Islam and a supplier of slaves. But that aside, Reade's representation of the history of Africa is characterized, like that of Du Bois, by a combination of chronological sequence and shifting geographical focus, beginning with Mediterranean Africa in ancient times, then shifting to the Muslim empires of the West African interior during medieval times, and finally ending with the Atlantic coast of Africa and the societies that were drawn into the Atlantic slave trade in the modern era. The parallel with Du Bois's vision is evident, and is probably more than mere coincidence, since Du Bois was certainly familiar with Reade's work.

In *The Negro* Du Bois quotes Reade, although only once, casually and without particular emphasis;[44] but in his later book *The World and Africa*, he makes more extensive citations. He seems to have drawn upon Reade principally with regard to Egypt and Ethiopia. He also utilized his work critically, or at least selectively, in particular rejecting Reade's view that the Nile valley civilizations had no connection with or influence upon sub-Saharan Africa. But in the later work, Du Bois refers to Reade in extravagantly approving terms: "One always turns back to Winwood Reade's *The Martyrdom of Man* for renewal of faith."[45] This formula suggests more than merely detailed empirical borrowings and supports the conclusion that Du Bois owed to Reade a significant intellectual debt.

Second, and more importantly, Leo Frobenius (1873–1935), was a distinguished pioneer of historical ethnology in Germany, who was in particular the principal discoverer of the famous brass and terracotta sculptures of the Yoruba kingdom of Ife (in Southwestern Nigeria), which he visited in 1910. Frobenius also is not usually highly regarded by historians of Africa; or, at least, to the extent that his work is judged to retain any value, it is normally only for the detailed empirical data he recorded, his "observations" rather than his "conclusions."[46] His most important and influential work was *Und Afrika Sprach* (1912), published in English translation the following year as *The Voice of Africa*.[47] This work is chiefly

---

[44] Du Bois, *Negro*, 18.

[45] Du Bois, *World and Africa*, x.

[46] See, e.g., J. M. Ita, "Frobenius in West African history," *Journal of African History* 13/4 (1972) 673–88.

[47] Leo Frobenius, *The Voice of Africa, being an account of the travels of the German Inner Africa Expedition in the years 1910–1912*, 2 vols. (1913; repr., New York: Arno Press, 1980).

remembered nowadays for its pioneering treatment of the archaeology and
art of Ife; yet it also dealt at length with the interior of West Africa,
especially its political institutions, including an influential model of "divine
kingship." Frobenius attributed the origin of this political tradition to
migration from Christian Nubia in the early seventh century CE. This
interpretation was based mainly on the traditions current widely in parts of
West Africa deriving the ancestry of their royal dynasties (and thus by
implication the origins of their institutions) from an ancestor called Kisra,
usually assumed to be derived from the Persian emperor Chosroes.
However, for the specific case of Yorubaland, Frobenius posited a different
(although also external) derivation, explaining the stylistic naturalism of its
art by the hypothesis of an ancient Etruscan maritime colonization of West
Africa (at some time prior to the thirteenth century BCE), also for good
measure identifying ancient Yorubaland with the legendary land of Atlantis.

This diffusionist explanation is nowadays regularly dismissed as
reflecting Frobenius's racial prejudice and support for European
colonialism. But this seems to me an anachronistic, or at least incomplete,
reading. In fact, the diffusionist model at this time was applied to human
history very generally, not to African history alone: for example, in Britain,
Stonehenge was also often supposed to have been built by ancient Egyptians
or Phoenicians.[48] Of course, diffusionism could readily be given a racist
twist, since attribution of the origins of anything that was thought
significant or praiseworthy in African history to foreign immigrants, could
be used to deny historical initiative and, by implication, potential for future
development to indigenous Africans, implicitly justifying European
imperialism. However, this was not a necessary implication of diffusionism,
and it is questionable whether it applies to the case of Frobenius. In fact, it is
clear that Frobenius himself saw the significance of his discoveries quite
otherwise. He presented his work as proving not that Africans had no record
of historical achievement but that Tropical Africa had a recoverable history
that, contrary to the then-dominant assumption (reproduced even by
Winwood Reade),[49] extended back into the pre-Islamic period—that is, a

---

[48] For the dominance of hyper-diffusionism (often in Egyptocentric versions) in early
archaeological thought, see, e.g., Glyn Daniel, *The First Civilizations: The archaeology
of their origins* (Harmondsworth: Penguin Books, 1971) 169–71.

[49] See Reade, *Martyrdom*, 130: "with the invasion of the Arabs the proper history of
[sub-Saharan] Africa begins."

vindication rather than a denial of Africa's place in history. As he himself observed in the conclusion to *The Voice of Africa*: "We no longer see a Continent which lay beyond the reach of interest in the history of the world, in a state of deplorable apathy, asleep to progress and dreaming its life away. What we see is that the African and his civilization are an important factor in transmitting forms of culture. The quickening pulse of universal history in Europe and Asia…had its echo in the hearts of African humanity."[50]

Here again, the work of Frobenius was evidently well-known to Du Bois, who cited *The Voice of Africa* extensively in *The Negro*. In his later work *The World and Africa*, Du Bois also cited a later work of Frobenius, the *History of African Civilization*, which was never available in English but was quoted from a 1936 French translation.[51] Du Bois did not treat Frobenius uncritically; in *The Negro* he characterized his identification of Yorubaland with Atlantis as "perhaps fanciful" and the derivation of its civilization from overseas as "far-fetched."[52] But Du Bois's citations of Frobenius are generally very positive. He cites Frobenius not only for detailed empirical material but also, explicitly, for his assertion that Africa had to be considered part of world history and as demonstrating the pre-Islamic origins, and hence by implication the "African" (rather than "Arab") character, of the civilizations of the West African interior.[53] In *The Negro* Du Bois commends Frobenius's work as "broad-minded and informing."[54] In the later *World and Africa* Du Bois offered what can only be called an encomium: "Frobenius is not popular among conventional historians or anthropologists…but he was a great man and a great thinker. He looked upon Africa with unprejudiced eyes and has been more valuable for the interpretation of the Negro than any other man I know." He characterized him, indeed, as no less than "this greatest student of Africa."[55]

Of course, Du Bois was selective in the use he made of Frobenius, as of Reade—obscuring for example the fact that Frobenius regarded the Yoruba as only "degenerate" successors of a high civilization and ignoring his

---

[50] Frobenius, *Voice of Africa*, ii, 680.

[51] Leo Frobenius, *Kulturgeschichte Afrikas* (Cultural History of Africa) (Zurich: Phaedon, 1933); *Histoire de la civilisation africaine* (History of African Civilization) (Paris: Gallimard, 1936).

[52] Du Bois, *Negro*, 63, 65.

[53] Ibid., 10, 49–50. Cf. Du Bois, *World and Africa*, 201.

[54] Du Bois, *Negro*, 244.

[55] Du Bois, *World and Africa*, x-xi, 79n22.

virulently derogatory remarks about Western-educated Africans. And likewise of course, we tend today to be equally selective in our use and evaluation of Du Bois himself. Robert Gregg, for example, interprets Du Bois's references in *The Negro* to racial mixture and the ambiguity of racial distinctions to present him as anticipating the view of race as a social construction,[56] which is perhaps a legitimate reading of the text but certainly a selective one that ignores for example Du Bois's obsessive interest in identifying Negroid features on Egyptian and other ancient monuments as proof of a biological Negro contribution to ancient civilizations. Likewise, I have highlighted the features of his representation of African history that seem to be progressive, in the sense of being congruent with later perceptions and priorities, and by implication dismissing those less congenial as reflecting only the general limitations of his age. But it is surely a legitimate exercise thus to contextualize any thinker, in order to distinguish the respects in which he was innovative from those in which he remained entrapped in contemporary limitations; just as Du Bois extended the generosity of this contextualization to Winwood Reade and Leo Frobenius, so we can and should extend it to him.

Works Cited

Bernal, Martin. *Black Athena: The Afroasiatic roots of Classical civilization.* Volume 1 of *The Fabrication of Ancient Greece, 1785–1985.* New Brunswick NJ: Rutgers University Press, 1987.

Blyden, Edward Wilmot. *African Life and Customs, Reprinted from "The Sierra Leone Weekly News".* 1908; repr. London, African Publication Society, 1969.

Bolt, Christine. *Victorian Attitudes to Race.* London: Routledge and K. Paul, 1971.

Bridges, Roy, editor. *An African Miscellany for John Hargreaves.* University of Aberdeen African Studies Group, 1983.

Burton, Richard F. *The Book of the Sword.* 1884; repr. New York: Dover Publications, 1987.

Curtin, Philip D. *The Atlantic Slave Trade: A census.* Madison: University of Wisconsin Press, 1969.

---

[56] Gregg, afterword to Du Bois, *Negro*, 264–67.

Daniel, Glyn. *The First Civilizations: The archaeology of their origins.* Harmondsworth: Penguin, 1971.

Davidson, Basil. *Old Africa Rediscovered.* London: Gollancz, 1959.

———. *The African Past: Chronicles from Antiquity to Modern Times.* Boston: Little, Brown & Co., 1964.

de Moraes Farias, P. F., and Karin Barber, editors. *Self-Assertion and Brokerage: Early cultural nationalism in West Africa.* Birmingham: Centre of West African Studies, University of Birmingham, 1990.

Du Bois, *Black Folk Then and Now: An essay in the history and sociology of the Negro Race.* 1939; repr. New York: Monthly Review Press, 1975.

--------. *The Negro.* New York/London: Home University Library of Modern Knowledge, 1915.

———. *The World and Africa: An inquiry into the part which Africa has played in world history.* Enlarged edition. 1965. Reprint, 1992].

Fage, J. D. "Continuity and Change in the Writing of West African history." *African Affairs* 70/282 (July 1971): 236–51.

———. "The Prehistory of African History." *Paideuma* 19/20 (1973/4): 146–61.

Ferguson, Adam. *An Essay on the History of Civil Society, 1767.* Edinburgh: Edinburgh University Press, 1966.

Frobenius, Leo. *The Voice of Africa, being an account of the travels of the German Inner Africa Expedition in the years 1910–1912.* 2 volumes. 1913. Reprint, New York: Aron Press, 1980.

Hair, P. E. H. "Ethnolinguistic continuity on the Guinea Coast', *Journal of African History*, vol.8, no.2 (1967), 247-68.

Hansberry, William Leo. "W. E. B. Du Bois's influence on African history." *Freedomways* 5 (1965): 73–87.

Hargreaves, J. D. "Winwood Reade and the Discovery of Africa." *African Affairs* 56/225 (October 1957): 306–16.

Hegel, Georg Wilhelm Friedrich. *The Philosophy of History.* Translated by J. Sibree. New York: Dover Publications, 1956.

Ita, J. M. "Frobenius in West African History." *Journal of African History* 13/4 (1972): 673–88.

Jedrej, Charles, Kenneth King, and Jack Thompson, editors. *Rethinking African History.* Edinburgh: Centre of African Studies, University of Edinburgh, 1997.

Jenkins, Paul, editor. *The Recovery of the African Past: African Pastors and African History in the Nineteenth Century*. Basel: Basler Afrika Bibliographien, 1998.

Johnson, J. C. deGraft. *African Glory: The Story of the Vanished Negro Civilizations*. London: Watts, 1954.

Kiernan, V. G. *The Lords of Human Kind: European Attitudes to the Outside World in the Imperial Age*. 1969. Reprint, Harmondsworth: Penguin, 1972.

Kirk-Greene, A. H. M., editor. *The Emergence of African History at British Universities: An Autobiographical Approach*. Oxford: Worldview Publications, 1995.

Law, Robin. "Early Yoruba Historiography." *History in Africa* 3 (1976): 69–89.

Lewis, David Levering. *W. E. B. Du Bois: Biography of a Race, 1868–1919*. New York: Henry Holt, 1993.

Lynch, Hollis R. *Black Spokesman: Selected Published Writings of Edward Wilmot Blyden*. London: Frank Cass, 1971.

Mann, Kristin, and Edna G. Bay, editors. *Rethinking the African Diaspora: The Making of a Black Atlantic World in the Bight of Benin and Brazil*. London and Portland: Frank Cass Publishers, 2001.

Masonen, Pekka. *The Negroland Revisited: Discovery and Invention of the Sudanese Middle Ages*. Helsinki: Finnish Academy of Science and Letters, 2000.

Ranger, T. O., editor. Emerging Themes of African History: Proceedings of the International Conference of African Historians held at University College, Dar es Salaam, October 1965. London: Heinemann Educational Books, 1968.

Reade, Winwood. *The Martyrdom of Man*, with an intro. by F.Legge. London: The Rationalist Press, 1924.

Winks, Robin W., editor. *Historiography*. Volume 5 of *The Oxford History of the British Empire*. Oxford: Oxford University Press, 1999.

Religious Animals, Refuge of the Gods, and the Spirit of Revolt: W. E. B Du Bois's Representations of Indigenous African Religion

David Chidester

In *Souls of Black Folk*, W. E. B. Du Bois insisted that the religious life of African Americans did not begin in America because it was built on "definite historical foundations," the religious heritage of Africa. Characterizing indigenous African Religion as "nature worship," with its incantations, sacrifices, and attention to good and evil spiritual influences, Du Bois invoked the African priest as both the guardian of African religious tradition and the mediator of religious change under slavery in America. As a result of colonization, passage, and enslavement, African social formations were destroyed, "yet some traces were retained of the former group life," Du Bois observed, "and the chief remaining institution was the Priest or Medicine-man." With the destruction of established African social relations of kinship and political sovereignty, which bore their own religious significance in Africa, the African priest represented a relatively mobile, transportable focus of religious life. Assuming multiple roles, operating as bard, physician, judge, and priest, the African ritual specialist "early appeared on the plantation and found his function as the healer of the sick, the interpreter of the Unknown, the comforter of the sorrowing, the supernatural avenger of wrong, and the one who rudely but picturesquely expressed the longing, disappointment, and resentment of a stolen and oppressed people." In these evocative terms, Du Bois recalled the creativity of the African priest, who deployed indigenous African religious resources under radically altered conditions.

Although the religion of the African priest came to be known by different names, such as "vodooism" or "obi-worship," Du Bois provocatively proposed that another name eventually adopted in America for indigenous African religion was "Christianity." Within the limits of the slave system, but also within the space opened by the African priest, "rose the Negro preacher, and under him the first Afro-American institution, the Negro Church." According to Du Bois, this church, in the first instance, was not Christian but African, since it only placed a "veneer of Christianity" upon the ongoing adaptation of indigenous African beliefs and practices under slavery. Suggesting that the Christianization of indigenous African religion should be regarded as a gradual process of religious transformation, Du Bois observed that "after the lapse of many generations the Negro church became Christian." In reviewing the "faith of the fathers" in *Souls of Black Folk*, Du Bois sought to establish a basic continuity in religious life from Africa to African America. The "study of Negro religion," he insisted, had to carefully track a transatlantic process of religious development "through its gradual changes from the heathenism of the Gold Coast to the institutional Negro Church in Chicago," which began with indigenous African religion. [1]

I want to look more closely at Du Bois' handling of the "definite historical foundations" of African religion. Among his many interests, Du Bois was an African historian. During the long course of his life, he took up the challenge of providing general historical overviews of Africa and the African diaspora in five books, *The Negro* (1915), *Africa: Its Place in Modern History* (1930), *Black Folk: Then and Now* (1939), *The World and Africa* (1947), and *Africa: An Essay Toward a History of the Continent of Africa and Its Inhabitants* (1963). Certainly, Du Bois's interest in writing these books was not strictly or merely historical, although his wide reading enabled him to synthesize a diverse range of historical and ethnographic sources into coherent narratives. In the process of providing accounts of African history, Du Bois engaged the African past as a basis for forging a Pan-African future. Looking back in order to look forward, Du Bois concluded his earliest account of African history in *The Negro* with the promise that the "future

---

[1] W. E. B. Du Bois, *The Souls of Black Folk* (1902; reprint, New York: Vintage Books, 1990) 141–42, 139.

world will, in all reasonable probability, be what colored men make it."[2] All of his histories of Africa were similarly focused on the African future.

In reconstructing the religious history of Africa, Du Bois had to have been tempted by prevailing forms of racial, ethnic, territorial, or geopolitical essentialism about Africans, African Americans, and the "dark continent" of Africa. Occasionally, he seems to have given in to those temptations. In *Souls of Black Folk*, he suggested that African Americans could essentially be defined by their inherent religiosity because the Negro is "a religious animal."[3] In his earliest historical overview of Africa, *The Negro*, he suggested that Africa is essentially a religious continent, the "refuge of the gods."[4] Reinforcing assumptions about wild Africans, the "religious animal," from the "refuge of the gods," he proposed that when their religion was transposed to America it inspired a "spirit of revolt."[5] As I hope to show, however, Du Bois's efforts to understand the role of indigenous African religion in Africa and the African diaspora went far beyond such essentialist stereotypes. By wrestling with the dilemma of representing indigenous African religion, Du Bois raised crucial issues for the study of religion in Africa and African religion in the Americas that remain salient and urgent.

By tracking the development of Du Bois's representations of indigenous African religion, I want to highlight three problems—humanity, divinity, and transatlantic continuity—that will recur in his historical overviews of Africa. These problems will appear under different terms in what follows, but they recur nonetheless. Put simply: Du Bois might have characterized the African as a "religious animal," but he also argued that Africans, enslaved, were dehumanized by being rendered as less than animals, since they were commodified as material objects, as trade goods in a capitalist economy. This is the problem of fetishism.

Du Bois might have referred to Africa as the "refuge of the gods," but he singled out one African deity, the Yoruba God Shango, as the exemplar of an African divinity, more powerful, he asserted, than any other, who certified political sovereignty. This is the problem of theology.

Du Bois might have suggested that indigenous African religion, transposed to the Americas, evoked a "spirit of revolt," but he became

---

[2] W. E. B. Du Bois, *The Negro* (New York: Henry Holt and Company, 1915) 242.

[3] Du Bois, *Souls*, 143.

[4] Du Bois, *Negro*, 9.

[5] Du Bois, *Souls*, 143.

increasingly skeptical of the efficacy of African religion in advancing revolutionary political projects either in America or in Africa. Despite academic interests in transatlantic continuity or discontinuity, with deference to positions associated with Herskovits or Frazier, this political problem with African language, culture, and religion is the problem of diaspora.[6]

In what follows, I explore these problems of humanity, divinity, and transatlantic continuity in Du Bois' historical writings about Africa. Tracing the shifts in his representations of indigenous African religion from 1915 to 1947, with some surprising effects, I hope to revisit the challenges he raised for our thinking about the role of religion not only in our representations of the past but also in our projects for the future.

The Negro

As a significant part of African cultural heritage, the indigenous religious life of Africa featured in *The Negro*. In his discussion of African religion, Du Bois seemed concerned with three things: the meaning of the fetish, the belief in God, and the continuity between the indigenous religion of Africa and African-American religion across the Atlantic.

Initially, Du Bois adopted a social evolutionary framework to account for religious development. Borrowing familiar terms from the scientific study of "savage" or "primitive" religion, Du Bois maintained that the "religion of Africa is the universal animism or fetishism of primitive peoples, rising to polytheism and approaching monotheism chiefly, but not wholly, as a result of Christian and Islamic missions."[7] By adopting the terms "animism" and "fetishism," Du Bois seemed to align his inquiry into African religion with the interests of European theorists who had been searching for the origin of religion in the fetishist's worship of material objects or the animist's attribution of spiritual life, agency, and power to material objects. A variety of evolutionary schemes, from Auguste Comte to E. B. Tylor, had identified this "primitive" religious materialism, whether characterized as fetishism, animism, or totemism, as the origin of religion.[8] For evidence of

---

[6] Melville J. Herskovits, *The Myth of the Negro Past* (New York: Harper & Brothers, 1941); E. Franklin Frazier, *The Negro Church in America* (New York: Shocken, 1963).

[7] Du Bois, *Negro*, 124.

[8] Eric J. Sharpe, *Comparative Religion: A History*, 2d ed. (La Salle IL: Open Court, 1986) 47–71; Edmund Leach, "Anthropology and Religion: British and French Schools,"

this "primitive" origin, they looked to reports by European travelers, traders, missionaries, and colonial agents about "savages" in Africa, the Americas, Asia, Australia, and the Pacific Islands. Through a remarkable intellectual sleight of hand, European theorists used reports about their living contemporaries, these "savages" on the colonized peripheries, as if they were evidence of the original "primitive" ancestors of all humanity. In the process, they speculated about an evolutionary trajectory, beginning in fetishism, that left both "primitives" and "savages" behind in the developmental process of human progress.[9]

Popular accounts of fetishism, however, did not always place the fetish at the origin of evolutionary progress. By stark contrast, European politicians, journalists, and especially Christian missionaries often represented fetishism not as the beginning of human evolution but as the end of human degeneration. For example, one of Du Bois's sources, the American Presbyterian missionary Robert Hamill Nassau, who had spent forty years in West Africa, insisted that fetishism was the primary cause of African degradation. In his monograph, *Fetichism of West Africa*, published in 1904, Nassau maintained that the fetish stood at the center of African religion. Fetishism, in Nassau's rendering, was a superstitious regard for the power of insignificant material objects that wove witchcraft and sorcery into every aspect of African thought, government, family, work, and daily life. Although meaningless, according to Nassau, the fetish nevertheless produced disastrous practical effects, leading to distrust, poisoning, secret societies, cannibalism, and depopulation, which effectively degraded Africans.[10]

Although he briefly deferred to an evolutionary theory of religion with the fetish at its origin, Du Bois seemed more concerned with countering this missionary account of Africa's fetishistic degradation. As if he were responding directly to Nassau's accusation, Du Bois sought to rehabilitate

---

in Ninian Smart et al., eds., *Nineteenth-Century Religious Thought in the West*, 3 vols. (Cambridge: Cambridge University Press, 1985) 3:215–62.

[9] Johannes Fabian, *Time and the Other: How Anthropology Makes Its Object* (New York: Columbia University Press, 1983).

[10] Robert Hamill Nassau, *Fetichism in West Africa: Forty Years' Observation of Native Customs and Superstitions* (New York: Scribner, 1904). See also Stephen Steptimus Farrow, *Faith, Fancies, and Fetich: or, Yoruba Paganism: Being Some Account of the Religious Beliefs of the West African Negroes, particularly of the Yoruba Tribe of Southern Nigeria* (Brooklyn: Athelia Henrietta Press, 1996).

the fetish. "It is not mere senseless degradation," he insisted. "It is a philosophy of life."[11] Instead of rendering fetishism as superstitious regard for material objects, he recast the fetish as the material focus of an indigenous African philosophy. According to Du Bois, the fetish represented both a logical and practical recognition of the dynamic forces of life, the positive and negative spiritual conditions within which Africans lived. "Fetish is a severely logical way of accounting for the world in terms of good and malignant spirits," he asserted.[12] Amplified by reports about the material spirituality of the Ewe of West Africa and the Xhosa of South Africa, Du Bois's account of fetishism placed the fetish in a positive light.[13] In recovering an African history of the fetish, therefore, Du Bois in 1915 suggested that fetishism was not superstitious ignorance, fear, or fraud but a coherent material philosophy of the spiritual dynamics of life.

Reinterpreting the fetish, however, was not sufficient to demonstrate that indigenous Africans had their own religion. Africans also believed in God. In this respect, Du Bois found the Yoruba as his privileged example of Africans who not only believed in God but also made that divinity the foundation of organized political life and state building. In *The Negro*, however, Du Bois deferred to the testimony of European reporters to establish indigenous African belief in God. "The African has a Great Over God," the explorer Mary Kingsley observed.[14] No matter how superstitious Africans might be, the missionary Robert Hamill Nassau found, "I do not need to begin by telling them that there is a God."[15] In Du Bois's account of indigenous African religion, European observers—the explorer, the missionary—were invoked as authorities on the indigenous theology of Africa. Effectively, they certified that Africans believed in God.

In the light of the evolutionary theory of religion Du Bois had cited, this assertion that Africans were not merely fetishists or animists but also theists was surprising. Supposedly representing a more advanced stage in the

---

[11] Du Bois, *Negro*, 124. On missionary theories of African religious degeneration, see David Chidester, *Savage Systems: Colonialism and Comparative Religion in Southern Africa* (Charlottesville: University Press of Virginia, 1996) 89–92.

[12] Du Bois, *Negro*, 125.

[13] See chapter 8 of *The Negro*, "African Culture," for Du Bois's discussion of the Ewe concept of "Kra," the immortal power of life, and the Xhosa concentration on the power of the dead to help or harm the living.

[14] Mary H. Kingsley, *West African Studies*, 2d ed. (London: Macmillan, 1901) 107.

[15] Nassau, *Fetichism*, 36.

development of religion, belief in God should not have mixed so easily with the earlier stage of religion's supposed origin. Perhaps by juxtaposing fetishism and theism, not in opposition but in counterpoint, Du Bois was working to undermine the developmental premises of religious evolution. As both material philosophy and spiritual theology, African religion could not so easily be claimed as the point of origin for the evolutionary progression of all humanity. Instead, African religion could be recovered as a different kind of origin for the development of the material and spiritual life of Africans in America.

Nevertheless, in *The Negro* Du Bois clearly relied upon the reports of outsiders—the European explorer, the Euroamerican missionary—to certify the existence of an indigenous African God. Certainly, such witnesses were problematic, since they were entangled in a complex history of repression, translation, and representation. Although searching for the "unknown God" all over the world, they often reported that such a deity was absent in Africa. In Southern Africa, for example, explorers and missionaries frequently testified to the absence of any belief in God among the Khoisan, the Xhosa, the Zulu, the Sotho-Tswana, and other people in the region.[16] The lack of African belief in God, as well as the absence of any trace of indigenous African religion, was reported by Richard Burton in the lake regions of central Africa, by James Grant on his "walk across Africa," and by René Caillié on his "travels to Timbuctoo."[17] Arguably, these insistent denials of religion, these recurring discoveries of religious absence, fit with broader colonial projects in representing Africa as an empty space for conquest and colonization. With no God, these denials seemed to suggest, Africans lacked any transcendent claim to political sovereignty.

In his handling of belief in God in *The Negro*, Du Bois seemed to recognize this link between theology and polity, observing briefly, in passing, that the Yoruba believed in a God who established the basis for royalty, sovereignty, and independent statehood. Nevertheless, he emphasized the authority of Kingsley and Nassau, the independent

[16] Chidester, *Savage Systems*, 39, 41, 47, 52, 88, 75, 78, 94, 96, 103, 120, 180–81, 190.

[17] Richard Burton, *Lake Regions of Central Africa*, 2 vols. (London: Longman, Green, Longman, and Roberts, 1860) 2:341–57; James Augustus Grant, *A Walk Across Africa; or Domestic Scenes from my Nile Journal* (Edinburgh: W. Blackwood, 1864) 145; René Caillié, *Travels through Central Africa to Timbuctoo*, 2 vols. (London: Colburn and Bentley, 1830) 1:303.

witnesses, in certifying indigenous African understandings of deity. Relying upon these reports, Du Bois was able to establish that belief in God was an indigenous feature of African religion that was not necessarily introduced by Muslim or Christian missions. Although he reviewed the importance of these missionizing religions in Africa, Du Bois appeared to regard them primarily as a disruption of African life, noting, for example, that the modern slave trade coincided with "the greatest expansion of two of the world's most pretentious religions."[18] Between the practical philosophy of the fetish and belief in God, however, African religion had its own integrity.

Crossing the Atlantic, Du Bois argued in *The Negro* for a basic continuity between African indigenous religion and African-American religion. In the transportation from Africa, the indigenous priest, responsible for religion and healing, carried that continuity. As he had proposed in *Souls of Black Folk*, Du Bois asserted in his account of African religion in *The Negro* that the African priest, even within the alien, alienating environment of the plantation system, continued to function as "the interpreter of the supernatural, the comforter of the sorrowing, and as the one who expressed, rudely but picturesquely, the longing and disappointment and resentment of a stolen people."[19] Not only transporting African religion across the middle passage, the priest also created a free space for transposing indigenous religious resources, even translating them into Christian terms.

Again, Du Bois held that the Black Church, "the first distinctively Negro American social institution," emerged directly from these indigenous African religious resources. "It was not at first by any means a Christian church," Du Bois insisted, "but a mere adaptation of those rites of fetish which in America is termed obe worship, or 'voodooism.'" Similar arguments of African continuity had been advanced. In his analysis of the fetish, for example, the missionary Robert Hamill Nassau had also proposed a direct continuity between Africa and America, but he complained that the religion of the fetish, "the evil thing that the slave brought with him," not only endured but actually grew under slavery.[20] Against the background of his rehabilitation of the fetish, however, Du Bois proposed that fetishism

---

[18] Du Bois, *Negro*, 150. For his overview of Muslim and Christian missions, see 128–30.

[19] Du Bois, *Negro*, 113.

[20] Nassau, *Fetichism*, 36.

was not an "evil thing" but the authentic religious inheritance from Africa. The philosophy of fetishism, with its attention to material signs of good and evil forces, provided the solid foundation for African religious life. Although eventually covered by a "veneer of Christianity," Du Bois argued, "the Negro church of to-day bases itself upon the sole surviving institution of the African fatherland," the indigenous religion of the fetish.[21]

Clearly, this formulation of transatlantic African religious continuity was important to Du Bois. With slight modification of phrasing, but almost word for word, the same account appeared in *Souls of Black Folk* (1903), *Negro Church* (1903), and even a section on historical background for a Carnegie-funded report, *Economic Co-operation among Negro Americans* (1907).[22] When he came to write his first history of Africa in *The Negro* (1915), Du Bois integrated this same account of African religion, tracing the essential religious continuity from African fetishism to African Christianity.

Although he certainly was not trying to advance a general theory of religion, Du Bois's intervention in representations of indigenous African religion carried significant implications for the history of religions. Poised between the evolutionary theory of religious progress and the missionary theory of religious degeneration, Du Bois's handling of the history of African religion could not be contained within either theoretical model. Implicitly, he challenged both the scientific evolutionists and the Christian missiologists. On the one hand, by attempting to rehabilitate fetishism as a viable material philosophy, he challenged the social evolutionary model that postulated a developmental trajectory from primitive fetishism to the modern material philosophy of science. On the other hand, by representing the Christian conversion of Africans in America as a veneer placed over the indigenous African religion of the fetish, he suggested that Christianization represented not progress but degeneration of authentic African religion. In either case, Du Bois placed indigenous African religion in a different kind of history, neither a speculative evolutionary history nor a missionary faith history, which he outlined in *The Negro* as a basic continuity, despite the radical disrupture of slavery, in fetishism, the material philosophy of spiritual influences.

---

[21] Ibid., 188–89.

[22] Du Bois, *Souls*, 142; *The Negro Church* (Atlanta: Atlanta University Press, 1903) 5–6; *Economic Co-operation among Negro Americans* (Atlanta: Atlanta University Press, 1907) 24; *Negro*, 188–89.

Black Folk

Nearly twenty-five years later, Du Bois substantially revised and expanded his earlier account of African history in *The Negro* for publication as *Black Folk: Then and Now* (1939). With respect to African indigenous religion, his discussion in *Black Folk* remained largely unchanged from his treatment of fetishism and God in *The Negro*, except for one dramatic alteration. Removing the explorer Kingsley and the missionary Nassau, who had reported on West African beliefs in God, Du Bois introduced the Yoruba God, Shango. Through this intervention, he effectively dismissed the authority of alien observers, however much they might have served his interests earlier, in preference for a direct appearance, almost a theophany in the text, of an indigenous African deity. No European explorer or Euroamerican missionary, he seemed to be saying in this erasure of Kingsley and Nassau, is necessary to certify the meaning and power of an indigenous African God. Shango, as he appears in *Black Folk*, is sufficiently powerful to display his own meaning in indigenous African religion. In place of alien authority, therefore, Du Bois in this account presented Shango.

In Yoruba religion, Shango (or Sango) is God of thunder and lightning. As the deity of such awesome heavenly power, Shango has been recognized as comparable to other West African gods, such as So among the Ewe or Ga among the Gua, but in Yoruba tradition Shango has also been regarded as a historical figure, the fourth king of Oyo, a dynasty that extended from Benin to Dahomey. As king, Shango discovered a ritual technique to summon lightning, but when he deployed this technique, the lightning destroyed his house and killed his family. In the aftermath of this destruction, Shango left the world, according to different accounts killing himself, ascending to the heavens, or descending under the earth, to control the spiritual forces of thunder and lightning. Besides exercising this heavenly power, Shango reinforced political authority in the world. Yoruba kings of Oyo, according to this tradition, could be traced back through a royal lineage to Shango. Within the priesthood of Shango, the head priest was responsible for initiating kings into the mysteries of this tradition. Synchronizing religion and politics, Shango stood as a transcendent deity of power among the Yoruba.[23]

In *Black Folk*, Du Bois introduced Shango as an African God of Thunder who "soars above the legend of Thor and Jahweh," thereby transcending the power of the European and Semitic thunder-gods. This assertion of the preeminence of an African God over the deities of Indo-European and Semitic tradition was a remarkable claim. During the nineteenth-century debates over what should be regarded as the original language, culture, and religion, biblically based assumptions about the preeminence of ancient Israel contended with new scholarly formulations of the priority of ancient Indo-European societies. Stretching from ancient Ireland to India, the Indo-European, Indo-Iranian, or Aryan represented a cultural zone that could be recovered in direct opposition to the Semitic culture of the Bible. As Maurice Olender has shown, defenders of Indo-European and Semitic origins asserted competing claims regarding not only human prehistory but also establishing access to the original "language of Paradise."[24] Almost casually, Du Bois dismissed this entire controversy by introducing Shango. Soaring above the Indo-European and Semitic deities, this indigenous African God left them far behind. By bringing Shango into the revised history of Africa that formed the text of *Black Folk*, therefore, Du Bois dismissed both alien authorities like Kingsley and Nassau and alien deities like Thor and Jahweh from his account of indigenous African religion.

As a textual effect, the introduction of Shango in *Black Folk* is also startling. Seeming to appear from nowhere, inserted as an unreferenced quotation, Shango simply registers as a force. Bringing death, giving life, causing fear, inspiring love—Shango is devastating and invigorating. Without providing any indication of the source of this profile of Shango, Du Bois announced the transcendent power of the African God: "He is the Hurler of thunderbolts, the Lord of the Storm, the God who burns down compounds and cities, the Render of trees and the Slayer of men; cruel and savage, yet splendid and beneficent in his unbridled action. For the floods

---

[23] William R. Bascom, *The Yoruba of Southwestern Nigeria* (New York: Holt, Rinehart & Winston, 1969); *Shango in the New World* (Austin: African and Afro-American Research Institute, University of Texas, 1972).

[24] Maurice Olender, *The Languages of Paradise: Race, Religion, and Philology in the Nineteenth Century*, trans. Arthur Goldhammer (Cambridge: Harvard University Press, 1992).

which he pours from the lowering welkin give life to the soil that is parched and gladden the fields with fertility. And, therefore, mankind fear him, yet love him."[25] Having dispensed with the European explorer and Christian missionary, Du Bois replaced their testimony with the awesome indigenous power of Shango, the violent destroyer of cities and compounds, sites of destruction that are tempting to read as colonial cities and native compounds. More powerful than alien gods, Shango—the destroyer, the source of life—registers as the most important indigenous divinity of Africa.

Certainly, Du Bois was not primarily interested here in working out an indigenous African theology. In revising his earlier account of African history, however, he inserted Shango as a deity of destruction, a God that configured the devastating destruction of slavery but also the potential for the liberating destruction of the enclosures of colonialism, slavery, and racist oppression. While Europeans were debating the racial superiority of Aryans or Semites, a debate disguised by deliberations over the history of language, culture, and religion, Du Bois simply asserted the transcendent power of the African deity, Shango, who soared above their pretensions.

Despite his celebration of the transcendent power of the African God, Du Bois was less confident in *Black Folk* about the historical development of African religion across the Atlantic. Turning to America, he revised his earlier account of transatlantic religious continuity. While he had observed in *The Negro* that slavery had not destroyed the religion of the fetish or the religious role of African priests, in *Black Folk* Du Bois stressed the radical disruption of kinship, community, and religion under slavery.

> The African family and clan life were disrupted in this transplantation; the communal life and free use of land were impossible; the power of the chief was transferred to the master, bereft of the usual blood ties and ancient reference. The African language survived only in occasional words and phrases. African religion, both fetish and Islam, was transformed. Fetish survived in certain rites and even here and there in blood sacrifice, carried out secretly and at night; but more often in open celebration which gradually became transmuted into Catholic and Protestant Christian rites. The slave preacher replaced the African medicine man and gradually, after a century or more, the Negro Church

---

[25] W. E. B. Du Bois, *Black Folk: Then and Now* (New York: Henry Holt & Co, 1939): 107–108.

arose as the center and almost the only expression of Negro life in America.[26]

In this revised version, by changing a few words, Du Bois charted the transatlantic crossing not as gradual continuity but as radical change. The cumulative effect of his key terms—disruption, impossibility, transference, bereavement, transformation, transmutation, and replacement—created a sense of complete disjuncture between Africa and African America. His earlier accounts, from 1902 to 1915, had tried to outline a historical development, from the indigenous religion of West Africa to the institutionalized church of Chicago, in which an underlying persistence of religious thematics could be discerned. In *Black Folk*, a revised version of the same story in 1939 emphasized loss.

As a revision of *The Negro*, the text of *Black Folk* bore two substantial erasures with respect to African religion. Besides deleting the testimony of Kingsley and Nassau, the alien explorer and missionary, as authoritative witnesses to African deity, Du Bois also removed any reference to the persistence of voodoo or obeah in America. Although "vodooism" and "obi-worship" had featured prominently in his earlier accounts of the continuity of African indigenous religion in America, they disappeared entirely in 1939. Traces of African heritage, he acknowledged, might be found in customs, literature, art, music, and dance, but further study would be required to establish historical connections. In *Black Folk*, Du Bois no longer seemed confident that the persistence of cultural resources, let alone religious resources, could be established. His language evoked a radical break between Africa and America.

In the case of the Black Church, which he had earlier identified as the "sole surviving institution of the African fatherland," Du Bois in *Black Folk* characterized the Black Church as an American institution that had become "almost the only expression of Negro life in America."[27] Again, Du Bois's language involved a subtle editorial change, but the shift from "sole surviving" to "almost the only," from "African fatherland" to "Negro life in America," hints at a broader shift in his structuring of the historical narrative. Instead of surviving the crossing from Africa as the "sole surviving institution," animated by the African priest, the fetish, and the material philosophy of Africa, indigenous African religion, whether it is called

---

[26] Du Bois, *Black Folk*, 198.

[27] Du Bois, *Negro*, 189; *Black Folk*, 198.

voodoo, obeah, or even Christianity, failed to take root in America. In *Black Folk*, Du Bois represented the Black Church not as a historical, developmental, or gradual continuity with African religion but as an American institution, almost the only one that had emerged in America, for the "expression of Negro life."

In his treatment of African religion in 1939, therefore, Du Bois highlighted destruction and discontinuity, the awesome destructive power of the Yoruba God Shango, and the radical discontinuity between indigenous African religious life and the Black Church in America. Still, his treatment of African fetishism, which he had developed in *The Negro*, remained entirely unchanged in his account of indigenous African religion in *Black Folk*. Surrounded by disputes about whether it represented the absence, origin, or degeneration of religion, the fetish presented a persistent problem in Du Bois's attempts to provide a historical account of indigenous African religion. The fetish might also have posed a dilemma in his thinking about continuity or disjuncture between African religion and the African-American religion of the Black Church. Celebrating the material philosophy of the fetish in his earlier accounts of African religious history, by 1939 Du Bois seems to have become reluctant to assert fetishism as the basis of African religion in America, removing any reference to fetish, voodoo, or obeah in the emergence of slave religion or the Black Church in America.

The World and Africa

In 1947, following the destruction of World War II, which signaled the "collapse of Europe," Du Bois returned to the challenge of writing a comprehensive history of Africa. In *World and Africa* (1947), he certainly devoted less attention to religion than he did in his previous histories of Africa. Nevertheless, if read against the background of his earlier accounts, Du Bois's interventions in the analysis of fetishism, divinity, and transatlantic connections are decisive and important for his historical reconstruction of African religion.

Most decisively, in *World and Africa* Du Bois demolished the fetish as a representation of African religion. By contrast to his earlier attempts in rehabilitating the fetish, Du Bois in 1947 vigorously denounced fetishism as an account of African indigenous religion. Citing the German anthropologist Leo Frobenius, who had observed, "I have seen in no part of Africa the Negroes worship a fetish," Du Bois rejected fetishism as a foreign, alien, and ultimately denigrating and dehumanizing characterization of African religion.[28]

Certainly, Frobenius was a controversial authority, an anthropologist, entrepreneur, and advocate of Africa whose theories and methods were not always accepted by his anthropological colleagues. In retrospect, Frobenius has often been accused of harboring a Germanic romanticism for the purity of languages, cultures, and religions in Africa. Nevertheless, with respect to the fetish, Frobenius displayed a capacity for critical analysis of material relations under colonial conditions. Explicitly, he linked colonial conquest, dispossession, and enslavement of Africans with the representation of Africans as fetishists. As part of the larger colonial, capitalist project of turning Africans into objects for the slave trade, Frobenius suggested, Europeans claimed that Africans were already less than objects since they were subject to fetishism, the worship of objects. According to Frobenius, therefore, the very term "fetishism" was implicated in European representations of Africans as commodities for the slave trade. The market in African slaves, Frobenius argued, "exacted a justification; hence one made of the Negro a half-animal, an article of merchandise. And in the same way the notion of fetish (Portuguese *feticeiro*) was invented as a symbol of African religion." Besides challenging the empirical validity of the concept by insisting that he had never witnessed Africans worshiping a fetish, Frobenius observed that European discourse about African fetishism was an integral part of colonizing projects in subjugating, dehumanizing, and commodifying Africans. Under the sign of fetishism, he concluded, "The idea of the 'barbarous Negro' is a European invention."[29]

By embracing and advancing this critique of fetishism, Du Bois recast African indigenous religion as a site of struggle over conflicting representations of materiality and humanity. As recent research on the history of the fetish has shown, the term emerged in West Africa during the

---

[28] W. E. B. Du Bois, *The World and Africa: An Inquiry into the Part which Africa has Played in World History* (New York: Viking Press, 1947) 79; Leo Frobenius, *Histoire de la civilization africaine* (History of African Civilization), trans. H. Back and D. Ermont (Paris: Gallimard, 1936) 79. The 1936 edition is a translation of Frobenius, *Kulturgeschichte Afrikas: Prolegomena zu einer historischen gestaltlehre* (Cultural History of Africa: Prolegomena to a historical morphology) (Zurich: Phaidon, 1933).

[29] Du Bois, *World and Africa*, 79; Frobenius, *Histoire*, 79.

eighteenth century within intercultural trading zones.[30] In these mercantile trading networks, Portuguese, Dutch, and English traders in West Africa dealt with African Christians, Muslims, and "fetishists," who, according to the English trader William Smith, "have no religion at all."[31] From this European Christian perspective, fetishists, allegedly lacking any trace of religion, had no stable system of value to assess material objects. Without religion, African fetishists were supposedly unable to evaluate objects. They overvalued trifling objects—a bird's feather, a pebble, a piece of rag, or a dog's leg—by treating them as "fetishes" for ritual attention, but they undervalued trade goods, showing a lack of interest in acquiring what European traders were interested in selling. Fetishism, therefore, emerged in the eighteenth century as a European mercantile theory not of the origin but of the absence of religion. In the context of incommensurable values in these intercultural trading relations, Europeans developed the stereotype of "fetishism" to characterize Africans who had no religion to organize the necessary relations of meaning, power, and value between human beings and material objects and thereby to organize relations among human beings in the exchange of objects. The discourse of fetishism, which cast Africans as incapable of properly valuing objects, as Frobenius suggested, could also be deployed to turn Africans themselves into objects, rendering them as suitable commodities for the slave trade.

Instead of representing the authentic origin of indigenous African religion, the term "fetishism" was implicated in the dehumanizing representations of Africans that had legitimated colonization and enslavement. Du Bois took this insight seriously. Although he referred briefly, in passing, perhaps accidentally, to the fetish at one other point in *World and Africa*, he erased all of his previous observations about African fetishism. Neither the basis of indigenous African religion nor the link between religious life in Africa and African America, the fetish was a European invention. When he considered African indigenous religion as an aspect of African history in 1947, therefore, he removed not only the European explorer and missionary but also the European category

[30] William Pietz, "The Problem of the Fetish, I," *Res* 9 (Spring 1985): 5–17; William Pietz, "The Problem of the Fetish, II," *Res* 13 (Spring 1987): 23–45; William Pietz, "The Problem of the Fetish, IIIa," *Res* 16 (Autumn 1988): 105–23.

[31] William Smith, *A New Voyage to Guinea* (London: Nourse, 1744) 26.

"fetishism" that had been deployed as an ideological instrument of African dehumanization and enslavement.

Generally, in *World and Africa* Du Bois showed much less interest in religion than he did in previous accounts. Within the limited scope he gave in this volume to reconstructing the indigenous religion of Africa, only Shango remained. However, amplifying on the power of Shango, Du Bois revealed his source, which had been omitted in *Black Folk*, as the German anthropologist Leo Frobenius. In the earlier volume, Shango seemed to appear from nowhere, the African God, more powerful than the Gods of ancient Israel or Europe, but also the God who needed no source, citation, reference, or footnote. In *World and Africa*, however, the source is duly cited, a citation that only gains force, however, by being linked to the critique of fetishism as a dehumanizing representation of Africans and African religion. Against this background, Du Bois expanded upon the divinity and power of the Yoruba God. In addition to highlighting Shango's destructive force and creative capacity, he emphasized the Yoruba deity's indigenous political role, which had been alluded to in previous accounts, by asserting that Shango is the supreme source of political power, authority, and sovereignty, father of royal rulers, whose "posterity still have the right to give the country its kings."[32] Having rejected the alien construction of fetishism, therefore Du Bois reinforced the indigenous African religious resources supporting independent and autonomous political sovereignty in Africa.

In his African history of 1947, Du Bois seems to have lost interest in the question of continuity or discontinuity with America. Besides the rejection of fetishism and the celebration of Shango, no other reflections on indigenous African religion or African-American religion remained. *World and Africa* did not contain any reprise or revision of the formulations of religious development from Africa to America that had featured in his early historical accounts. Instead, he devoted his attention in *World and Africa* to actively building a Pan-African solidarity. Du Bois's reconstructions of indigenous African religion, however, were part of the project, sometimes in unexpected ways. For example, the problem of African fetishism, with which Du Bois wrestled from 1915 to 1947, moving from imaginative rehabilitation in *The Negro* to critical rejection in *World and Africa*, became a point of departure for the anti-colonial work of Aimé Césaire, who drew

---

[32] Du Bois, *World and Africa*, 158; Frobenius, *Histoire*, 56.

inspiration for his *Discourse on Colonialism* from the same passage by Frobenius that Du Bois cited to reject fetishism: "the idea of the barbaric Negro is a European invention."[33] If that inspiration was linked to Frobenius's critique of European inventions of the "barbaric Negro," it was also situated in the struggle to come to terms with the fetish and fetishism that provided the context for Frobenius's statement and Du Bois's transition from rehabilitating to rejecting the fetish as the defining feature of African indigenous religion.

Writing African Religion

It is tempting to locate Du Bois' changing representations of indigenous African religion in relation to his broader intellectual biography, linking his shift from rehabilitating to rejecting fetishism, for example, to his transition from a racialized to a radicalized Pan-Africanism. Although such connections might be established, I want to conclude with methodological rather than biographical observations arising from this brief review of Du Bois's handling of three features of indigenous African religion—fetishism, God, and transatlantic continuity—in his historical writings about Africa.

First, with respect to fetishism, we have seen that Du Bois consistently rejected the two standard accounts that placed the fetish either at the origin of religious evolution or at the end of religious degeneration. Emphatically, he countered the missionary slander of degradation, but he initially seemed to adopt the evolutionary model the emerged in late-nineteenth-century anthropology of religion. Although he seemed to defer briefly to an evolutionary progression of religious development from fetishism, through polytheism, to monotheism in *The Negro*, repeating that formulation in *Black Folk*, Du Bois actually did not accept that model's primary premise, which asserted that the origin of religion—fetishism—was essentially a mentality, a primitive psychology that mistakenly attributed life to inanimate objects. In

---

[33] As Robin D. G. Kelley has observed, Césaire, Senghor, and others in the Négritude movement drew inspiration from Frobenius. See Kelley, "A Poetics of Anticolonialism," *Monthly Review* 51/6 (November 1999) 21, footnote 19. See Suzanne Césaire, "Leo Frobenius and the Problem of Civilization," in Michael Richardson, ed., *Refusal of the Shadow: Surrealism and the Caribbean*, trans. Michael Richardson and Krzysztof Fijalkowski (London: Verso, 1996) 82–87; L. S. Senghor, "The Lessons of Leo Frobenius," in E. Haberland, ed., *Leo Frobenius: An Anthology* (Wiesbaden: Franz Steiner Verlag, 1973) vii.

social evolutionary theories of religion, fetishism was defined as a "frame of mind," as John Lubbock put it in the 1870s, that induced dogs, children, and savages to think that objects were alive.[34] As a primitive mentality, according to Edward Clodd, fetishism was the "confusion inherent in the savage mind between things living and not living."[35] Standard evolutionary theories of religion repeated this premise that fetishism was a primitive, childish, or uncultured psychology, a "low grade of consciousness," as A. C. Haddon proposed, because it imagined that material objects were alive.[36] Arguably, Placide Tempel's "Bantu philosophy," with its spirituality of "vitalism," continued this tendency to cast indigenous African religion as a mentality, psychology, or spirituality that attributed life to inanimate material objects.[37]

By contrast, Du Bois refused to render fetishism as a primitive psychology. Consistently, he wrestled with fetishism as a "material philosophy," from his early attempt to validate an indigenous African logic of material signs of spiritual forces to his later rejection of fetishism as an alien European logic for turning spiritual beings into material commodities. Du Bois seemed to recognize, in William Pietz's phrase, the fetish's "irreducible materiality."[38] Instead of seeing the fetish as the symptom of a primitive African mentality, he focused on material conditions—from an indigenous African "material philosophy" to the alien forces of slavery, colonization, and capitalism, with its own fetishism of commodities, "abounding in metaphysical subtleties and theological niceties," as Marx insisted, in which the meaning and value of being human were at stake.[39] By 1947, therefore, Du Bois had realized that fetishism, far from representing a primitive mentality that turned dead objects into living beings, was a term that provided ideological cover for capitalist transformations of living beings into objects. For the history of indigenous African religion, this focus on

---

[34] John Lubbock, *The Origin of Civilization and the Primitive Condition of Man*, 5th ed. (London: Longmans, Green, 1889) 205–10.

[35] Edward Clodd, *Myths and Dreams* (London: Chatto and Windus, 1885) 13.

[36] Alfred C. Haddon, *Magic and Fetishism* (London: Archibald Constable, 1906) 84–85. For similar renderings, see Frank Byron Jevons, *An Introduction to the History of Religion*, 8th ed. (London: Methuen, 1921) 28.

[37] Placide Tempels, *Bantu Philosophy*, trans. Colin King (1945; repr., Paris: Presence Africaine, 1959).

[38] Pietz, "Fetish I," 7.

[39] Karl Marx, *Capital*, 2 vols., trans. Samuel Moore and Edward Aveling (1867; repr., London: Lawrence and Wishart, 1974) 1:81.

materiality, rather than spirituality, advanced a critical perspective on the contingent, contested zones of religious production.

Second, with respect to God, Du Bois dealt with African divinity not as a theological problem but as a political problem. By stark contrast to the prevailing religious interests of Christian missionaries, Du Bois was not concerned with establishing theological principles of translation between African and Christian concepts of God.[40] Although, as we recall, he invoked missionary testimony for the existence of an African God, which was supposedly just like the Christian God, the Christian assertion of translatability in *The Negro* (1915) was erased when the text was revised for publication in 1939 as *Black Folk*. In place of the missionary's claim about the inherent intelligibility of the Christian God in Africa, Du Bois inserted Shango, an African deity with at least three features—locality, specificity, and sovereignty—that could not be easily subsumed in the Christian deity. Instead of representing the vague, generalized "Great Over God," to use the explorer Mary Kingsley's phrase, Shango was God of a definite place, with a specific identity, even a biography, which reinforced the claims of a royal lineage to political sovereignty. By 1939, asserting that Shango was greater than the deities of either European paganism or the Bible, Du Bois suggested that such a deity could not be translated or assimilated into the God of Christianity.

In the missionary literature on indigenous African concepts of God, the overriding concern has been the theological translation of the "unknown God" of Africa into the Christian God. This theological interest only continued to be developed in academic accounts of African deities such as Edwin Smith's *African Ideas of God* (1950), John S. Mbiti's *Concepts of God in Africa* (1970), and Malcolm J. McVeigh's *God in Africa: Conceptions of God in African Traditional Religion and Christianity* (1974).[41] Even in sociological formulations, such as Robin Horton's analysis of the conversion from

---

[40] On Christian translation, see Lamin Sanneh, "Missionary Translation in African Perspective: Religious and Theological Themes," in *Translating the Message: The Missionary Impact on Culture* (Maryknoll NY: Orbis, 1996) 157–91; Andrew F. Walls, "The Translation Principle in Christian History," in *The Missionary Movement in Christian History* (Maryknoll NY: Orbis, 1996) 26–42.

[41] Edwin W. Smith, ed., *African Ideas of God: A Symposium* (London: Edinburgh House Press, 1950); John S. Mbiti, *Concepts of God in Africa* (London: SPCK, 1970); Malcolm J. McVeigh, *God in Africa: Concepts of God in African Traditional Religion and Christianity* (Cape Cod: C. Stark, 1974).

African "microcosmic" worldviews to Christian or Islamic "macrocosmic" worldviews, the question of theological translatability from local deities to the translocal deities of "world religions" has been prominent in the analysis of the history of African understandings of God.[42] By invoking Shango, however, Du Bois effectively asserted that the problem of God in Africa was political rather than theological. Not a primitive high god, a Christian-like supreme being, or a world religion's macrocosmic deity, Shango was a local deity of political sovereignty, bearing the "right to give the country its kings," who "soars above the legend of Thor and Jahweh," not by transcending the world but by being imminent, situated, and forceful in a specific world.

Third, the question of transatlantic continuity between Africa and African America, of course, also raised the problem of translatability, but with an entirely different valence. Rather than a universal, macrocosmic worldview assimilating a local, microcosmic worldview, the transatlantic passage entailed the challenges of translation posed by transportation, enslavement, and alienation in America. In his earliest formulations, Du Bois identified the indigenous African priest as the nexus of transatlantic translation. Generally, under colonial conditions within Africa, indigenous ritual specialists, with specialized knowledge and techniques of healing, divination, and sacred power, were best equipped to survive the displacements of the religion of the home and the destruction of the religion of the polity that dramatically altered the terrain of indigenous African religion. As Du Bois suggested, the knowledge and power of African religious specialists had a kind of portability that could even cross the Atlantic. By focusing on the African priest, along with the indigenous religious resources of voodoo or obeah, Du Bois advanced the challenging assertion that Christianity did not convert Africans but was actually converted by Africans into indigenous African religion.

Although Du Bois seems to have lost confidence in this formula by 1947, no longer showing an interest in tracing African religion "from the heathenism of the Gold Coast to the institutional Negro Church in Chicago," the second half of the twentieth century witnessed a dramatic

---

[42] Robin Horton, "African Conversion," *Africa* 41/2 (April 1971): 85–108. See Terence Ranger, "The Local and the Global in South African Religious History," in *Conversion to Christianity: Historical and Anthropological Perspectives on a Great Transformation*, ed. Robert W. Hefner (Berkeley: University of California Press, 1993).

vitality of African-American religion with explicitly African roots. Shango, for example, was alive and well in America, flourishing in Haitian Voodoo, Cuban Santeria, Brazilian Candomblé, and the Shango movement in Trinidad. Although these religious movements certainly involved translation, identifying Shango with the Christian Saint Barbara in Cuba, with the Christian Saint John in Trinidad, for example, such interreligious translations were obviously not controlled by any Christian orthodoxy.[43] These translations arose, as Du Bois had suggested, out of the portable resources of the African priest—with his or her capacity to heal the sick, interpret the unknown, comfort the sorrowing, and avenge wrongs—but also out of the locality, specificity, and contested sovereignty of an African, American, and transatlantic politics of religion. That religious politics, as Du Bois proposed, operates within the symbols, myths, and rituals that configure the "longing, disappointment, and resentment of a stolen and oppressed people," but can this religious politics also serve political projects against oppression or for liberation from oppression?

This is a difficult question. It must not have an easy answer. Profoundly, the question tests the materiality, locality, and translatability of religion not only in political relations but also in any politics of social, economic, and human transformation. In conventional terms, politicians, even radical politicians, might ask whether indigenous religion is progressive or reactionary. With its material fetishes, its local gods, and its resistance to translation into any universal intelligibility, indigenous religion can easily appear as wild religion, a religion beyond the bounds of any political project. In *Souls of Black Folk*, Du Bois touched briefly on the capacity of this wild religion for rebellion. Drawing on an indigenous African religious inheritance, with its gods and devils, elves and witches, and other spiritual influences, the African in bondage in America could only conclude that the evil had triumphed. "All the hateful powers of the Under-world were striving against him," Du Bois wrote, "and a spirit of revolt and revenge filled his heart." Acting out that spirit of revolt, as Du Bois related, Africans "called up all the resources of heathenism," but those religious resources

[43] Bascom, *Shango in the New World*; Leonard E. Barrett, *Soul Force: African Heritage in Afro-American Religion* (Garden City NY: Anchor Press, 1974); George Eaton Simpson, *The Shango Cult in Trinidad* (Rio Piedras: Institute of Caribbean Studies, University of Puerto Rico, 1964); *Sacred Possessions: Voodoo, Santeria, Obeah, and the Caribbean*, ed. Margarite Fernandez Olmos and Lizabeth Paravisini-Gebert (New Brunswick NJ: Rutgers University Press, 1997).

were rituals, sacrifices, spells, "weird midnight orgies and mystic conjurations."[44] Certainly, these religious practices gave expression to the situation of oppression, even expressing a "spirit of revolt" against oppression, but they did not seem like ingredients in any viable political revolution against oppression.

Du Bois's decreasing interest in transantlantic African religious continuity was perhaps connected to his failing confidence in the efficacy of indigenous African religion, especially wild religion, in serving the goals of any emancipatory political project. Certainly, this political problem of the role of an indigenous African religious heritage was inherited by other African revolutionaries. In *Wretched of the Earth*, for example, Frantz Fanon largely ignored religion, whether Islam in Algeria or Christianity, Islam, and indigenous African religion in West Africa, but he did reflect on revivals of wild religion—with its "terrifying myths," populated by maleficent spirits, the "leopardmen, serpent-men, six-legged dogs, zombies"—that generated an imaginary world of spiritual powers and prohibitions that were "far more terrifying than the world of the settler."[45] As both psychological displacement and political distraction, this wild religion could not be coordinated with a revolutionary political project.

"At the intersection of religious practices and the interrogation of human tragedy," as Achille Mbembe has recently observed, "a distinctively African philosophy has emerged."[46] But that African philosophy of tragedy, with its roots in slavery, colonization, and apartheid, has engaged religion in different ways. Against the radical dismissal of the viability of indigenous religion for revolutionary, national, or postcolonial projects, nativist positions, with their "reenchantment of tradition," have sought to recover the authentic precolonial religious resources of Africa as a foundation for the future. At the same time, these philosophical alternatives, radical and nativist, have had to maneuver within rapidly changing, globalizing conditions, which have transformed religion, even wild religion, within new political economies of the sacred. For example, in the name of an African Renaissance, with its promise of revitalizing an indigenous African heritage,

---

[44] Du Bois, *Souls*, 143.

[45] Frantz Fanon, *The Wretched of the Earth*, trans. Constance Farrington (London: Penguin, 1967) 43.

[46] Achille Mbembe, "African Modes of Self-Writing," *Public Culture* 14/1 (Winter 2002): 239.

formerly radical political interests can align with the global financial structures of the World Bank, the International Monetary Fund, the European Union, and the United States.[47] At the same time, a devoted African nativist, such as the self-proclaimed Zulu witchdoctor, later sangoma, and now shaman Credo Mutwa, can establish transatlantic continuity as featured artist on the website African.com, "the website of the African diaspora," for depicting the website's patron, the Yoruba God Shango.[48] As Mbembe has suggested, indigenous African religion, which has not been adequately captured either by radical dismissals or nativist reconstructions, has to be regarded as a modality of self-writing, self-styling, and self-practice. In writing about the history of Africa, Du Bois was engaged in precisely such a struggle of self-formation, but he was also trying to make sense of a political project initially located in the United States but increasingly global in scope. Writing about indigenous African religion, in this context, was a way of writing not only about a religious heritage but also about a changing world.

Works Cited

Barrett, Leonard E. *Soul Force: African Heritage in Afro-American Religion.* Garden City NY: Anchor Press, 1974.

Bascom, William R. *Shango in the New World.* Austin: African and Afro-American Research Institute, University of Texas, 1972.

———. *The Yoruba of Southwestern Nigeria.* New York: Holt, Rinehart & Winston, 1969.

Burton, Richard. *Lake Regions of Central Africa.* 2 volumes. London: Longman, Green, Longman, and Roberts, 1860.

Caillié, René. *Travels through Central Africa to Timbuctoo.* 2 volumes. London: Colburn and Bentley, 1830.

Chidester, David. *Savage Systems: Colonialism and Comparative Religion in Southern Africa.* Charlottesville: University Press of Virginia, 1996.

Clodd, Edward. *Myths and Dreams.* London: Chatto and Windus, 1885.

---

[47] Malegapuru William Makgoba, ed., *African Renaissance: The New Struggle* (Tafelberg South Africa: Mafube, 1999).

[48] The African.Com (<http://theafrican.com/AboutUs.htm>). Mission, 1998, accessed April 14, 2004.

Du Bois, W. E. B. *Black Folk: Then and Now*. New York: Henry Holt and Company, 1939.

———. *Economic Co-operation among Negro Americans*. Atlanta: Atlanta University Press, 1907.

———. *The Negro Church*. Atlanta: Atlanta University Press, 1903.

———. *The Negro*. New York: Henry Holt and Company, 1915.

———. *The Souls of Black Folk*. New York: Vintage Books, 1990.

———. *The World and Africa: An Inquiry into the Part which Africa has Played in World History*. New York: Viking Press, 1947.

Fabian, Johannes. *Time and the Other: How Anthropology Makes Its Object*. New York: Columbia University Press, 1983.

Fanon, Frantz. *The Wretched of the Earth*. Translated by Constance Farrington. London: Penguin, 1967.

Farrow, Stephen Steptimus. *Faith, Fancies, and Fetich: or, Yoruba Paganism: Being Some Account of the Religious Beliefs of the West African Negroes, particularly of the Yoruba Tribe of Southern Nigeria*. Brooklyn NY: Athelia Henrietta Press, 1996.

Frazier, E. Franklin. *The Negro Church in America*. New York: Shocken, 1963.

Frobenius, Leo. *Histoire de la civilization africaine*. (History of African Civilization) Translated by H. Back and D. Ermont. Paris: Gallimard, 1936.

———. *Kulturgeschichte Afrikas: Prolegomena zu einer historischen gestaltlehre*. (Cultural History of Africa: Prolegomena to an historical morphology) Zurich: Phaidon, 1933.

Grant, James Augustus. *A Walk Across Africa; or Domestic Scenes from my Nile Journal*. Edinburgh: W. Blackwood, 1864.

Haberland, E., editor. *Leo Frobenius: An Anthology*. Wiesbaden: Franz Steiner Verlag, 1973.

Haddon, Alfred C. *Magic and Fetishism*. London: Archibald Constable, 1906.

Hefner, Robert W., editor. *Conversion to Christianity: Historical and Anthropological Perspectives on a Great Transformation*. Berkeley: University of California Press, 1993.

Herskovits, Melville J. *The Myth of the Negro Past*. New York: Harper & Brothers, 1941.

Horton, Robin. "African Conversion." *Africa* 41/2 (April 1971): 85–108.

Jevons, Frank Byron. *An Introduction to the History of Religion*. Eighth edition. London: Methuen, 1921.

Kelley, Robin D. G. "A Poetics of Anticolonialism." *Monthly Review* 51/6 (November 1999): 1–21.

Kingsley, Mary H. *West African Studies*. Second edition. London: Macmillan, 1901.

Lubbock, John. *The Origin of Civilization and the Primitive Condition of Man*. Fifth edition. London: Longmans, Green, 1889.

Makgoba, Malegapuru William, editor. *African Renaissance: The New Struggle*. Tafelberg South Africa: Mafube, 1999.

Marx, Karl. *Capital*. 2 volumes. Translated by Samuel Moore and Edward Aveling. London: Lawrence and Wishart, 1974.

Mbembe, Achille. "African Modes of Self-Writing." *Public Culture* 14/1 (Winter 2002): 239.

Mbiti, John S. *Concepts of God in Africa*. London: SPCK Publishing, 1970.

McVeigh, Malcolm J. *God in Africa: Concepts of God in African Traditional Religion and Christianity*. Cape Cod MA: C. Stark, 1974.

Nassau, Robert Hamill. *Fetichism in West Africa: Forty Years' Observation of Native Customs and Superstitions*. New York: Scribner, 1904.

Olender, Maurice. *The Languages of Paradise: Race, Religion, and Philology in the Nineteenth Century*. Translated by Arthur Goldhammer. Cambridge: Harvard University Press, 1992.

Olmos, Margarite Fernandez, and Lizabeth Paravisini-Gebert, editors. *Sacred Possessions: Voodoo, Santeria, Obeah, and the Caribbean*. New Brunswick NJ: Rutgers University Press, 1997.

Pietz, William. "The Problem of the Fetish, I." *Res* 9 (Spring 1985): 5–17.

———. "The Problem of the Fetish, II. *Res* 13 (Spring 1987): 23–45.

———. "The Problem of the Fetish, IIIa." *Res* 16 (Autumn 1988): 105–23.

Richardson, Michael, editor. *Refusal of the Shadow: Surrealism and the Caribbean*. Translated by Michael Richardson and Krzysztof Fijalkowski. London: Verso, 1996.

Sanneh, Lamin. *Translating the Message: The Missionary Impact on Culture*. Maryknoll NY: Orbis, 1996.

Sharpe, Eric J. *Comparative Religion: A History*. Second edition. La Salle, IL.: Open Court, 1986.

Simpson, George Eaton. *The Shango Cult in Trinidad*. Rio Piedras: Institute of Caribbean Studies, University of Puerto Rico, 1964.

Smart, Ninian, et al., editors. *Nineteenth-Century Religious Thought in the West*. 3 volumes. Cambridge: Cambridge University Press, 1985.

Smith, Edwin W., editor. *African Ideas of God: A Symposium*. London: Edinburgh House Press, 1950.

Smith, William. *A New Voyage to Guinea*. London: Nourse, 1744.

Tempels, Placide. *Bantu Philosophy*. Translated by Colin King. Paris: Presence Africaine, 1959.

The African.com (http://theafrican.com/AboutUs.htm). Mission, 1998, accessed April 14, 2004.

Walls, Andrew. *The Missionary Movement in Christian History*. Maryknoll NY: Orbis, 1996.

The Intellectual and Pragmatic Legacy of Du Bois's Pan-Africanism in Contemporary Ghana[1]

Jesse Weaver Shipley
Jemima Pierre

> Ghana must...be the representative of Africa, and not only that, but of Black Africa below the Sahara desert...Ghana should lead a movement of black men for Pan-Africanism....
> —W. E. B. Du Bois, 1957[2]

Hidden in Cantonments neighborhood, the former British colonial residential area of Accra, Ghana, is the W. E. B. Du Bois Memorial Centre for Pan-African Culture. This centre was established in 1985 as a tribute to "the father of Pan-Africanism" (who moved to Ghana in 1961 at the age of 91) "and to all who are committed to the struggle of African peoples for a better life."[3] Based in the house where W. E. B. Du Bois spent the final two

[1] We would like to thank the Carter G. Woodson Institute for Afro-American and African Studies and the University of Virginia for generously supporting the research and writing of this paper, as well as the Wenner-Gren Foundation for funding part of the research. We also want to thank Mohammed Ben Abdallah for giving us insight into Pan-Africanism during the Rawlings years.

[2] W. E. B. Du Bois, 1957. "A Future for Pan-Africa: Freedom, Peace, Socialism" in Julius Lester, ed., *The Seventh Son: The Thought and Writings of W. E. B. Du Bois, Volume II*. New York: Random House, p. 648. This was Du Bois's greeting to Kwame Nkrumah in 1957 when Ghana gained its independence from Britain. Although invited by Nkrumah, Du Bois was prevented by the US government from attending (Lester 1971: 648)

[3] W. E. B. Du Bois Memorial Centre program description for Pan-African Culture, produced for the 8th Du Bois-Padmore-Nkrumah Pan African Lectures on the topic "Pan-

years of his life, the memorial serves as a contemporary site of pilgrimage for scholars, artists, tourists, and students, mostly from Africa and the African diaspora. While originally buried with full military honors at Osu/Christianborg Castle in 1963—a former slave trading fort and the current seat of government—Du Bois was re-memorialized in 1985 in another official state ceremony.[4] Du Bois's reburial was followed in 1992 by the reburial of Trinidadian Pan-Africanist George Padmore and the renaming of a memorial library in his honor[5] as well as by the construction of a memorial park and the reinterment[6] of Pan-Africanist and first president of Ghana, Kwame Nkrumah. The establishment of these public memorials in Accra signaled the state's self-conscious recuperation of Ghana's legacy of Pan-Africanism. It also, at least symbolically, invoked (and reestablished) the intellectual and pragmatic legacy of W. E. B. Du Bois for a new generation of Ghanaians, Africans, and people of African descent in the diaspora.

We suggest, in this essay, that the state reincorporation of W. E. B. Du Bois (and later Padmore and Nkrumah) into the national historical, political, and cultural imagination represents a significant moment in the contemporary articulation of Pan-Africanism. Indeed, we argue that the explicit deployment of the figure of Du Bois at this historical juncture serves two particular and important functions. First, re-invoking Du Bois's political and personal ties to the country and his lifetime of work towards global Black emancipation recalls, for the contemporary moment, Ghana's position as the symbolic center of Pan-African politics and practice. Relatedly (and second), it has allowed for the emergence and reinterpretation of specific practical manifestations of the cultural and political relationships between

---

Africanism in the Era of Globalization," given by Ali Mazuri, 3–8 August 2001. Ali A. Mazrui. "Pan-Africanism and the Origins of Globalizations," November 2001. http://igcs.binghamton.edu/igcs_site/dirton12.htm. Date of Access: February 12, 2002.

[4] The Ghanaian government, under the leadership of its first president, Kwame Nkrumah, had given W. E. B. Du Bois a state funeral on 29–30 August 1963 and had buried his body next to the walls of Christianborg/Osu Castle in Accra.

[5] George Padmore died in 1959 and was also buried at Christianborg/Osu Castle. Initially a library had been dedicated to Padmore; however, during the Second Republic of Ghana under the leadership of K. Busia, Padmore's name was removed.

[6] This was the second time Nkrumah's remains would be reinterred. His remains were first repatriated from Guinea (Nkrumah died in 1972 in exile after the 1966 coup d'etat that deposed his government) and buried in his hometown in Nkroful, Ghanna.

African continental and diaspora peoples. This contemporary recuperation
of Pan-Africanism has occurred, however, within the specific context of the
liberalization of the global political economy and the concomitant
restructuring of the Ghanaian state's economic policies from the 1980s. As
we show below, the Ghanaian state has deployed Pan-Africanism with
particular intentions that reveal its ambivalent relationship to both free-
market capitalism a nd the liberational political trajectory of Pan-
Africanism. In this ambivalent space, the resultant contemporary Pan-
Africanism—particularly as it is *practically* manifest—highlights the ongoing,
complex, and yet interdependent African/diaspora relationship envisioned
by Du Bois. This contemporary Pan-Africanism offers a new set of symbols,
economies, and practices around which peoples of Africa and the diaspora
continue to forge and contest political, economic, intellectual, and cultural
connections. In this context, such a deployment also serves to signal a
realignment of identifications around notions of nation and state,
economies, and culture.

Using historical and ethnographic analyses, this essay first examines the
specificities of Du Bois's influence on the trajectory of Pan-Africanism,
particularly its later formulation in the postwar period as it focused on
decolonization and continental African liberation. Next, we show the ways
in which Ghana becomes the practical and ideological center of Pan-
Africanism in light of first president Kwame Nkrumah's political and
ideological projects and the symbolic significance of Du Bois's move to the
country. We then discuss Du Bois's legacy in contemporary Ghana by
focusing on the state-sponsored Pan-African Theatre Festival (PANAFEST)
and Emancipation Day and the politics of the return of diaspora peoples to
Ghana, where race, African identity, and nationalism are pragmatically
reconfigured. Our discussion shows that an important aspect of Du Bois's
legacy is the recognition that Pan-African and diasporic political, cultural,
and intellectual connections have always been central to African politics.
These connections are indicative of what J. L. Matory calls a "live Afro-
Atlantic dialogue," in which "the diaspora and Africa itself are united by a
'discontinuous' and mutually influential dialogue that has continued long
beyond the end of slavery."[7] Such Pan-African connections and practices

---

[7] J. Lorand Matory, 1999. "Afro-Atlantic Culture: On the Live Dialogue Between
Africa and the Americas" in Kwame A. Appiah and Henry L. Gates, eds, *Africana: The*

ultimately have ramifications that extend beyond intellectual dialogue and explicit political movements; they have produced significant transformations of daily life, symbols, and practices on *both* sides of the Atlantic.[8] It is these pragmatic/practical aspects—the effects of the deployment of Du Bois's legacy in Ghana—with which we are concerned.

Our argument stands in contradistinction to the particular trend in Pan-Africanist historiography that locates Pan-Africanism's significance primarily in explicit intellectual articulations and political movements. However, as P. Olisanwuche Esedebe accurately demonstrates, the definition of Pan-Africanism is notoriously amorphous, a fact that has complicated the development of scholarship on the subject, particularly efforts to delineate both its significance and its complexity[9]. Many scholars have argued that only self-consciously "Pan-Africanist" intellectual (and later, political) activity such should be considered under the rubric Pan-Africanism as a historical movement.[10] Others point particularly to the inability of early-twentieth-century Pan-Africanism to find a common point of articulation and action. These scholars seem most adept at delineating the discontinuities and contradictions of this movement. In this sense, if Pan-Africanism is considered as a movement at all it becomes a series of disparate vaguely connected projects.[11] George Shepperson and others have attempted to come to terms with the "diverse and cross-fertilized black traditions and resistance and anticolonialism."[12] Shepperson in particular distinguishes between Pan-Africanism (with a capital "P"), which points to explicit movements (such as the Pan-African Congresses), and pan-Africanism (with a lowercase "p"), which he considers not as a coherent movement but a

---

Encyclopedia of the African and African American Experience. New York: Basic Civitas Books, pp. 36-44.

[8] Ibid.

[9] P. Olisanwuche Esedebe, 1982. *Pan-Africanism: The Idea and Movement, 1776-1963*. Washington, D. C.: Howard University Press

[10] St.Clair Drake, 1982. "Diaspora Studies and Pan-Africanism," in Joseph Harris, ed. *Global Dimensions of the African Diaspora*. Washington, D.C.: Howard University Press.

[11] William Ackah, 1999. *Pan-Africanism: Exploring the Contradictions: Politics, Identity, and Development in Africa and the African Diaspora*. Brookfield, VT: Ashgate.

Imanuel Geiss, 1974. *The Pan-African Movement: A History of Pan-Africanism in America, Europe, and Africa*. New York: Holmes & Meier Publishers.

[12] Brent Edwards, 2001. "The Uses of Diaspora," *Social Text* 19 (1): 45-73.

group of activities with a cultural bent.[13] Even St. Clair Drake, Pan-African
and diaspora theorist, suggests a difference between "traditional" and
"continental" Pan-Africanism, linking the "traditional" to an explicit Black
international "racial" program. Indeed, the Pan-Africanism undergirded by
the series of five Pan-African Congresses (dated from 1919 to 1945),
primarily organized and presided over by Du Bois, has been seen as distinct
from other activities that may be considered Pan-Africanist, and often
without understanding the broader historical forces which connect them.

While recognizing the need to address the complexity—particularly the
ideological and political differences among different strains of thought and
practice—of Black internationalism, we understand Pan-Africanism in its
broadest terms. As Du Bois made clear, both in his scholarship and through
his political and practical activities, Pan-Africanism is a broadly conceived
set of intellectual, political, economic, cultural, and spiritual meanings and
practices. It is a movement structured by the history of global racial
inequality—beginning with the slave trade, the development of global
commerce, colonialism, and capitalist expansion—but is certainly not
reducible to it[14] Further, we follow Horace Campbell, who explains that,
despite its various forms, Pan-Africanism "has been most clearly articulated
in the project of achieving liberation of the continent of Africa and the
dignity and self-respect of all Africans."[15] What is most important to us are
the particular practices engendered by Black international interaction (as Du
Bois conceived it) and their role in structuring new understandings of Pan-
Africanism. Here, then, we focus on pragmatic, on-the-ground effects of the
Du Boisian legacy, particularly as it is reformulated by the practices of the
Ghanaian state.

We also feel that a problematic side effect of the continuing
segmenting of Pan-Africanist activities is the tendency of many scholars to
overemphasize a shift in Pan-Africanism in 1945 (at the Fifth Pan-African
Congress in Manchester, England), often suggesting that diaspora Africans

---

[13] George Shepperson, 1965. "The African Abroad or the African Diaspora," in
Terence O. Ranger, ed. *Emerging Themes of African History.* London: Heinemann
Educational Books Ltd.

[14] Thus we argue that Pan-Africanism is manifest not only in explicit political and
intellectual movements but also in daily practices, symbols, and actions.

[15] Horace Campbell, 1994. "Pan-Africanism and African Liberation" in Sidney J.
Lemelle and Robin D. G. Kelley, eds. *Imagining Home: Class, Culture, and Nationalism
in the African Diaspora.* New York: Verso.

suffered some sort of abnormal racial parochialism. As conventionally articulated in the literature, Pan-Africanism saw an important shift in 1945 where historical and political imperatives mandated that continental Africans turn to decolonization and nation-building while those in the diaspora continue the explicit struggle against localized racial oppression. For example, Kwame Anthony Appiah states that post-World War II Pan-Africanist thought saw African identity as a "more geographical idea."[16] He continues that for Kwame Nkrumah, African unity was "the unity of those who shared the African continent." He further argues that the split with continental Pan-Africanism was fostered as those in the diaspora were "taken up with the questions of civil rights."[17]. This shift in strategy, as it is argued, forced those in the diaspora outside the discussion of (continental) Pan-Africanism as they are said to have remained focused on the narrow problem of race. The obvious—and, we insist, incorrect—suggestion here is that diaspora peoples narrowly (and wrongly) focused on racial oppression to the exclusion of global connections *and* more complex analyses of Western imperialism. As we show below, particularly by examining Du Bois's relationship to Africa and decolonization, Pan-African forms of racial consciousness have been an important and direct result of the global structuring of white racial dominance and the struggle of African diasporic peoples against these interconnected forms of inequality. Furthermore, African liberation from colonial rule was always seen in terms of its global implications and was always at the forefront of the diasporic struggle for Black emancipation. Bernard Magubane, for example, makes this point explicit when he asserts: "The American blacks who initiated the idea of Pan-Africanism…made African independence a part of the political consciousness of the world, a consciousness which has grown in time."[18]

In fact, we see the conventional representation of the purported diaspora brand of Pan-Africanism—juxtaposed against continental Pan-Africanism that was presumed non-racial, particularly after 1945—as thoroughly (and unnaturally) "racialist" and intellectually disingenuous, if not historically inaccurate. This trend, we believe, reflects the continued

---

[16] Kwame A. Appiah, 1998. "Pan-Africanism." In E. Craig (Ed.), *Routledge Encyclopedia of Philosophy*. London: Routledge. Retrieved September 28, 2006, from http://www.rep.routledge.com/article/Z018

[17] Ibid., 6.

[18] Bernard Magubane, The *Ties that Bind: African-American Consciousness of Africa* (Trenton NJ: Africa World Press, 1994) 144.

refusal—in some aspects of the scholarship on Pan-Africanism, as well as liberal studies of Africa more generally—to recognize the crucial role of Africa/diaspora connections in decolonization movements and African politics.[19] In effect, it is a denial of the global forms of racial oppression and the links between the United States's internal "problem of race," the history of the slave trade and colonialism, and contemporary global politics. It further contributes to a not-so-benign form of liberal anthropology and historiography, which, ignoring many aspects of global political, economic, and cultural history, naively sees race as an "American" (and, by extension, "diasporic") problem.[20] Du Bois, however, had a much more complex understanding of these relationships. He "was well aware of the international nature of the race question, and his insights led him to play an important role in [Pan-Africanism]."[21] Thus, we present a reading of Du Bois's multifaceted legacy in Ghana that reveals a shifting set of relationships between the African diaspora and the continent; indeed, we present a new reading of practices (historical and contemporary) that highlight the continuities—rather than the discontinuities—of the complex history of Pan-Africanism.

Du Bois, Pan-Africanism, and Nkrumah's Ghana

Few studies focus explicitly on the particularities of the Du Bois's legacy in Africa. Ghanaian scholar Daniel Agbeyebiawo makes this point clear in his biography of Du Bois: "Although Dr. Du Bois achieved so much for the African continent in general, and Ghana in particular, little is known about him...Not even the academics of Africa know much about him...[Yet] Dr. Du Bois was very instrumental in the decolonization process in Africa...[by] making known to the International Community, the plight of colonized

---

[19] Bernard Magubane makes the important point that "At the turn and the early part of this century, American blacks stood alone as advocates of African nationalism, independence and Pan-Africanism. In the panorama of Afro-American advocates of African independence stand Garvey, W. E. B. Du Bois, George Padmore, Aime Cesaire, Bishop Turner, and others" (*Ties that Bind*, 98).

[20] See Pierre Bourdieu and Loic Wacquant, "On the Cunning of Imperialist Reason," *Theory, Culture & Society* 16/1 (February1999): 41-58.

[21] Magubane, *Ties that Bind*, 151.

Africa.[22] It is significant that many have not recognized Du Bois's multi-pronged approach to global Black emancipation. He was, in fact, one of the earliest Africanist historians, providing studies of African societies and cultures when the continent was considered unworthy of sociological and historical analysis. The entire corpus of Du Bois's work shows an explicit and intellectual concern with Africa, with five particular works focused in large part on Africa itself—*The Negro* (1915); *Africa, Its Geography, People and Products* (1930); *Africa—Its Place in Modern History* (1930); *Black Folk Then and Now* (1939); and *The World and Africa* (1947).[23] In addition, the *Encyclopedia Africana* project—which Du Bois embarked on, with Nkrumah's patronage, when he moved to Ghana—was explicitly Africa-focused. In recounting his motivations for the project, Du Bois states that his idea had been "to prepare and publish an encyclopedia not on the vague subject of race, but on the peoples inhabiting the continent of Africa…[The encyclopedia should be] mainly edited by African scholars…to have included among its writers the best students of Africa in the world."[24] With such a collection—though modest by Du Bois's own admission—it is a wonder that W. E. B. Du Bois is often not associated with African history (or anthropology). Rather (and tellingly), he is associated primarily with the "Negro" problem in the United States and with Pan-Africanist activities (but mostly in terms of how they concern diaspora blacks). Yet, it is clear that W. E. B. Du Bois conceptualized Africa and the diaspora within the same sociopolitical and cultural framework—linking histories of the slave trade and colonialism to global black exploitation and inequality. Indeed, Herbert Aptheker asserts that Du Bois's essays often insisted on the "integral relationship of the Afro-American and African struggles for freedom."[25] And, though Du Bois recognized his own reality as an African American and the necessity of black liberation in the United States, he saw this relationship as tied to the African struggle for liberation.[26]

---

[22] Daniel Agbeyebiawo, *The Life and Works of W. E. B. Du Bois* (Accra: Stephil Printing Press, 1998) 64.

[23] *Correspondence of W. E. B. Du Bois 1877–1963*, ed. Herbert Aptheker, 3 vols. (Amherst: University of Massachusetts Press, 1973) vol. 1.

[24] Herbert Aptheker, ed., 1973. *The Correspondence of W. E. B. Du Bois, 1868-1963*, Vol 2: 389

[25] *Correspondence,* ed. Aptheker, Vol. 1: xi.

[26] Ibid.

In this context, then, Du Bois's articulation of Pan-Africanism foregrounded this integrated understanding of Africa and the diaspora. For him, "Pan-Africa means intellectual understanding and co-operation among all groups of Negro descent in order to bring about at the earliest possible time the industrial and spiritual emancipation of the Negro peoples."[27] Du Bois thus always made sure he linked his work for Negro emancipation in the United States to the struggle in Africa. In a review of his ten-year coverage of the "Negro problem" in *Crisis* magazine, he stated: "We have considered all these matters in relation to the American Negro but our underlying thought has been continually that they can and must be seen not against any narrow, provincial or even national background, but in relation to the great problem of the colored races of the world and particularly those of African descent."[28]

As Kathy Ogren has argued, the Pan-Africanism Du Bois insisted on for the elimination of colonial and capitalist domination. While recognizing the complex intertwined nature of development and culture, Africanity and Western society, Du Bois also called for extending the structures of modern society to Africans so that African societies could develop on their own terms. Thus, in "content, metaphor and program, [Du Bois] stressed connections between America, Africa and the rest of the world."[29] At the same time, Du Bois conceptualized Pan-Africa in a way that allowed for individual and particular struggles—he appreciated the need for various Black populations to work out their specific problems. This was explicitly demonstrated in his advocacy of African leadership of continental affairs[30] as well as his realization that Pan-Africa had to work together "through independent units."[31]

---

[27] W. E. B. Du Bois, 1933. "Pan-Africa and New Racial Philosophy." In Julius Lester, ed., *The Seventh Son: The Thought and Writings of W. E. B. Du Bois, Volume II.* New York: Random House, p. 208.

[28] Du Bois, quoted in *Seventh Son*, ed. Lester, 206.

[29] Kathy Orgen, 1994. "What Africa is to Me? African Strategies in the Harlem Renaissance" in Sidney J. Lemelle and Robin D. G. Kelley, eds. *Imagining Home: Class, Culture, and Nationalism in the African Diaspora.* New York: Verso.

[30] This was particularly true in terms of having African scholars work on the *Encyclopedia Africana* project, as well as Du Bois's hesitancy at Nkrumah's desire to appoint certain expatriate whites to leadership positions in newly independent Ghana.

[31] *Seventh Son*, ed. Lester, 649.

Du Bois's international crusade for African (black) liberation—spanning many decades—also led to the development of personal relationships with many African and diaspora political leaders. In fact, Du Bois had been in contact with, and influenced, many of the future African heads of state at the height of the decolonization movement. His relationship to Ghana in general, and Kwame Nkrumah in particular, stands as a key example: Nkrumah considered Du Bois one of his primary mentors and, in that capacity, Du Bois exerted a certain kind of influence in the affairs of the new independent state. In a broader sense, Du Bois's intellectualism and radical political views inspired Nkrumah (as well as many others) in the fight against colonialism. Nkrumah considered Du Bois a "real friend and father" and admired the "intellectual honesty and integrity"[32] of this great "father of Pan-Africanism."

In fact, no other name resonates more with the early development of Pan-Africanism than that of W. E. B. Du Bois. He organized and presided over four Pan-African congresses and was the honorary chair of the 1945 Fifth Pan-African Congress. Taking up the mandate initiated in 1900 by Henry Sylvester Williams, who organized what should reasonably be called the first Pan-African Congress, Du Bois structured an international movement that was to influence generations to come. Initially his program of Pan-Africanism was not a direct plan of action but a set of periodical conferences and free intellectual discourse. This, he felt, "was a necessary preliminary to any future plan of united or separate action,[thus] the resolutions adopted by the successive Congresses were many statements urging united action, particularly in the matter of race discrimination."[33]

By the 1945 Fifth Pan-African Conference, however, the intellectual and ideological mandates of Pan-Africanism became manifested in concrete action and popular movements toward independence as the growing participation of young leaders and union organizers from the African continent (still under colonial rule) changed the practical contours of these congresses—the same way they would later change the political scene of the continent. At this fifth congress, Du Bois's intellectual influence, particularly his increasing adoption of a strong critique of colonial/imperial rule, was

---

[32] Afari-Gyan, Kwadwo, 1991. "Kwame Nkrumah, George Padmore and W. E. B. Du Bois." *Institute of African Studies Research Review* 7 (1 & 2): 1 – 21.

[33] Eric Sundquist, editor. *The Oxford W. E. B. Du Bois Reader* (Oxford: Oxford University Press, 1996) 664.

significant in the nascent African nationalist movements throughout the continent. However, it is also at this moment, that the legacy and the symbolic leadership of Pan-Africanism shifted from the elder statesman of Du Bois to the rising stars of George Padmore and especially Kwame Nkrumah. As Sinclair Drake points out, after World War II Nkrumah became the "virtual symbol of Pan-Africanism as Afro-Americans and West Indians understood the term."[34] Du Bois would later confirm Nkrumah's role as the new paragon of African/diaspora cooperation in his congratulatory letter to the new president of Ghana during the country's independence celebrations. In fact, in this letter Du Bois symbolically bestowed on Nkrumah the title of "President of the Pan-African Congress," relinquishing his lifelong role. As suggested by our epigraph, Du Bois expected Ghana to take up the mantle of Pan-Africanism and proscribed a program of political, intellectual, and cultural activities that included periodic conferences (on the African continent), the establishment of cultural centers, and the generation of research agendas that would counter hegemonic, racist representations of blacks with deeply historical understandings of the socioeconomic constructions of racial constructions and identifications.

As the first prime minister of the newly independent Ghana, Nkrumah was to forge the nation-state through this Du Boisian legacy of Pan-Africanist vision of liberation and international cooperation. In so doing, Nkrumah helped place Ghana at the center of global discourses on African politics and global racial liberation. Nkrumah's Ghana came to reflect the broadly humanistic understanding of Pan-Africanism that underlay Du Bois's intellectual and political work, which he articulated as early as 1915 in *The Negro*, stating, "A belief in humanity means a belief in colored men."[35] In this sense, Du Boisian Pan-Africanism became manifest both in explicit state ideologies as well as cultural and political economic practices. Nkrumah demonstrated the strength of his commitment to this on the eve of independence when he proclaimed that the independence of Ghana was meaningless unless linked to the total liberation of the African continent. Indeed, the very institutions and ideologies of the state were produced through a recognition of the need to maintain the links between African politics and the diaspora. It seemed that Nkrumah, on many levels, heeded

---

[34] Drake, St.Clair, 1982. "Diaspora Studies and Pan-Africanism," p. 460.

[35] Du Bois, *Negro*, 146.

Du Bois's vision. And while early on Nkrumah focused on the liberation of the African continent, his Pan-Africanist thinking increasingly recognized that there were intrinsic links between "imperialism and racism as a 'basic factor of instability in Africa'"[36] In fact, the constitution of the Republic of Ghana explicitly prohibited racial, religious, and sexual discrimination[37]. The new state sponsored a number of Pan-Africanist events, most notably the 1958 All Africa Peoples Conference in Accra, which, in many ways, laid the foundation for the founding of the Organization of African Unity in 1963. At the opening ceremony to the All Africa Peoples Conference, Nkrumah expressed his delight to see "so many of our brothers from across the sea," adding, "we must not forget that they are a part of us."[38]

In fact, earlier in the year, Nkrumah had visited the United States and, at a speech in Harlem to a capacity crowd, proclaimed that "Africans and African Americans were held together by 'bonds of blood and kinship' and appealed to 'doctors and lawyers and engineers to come and help us build our country.'"[39] Nkrumah encouraged the return to Ghana of those from the diaspora to help in the immediate project of developing the new Ghanaian nation in particular and the ultimate liberation of African peoples in general. As Ghana's independence had served as a highly visible symbol for diaspora blacks of global black emancipation, many repatriated to Ghana. A number of these repatriates became involved in Nkrumah's government and held highly public positions. This movement of peoples shows the continual dialogue that developed in the context of Nkrumah's leadership. George Padmore came to Ghana and became Nkrumah's key advisor and a crucial political figure behind the scenes. A sizable African-American and West-Indian community of artists, professionals, and others developed in Accra, which included its acknowledged leader, the writer Julian Mayfield, who also

---

[36] Kwame Nkrumah, quoted in Ronald W. Walters, *Pan Africanism in the Diaspora: An Analysis of Modern Afrocentric Political Movements* (Detroit: Wayne State University Press, 1993) 99–100.

[37] *Pan Africanism*, ed. Walters, 99–100.

[38] Kwame Nkrumah, 1958. Opening address at the "All African Peoples Conference" in Accra, Ghana. In *All-African Peoples Conference Secretariat. News Bulletin Vol 1 (1-7) (Text of speeches, etc.)*. Accra, 1959, p. 59

Joseph Harris and Slimane Zeghidour, 1993. "Africa and its Diaspora Since 1935" in Ali A. Mazrui, ed., *General History of Africa, Vol. 3: Africa Since 1935*. Berkeley: UNESCO/Heinemann

[39] Nkrumah, quoted in *Pan Africanism*, ed. Walters, 98.

worked in government; poet Maya Angelou; and Dr. Alphaeus Hunton and his wife Dorothy, among others.[40] Furthermore, publicized visits by Malcolm X and other dignitaries from the diaspora to Ghana highlighted the new nation as a symbol of racial and radical consciousness. These transatlantic movements demonstrate the complex and overlapping relationships between diasporic and continental African political struggle.

Of course, the highlight of the repatriation of peoples from the diaspora was that of W. E. B. Du Bois himself, who spent the final two years of his life in Ghana as a Ghanaian citizen working on the state-sponsored Pan-Africanist project, the *Encyclopaedia Africana*. His wife Shirley Graham Du Bois later became the first head of the Ghana Broadcasting Corporation (GBC). Du Bois's presence affirmed the new nation's symbolic power as the leading light of Pan-Africanism. His personal relationship with Nkrumah, coupled with his professional role in Ghanaian intellectual and political circles, contributed to the concretization of black transatlantic links. David Levering Lewis stresses that while in Ghana Du Bois "discharged his role as oracle and symbol consummately...encouraging [Nkrumah's] regime with generalities, presiding over an international conference of scholars at the Legon campus of the University of Ghana, granting audiences" to many local and international visitors at his Accra home.[41] Even in death, Du Bois reinforced the global connections of all with comparable experiences of racial inequality and its attendant economic marginalization. Ghana staged a massive funeral with full state and military honors while numerous cables of salutation and condolence from all corners of the African continent and abroad poured into the country.[42] His death was also announced during the 1963 civil rights march on Washington just before Dr. Martin Luther King, Jr.'s famous "I Have a Dream" speech. As Levering Lewis points out, "The state funeral for W. E. B. Du Bois...on August 29, 1963 was meant to celebrate and symbolize Ghana's claim to Pan-African leadership."[43] It highlights the fact that Du Bois represented for Ghana and the black world a legacy of Pan-Africanism that stressed the connections between the African continent and the diaspora.

---

[40] *Pan Africanism*, ed Walters, 89-126.

[41] David Levering Lewis, *W. E. B. Du Bois: The Fight for Equality and the American Century: 1919–1963* (New York: Henry Holt and Company, 2000) 568-69.

[42] The United States Embassy, most notably, neglected to pay their respects at Du Bois's funeral.

[43] Lewis, *Fight for Equality*, 5.

As we have described, Du Bois's particular influence was a crucial, if under-recognized, aspect of the movement for African decolonization. In this sense Du Bois concretized the links between African continental political liberation and the diaspora—and indeed the world—liberation struggles. The early years of independence in Ghana, as with many African states, were marked by a continued intellectual and political understanding of connections between colonialism, African political liberation, and global racial inequality by both African and diaspora political leaders. As St. Clair Drake argues, "Nkrumah had always been adept at keeping continental Pan-Africanism central but not neglecting what he conceived of as the legitimate concern of Africans for the fate of people in the diaspora."[44] His actions then affirmed the continuation of the "live dialogue" between the continent and the diaspora that, in turn, structured the personal, political, sociocultural, and practical relationship between these groups of peoples.

By the mid-1960s much of the continent had achieved political independence. However, the series of military coups that followed, particularly the overthrow of Nkrumah's regime in 1966, destabilized the ideological unification of African political liberation struggles as well as their connections to African diasporic civil rights structured through a Pan-Africanist vision. In particular, the Ghanaian state's explicit policy of reaching out to diaspora blacks in developing the nation waned as various military governments became preoccupied with consolidating power.[45] As a result, the relationships that were cultivated between the continent and the diaspora at the height of Nkrumah's Pan-Africanist rule suffered. Many of those from the diaspora who settled in Ghana, including W. E. B. Du Bois's widow Shirley Graham Du Bois, became disillusioned and left the country. The explicit connections between African liberation and diaspora struggles were, therefore, bracketed in the face of internal African political struggles.

---

[44] St.Clair Drake, 1982. "Diaspora Studies and Pan-Africanism," p. 469.

[45] This shift in focus can partly be attributed to the conditions under which Nkrumah was deposed and the general anti-Nkrumah sentiments throughout Ghana at the time. In fact, there was mass destruction of all things associated with Nkrumah, and the political climate of the country at the time worked against any acknowledgement of Nkrumah's successes and ideological positions. In particular, many Ghanaians blamed Nkrumah for focusing too many economic and political resources on Pan-Africanist visions of African liberation and the international fight against imperial domination. It is telling that Nkrumah was overthrown while on a trip to consult with the Chinese government on topics including the American intervention in Vietnam.

These linkages around black international cooperation, however, would later be rekindled by the recognition of the continuation of the basic global exploitative political economic relations of the (post) colonial world. But with the passing of Nkrumah and his generation of politicians, the explicit critique of neocolonialism and the attendant calls for (black) international cooperation became less central to political practice and ideology. The explicit links, then, between African political sovereignty and global racial(ized) liberation—which Nkrumah and Du Bois had emphasized— were sidelined. There was not the opportunity—or will—for Ghana's set of successive military governments to make such connections. The result was that, both on the intellectual and the political level, critiques of the African nation-state and the predicament of the continent and its peoples turned inwards, sidelining internationalist insights into the global historical nature of racial capitalism. While African Americans and West Indians maintained spiritual and cultural affinities with the African homeland, the explicit connections around political struggle seemed to become less prominent in the post-Civil Rights era.

Nevertheless, as Joseph Harris suggests, diaspora "links to Africa...continued."[46] There were a number of intellectual projects and cultural events, from the continued publication of *Présence Africaine* in the Francophone world to various cultural conferences, including the 1957 world conference of black writers in Paris—out of which emerged the Société Africaine de Culture, with its United States branch, the American Society of African Culture[47] and the 1966 Festival of Negro Arts in Dakar. Thus, cultural festivals like the Festival of Black and African Arts and Culture (FESTAC) in Lagos (1977), musical and sporting events such as *Soul to Soul* in Accra (1971) and the Rumble in the Jungle in Kinshasa (1974) and the visits of popular cultural figures to Africa such as James Brown, Wilson Pickett, and Mohammed Ali became the representative statement of black international interaction. In many ways the popular styles and music of Black America became signs of racial solidarity for Africans, while conversely symbols of Africa including kente cloth, jewelry, artistic representations of the continent, etc. played a similar role for African Americans. For diaspora peoples, Africa became a set of cultural symbols

---

[46] Joseph Harris, ed., *Global Dimensions of the African Diaspora* (Washington DC: Howard University Press, 1993) 714.

[47] Ibid.

invoked through individual, emotional connections with Africa. As this implies, solidarity began to be put in terms of the consumption of African-oriented symbols and cultural products. Thus, while the forms of Pan-Africanist articulations—as well as their interpretations by scholars—have taken different forms, our point here is to show that connections around black identifications and their implicit unity of purpose and global cooperation have been continually maintained. This particular movement of various forms of Pan-Africanist interaction, in fact, confirms our broader point that the global sociohistorical experience of racialized identities, while explicitly manifest in diffuse ways, is embedded within the practical experience of black peoples and lays the basis for ongoing global dialogue.

The Contemporary Recuperation of Du Boisian Pan-Africanism

From the 1980s there was a renewed and explicit focus on Pan-Africanism in Ghana. Initiated by the then-Provisional National Defense Council (PNDC) under the leadership of its chairman, flight lieutenant Jerry John Rawlings, this revival of the Pan-Africanist legacies of Du Bois (and Nkrumah) occurred partially as a response to the changing landscape of global political economy. The PNDC had assumed control of the country through a military coup d'etat in 1981. Through the influence of left-oriented intellectuals,[48] the PNDC once again made explicit Nkrumah's critiques of neocolonialism and its crippling effect on African polities. At first, Rawlings, a charismatic and outspoken young Air Force officer, was publicly committed to populism as a political principle (though from the beginning, his new administration was fraught by internal, contrasting political philosophies and goals). In his initial radio address (after taking power), Rawlings denounced the corruption of previous regimes and their collusion with the dominant world economic order. He vehemently proclaimed, "I ask for nothing less than a revolution. Something that would transform the social and economic order of this country." In this revolutionary moment, Rawlings invoked the political legacy of Nkrumah and Ghana's position at the center of African liberation struggles: "…Ghana may not be that rich but she is the political light to Africa…[A]s soon as Ghana realises her social and economic democracy, the rest of Africa will

---

[48] These included Kojo Tsikata, Kwesi Botchwey, and Mohammed Ben Abdallah.

follow and will be on the road to a continental unity...."[49] In another radio address several days later, Rawlings more explicitly invoked Pan-Africanist sensibilities when he recalled Nkrumah's appeal to people and institutions in the diaspora to support Ghana. He further demonstrated his recognition of the links between Ghanaian sovereignty and global political liberation across the continent and beyond: "We are appealing to the African peoples, our neighbours in particular, and their governments to show solidarity with us in these critical times even as they did in our better times. Our solidarity with the peoples of Southern Africa[50] in their struggles to free themselves from alien domination is naturally strengthened by our new commitments...."[51]

Building on ideas of cultural nationalism from the Nkrumah era, the Rawlings government, in its early years, argued that African and Ghanaian culture and civilization needed to be the basis for African political liberation. In this sense, the new government reestablished the links made, through the legacy of Du Bois in Ghana, between global (racial) inequality and Pan-African cultural nationalism. The revival of this legacy, in addition, reawakened and encouraged critiques of the structural power of Africa's neocolonial political economy.[52]

The Rawlings administration took power under the aegis of a populist revolution and several of its advisors had strong Marxist, as well as Pan-

---

[49] Radio broadcast to the nation, Thursday, 31 December 1981, reprinted in *A Revolutionary Journey: Selected Speeches of Flt. Lt. Jerry John Rawlings Chairman of the PNDC, Dec. 31st 1981– Dec. 31st 1982, Volume One.* Reprinted in: Rawlings, Jerry John, 1982. *A Revolutionary Journey: Selected Speeches of Flt. Lt. J. J. Rawlings Chairman of the Provisional National Defence Council December 31, 1981 – December 31, 1982.* Accra: Information Services Department, Ghana Publishing Corporation.

[50] Rawlings's regime expressed African political solidarity by aiding in the struggles against the repressive white regimes in Southern Africa in a number of ways, including helping with military training as well as issuing Ghanaian passports to South Africans who were unable to travel internationally using their own national affiliations.

[51] Radio and television broadcast to the nation, Tuesday, 5 January 1982, reprinted in *A Revolutionary Journey: Selected Speeches of Flt. Lt. Jerry John Rawlings Chairman of the PNDC, Dec. 31st 1981– Dec. 31st 1982, Volume One.*

[52] Personally, Rawlings had an ambivalent relationship with the Nkrumah's politics and personality, in some ways feeling overshadowed by the first president. However, he also felt that appropriating Nkrumah's political and intellectual legacy was instrumental for maintaining power as well as crucial to the development of the Ghanaian state ("Personal Telephone conversation between Jesse Weaver Shipley and an ex-PNDC official, 12th February 2002.").

Africanist, ideals and intentions.[53] In keeping with this populist stance, the PNDC called for reforming government practices to allow for the truly democratic incorporation of the masses into the political process. However, by the mid-1980s Ghana was forced, by dire economic circumstances, to accept financial assistance from the International Monetary Fund (IMF) in exchange for the realignment of the state's policies in terms of liberal, free-market capitalism and the divestment of state enterprises. An effect of this restructuring was the government's gradual abandonment of its more radical critiques of Western capitalism and neocolonialism. As a result of these liberalizing reforms, which continued into the 1990s, Pan-Africanism and cultural nationalism became, instead, sites of income generation for the state as well as the private sector. With the help of international organizations such as UNESCO, Ghana's many cultural and historical sites became increasingly commodified through heritage tourism. In the face of increasing protest and criticism from the economically depressed population, the administration turned to Pan-Africanist rhetoric as a way to critique its economic predicament and absolve the government of blame. In this context, however, the appropriation of Pan-African ideals, particularly in its Du Boisian (and Nkrumahist) form of African/diasporic cooperation, occurred in terms of the full development of Ghana's heritage tourism industry—currently the country's third-largest source of income. Thus, in an about-face from Rawlings's professed populism, the state and private industry began to capitalize on Ghana's history of Pan-Africanism.

The government's appropriation of the country's early legacy of Pan-Africanism took on many forms: the promotion of repatriation and tourism of diaspora peoples;[54] the development of international African cultural festivals; the restoration, and later, promotion of the former slave trading castles along the coast; the establishment of public memorials and research centers in honor of Du Bois, Padmore, and Nkrumah; the support of foreign research scholars and students in study abroad programs; the development of private investment; and the encouragement of diaspora peoples to purchase land in Ghana. These activities, though largely articulated in terms

---

[53] There were, of course, many internal ideological and practical disagreements regarding the means of achieving the sought-after radical changes, which we are not able to discuss fully in this essay.

[54] In the 1990s, Ghana Airways began to fly non-stop from New York and Washington DC with the explicit intent of encouraging African American tourism.

of commodified forms and consumer practices, nevertheless tapped in to the practices and connections that, arguably, had continued from the early twentieth century through to the 1970s. They ultimately worked to reestablish the significant links between Africa and the diaspora through, admittedly, complex and contradictory economic and cultural means.

These forms of Pan-Africanist activities during the Rawlings era have been most clearly articulated through the state's initial sponsorship of PANAFEST (Pan African Historical Theatre Festival) and Emancipation Day celebrations. We argue that, though these festivals are structured within the particularities of state politics and are shaped by the global political economy of the 1990s, they are embedded in the legacy of Du Bois's Pan-Africanism in Ghana. Specifically, they (re)articulate Ghana as the center of Pan-Africanist thinking and paradoxically reaffirm the connections between continental African and diasporic struggles against marginalization and racial oppression.

PANAFEST was launched in 1992 as a state-sponsored festival of African and African-diaspora culture under the theme "Re-Emergence of African Civilization." In the tradition of earlier celebrations such as the 1966 Festival of Negro Arts in Dakar and the 1977 Festival of African and Black Arts in Lagos, PANAFEST began as a "vision for uplifting and reuniting African peoples through the arts."[55] The festival was initiated by Ghanaian dramatist, writer, and Pan-Africanist Efua Sutherland, who was also instrumental in the founding of both the Du Bois Memorial Centre and, in the 1960s, the Ghana National Theatre Movement. Bringing together Pan-Africanist identifications, ideas of cultural affinities, and notions of economic development, the festival has over time gained international popularity, attracting more and more people from Africa and the African diaspora. In 1997, 1,400 participants from twenty-seven countries, primarily from the United States, Nigeria, United Kingdom, and Jamaica, came under the theme "Uniting the African Family for Development." In 1999 there were 5,000 participants from forty countries. PANAFEST has endeavored to use, as a basis of mutual political and economic progress, the links between expressive culture, intellectual thought, and African civilizations around the globe. Its stated aims are to: (1) use African arts and culture to vindicate Africa's pride in its history; (2) provide a forum for promoting unity between

[55] "Panafest Ghana," 2001. Retrieved February 20, 2002, from http://www.panafest.org/history.html.

Africans on the continent and those in the diaspora; and (3) affirm the common heritage of continental and diaspora Africans and define Africa's contribution to world civilization.[56]

As a result, PANAFEST further concretizes Ghana's role as the leading Pan-Africanist state on the African continent and, indeed, across the globe. Over the years, the festival has attempted to bring together artists, musicians, theater groups, dancers, students, intellectuals, and returnees from the African diaspora to perform, exchange ideas, and strengthen the bonds of brotherhood between Africans and black people in the diaspora. Well-known African-American artists such as Stevie Wonder and Isaac Hayes, for example, have come to perform for the celebrations. The festival has also attracted other famous personalities, including Denzel Washington, Danny Glover, and Rita Marley. In addition, participants and performers have come from across the African continent. The festival has revolved around several days of theatrical, musical, and dance performances from around the continent and the diaspora, which are juxtaposed to show the historical continuities embedded in these different forms of expression. The events have also included durbars (Durbars are large state ceremonial gatherings of officials and dignitaries. They have their origins in the British colonial period where local officials gave formal receptions for visiting British rulers.) of chiefs that display the wealth and grandeur of Ghanaian chieftaincy; Akan naming ceremonies in which African names are ceremonially given to people from the diaspora; and candle-lit services, enacted in the former slave trading forts Elmina and Cape Coast Castle, in memory of the horrors of the Atlantic slave trade.[57] Additionally, various academic colloquia have been held, bringing together scholars and writers of African decent.

The establishment of Emancipation Day as a national holiday in Ghana was inspired by former president Rawlings's visit to Jamaica on 1 August 1997 where he participated in celebrations commemorating the 1834 abolition of slavery throughout the British empire. Official annual celebrations commemorating this event began in Ghana in 1998 as a rallying point "for Africans on the continent and in the diaspora...to defy any form

---

[56] Ibid.

[57] UNESCO has established several slave castles as World Heritage sites and has given financial and practical resources to aid in the preservation of cultural heritage and the encouragement of cultural tourism.

of oppression, slavery, or colonialism against the African people...."[58] At the
opening ceremony that year, Rawlings again called for unity between those
in Africa and those in the diaspora, saying, "If the nations and peoples of
Africa and the Diaspora can come together with determination to build a
strong economic base, our people can live in peace and dignity."[59] The nine-
day celebrations occurred under the theme "Our Heritage, Our Strength,"
and, like PANAFEST, brought together a number of black peoples from
across the globe. The opening ceremonies culminated in the solemn
repatriation of the remains of two former enslaved Africans, Crystal from
Jamaica and John Carson from the United States.[60] Thus, clearly linking
slavery and colonialism to the present situations of African peoples,
Emancipation Day also became a focal point of diasporic African interest in
and contact with Ghana.

In August of 2001, the PANAFEST and Emancipation Day
Celebrations—previously celebrated separately—were united under the
auspices of the Ministry of Tourism.[61] Bringing together cultural and
political forms of Pan-Africanism, PANAFEST and Emancipation Day both
began as state-sponsored projects in which Pan-Africanism was deployed in
the name of state politics and development. This gave way to a particular
trajectory where state concerns with practical notions of development led to
a more consumer-centered approach to these celebrations. With the global
turn towards cultural heritage tourism, PANAFEST has become a popular
tourist destination for those of African descent in the diaspora. In fact, while
Ghanaian intellectuals and artists have participated and local businesses have
benefited economically from the festivals, the local Ghanaian population
has, in general, not been major participants of such Pan-Africanist
celebrations.

---

[58] Reuters, 1998. "Ghana hosts first Black Emancipation Day in Africa." Retrieved
March 1, 2002 from http://www.ghanaforum.com/news/reuters073098.htm

[59] Pan African News Agency, July 31, 1998. "Rawlings Calls For Unity Of The
Black   Race."   Retrieved   December   24,   2006   from
http://www.interchange.org/nsagislist/NL08249812.html

[60] Ibid.

[61] While both festivals had been initially state-organized projects, by the late 1990s
they involved significant private sponsorship, though the state maintained a certain
amount of control over the events, used them for government propaganda, and made
them appeare to the public as if they were state-run projects.

By the late 1990s, while still maintaining a certain ideological commitment to the principles of Pan-Africanist liberation these events became more oriented towards the instrumental capital to be earned through tourism. For example, whereas the 2000 Emancipation Day celebrations were well advertised to communities outside of the country on the internet and through global organizations, advertising for these same celebrations within Ghana did not occur until the first day of the weeklong activities *and* with much less fanfare. There was hardly any local discussion of the events—either in the popular press or on radio stations. Ghanaians, for the most part, were left completely unaware. Furthermore, the cost of and lack of accessibility to many of the events[62] made it impossible for most Ghanaians to attend. Some Ghanaians have been cynical about these festivals, arguing that the state has used Pan-African ideology for nationalist propaganda and for its own economic gains at the expense of those from the diaspora. At the same time, those from the diaspora are seen, by some members of the local population, as wealthy benefactors with the personal financial ability to help alleviate Ghana's economic woes.

Despite these complex, ironic, and sometimes contradictory reactions, there has been, throughout the 1990s, a steady growth in diaspora returns to Ghana. These festivals; the memorials to Du Bois, Nkrumah, and Padmore; and the memorialization of the former slave-trading forts continue to give concreteness to the view of Africa as the ancestral homeland. They have opened up spaces for maintaining artistic, intellectual, economic, and political dialogues across the diaspora. Echoing state officials, some African Americans residing in Ghana have explicitly articulated the links between attracting diaspora returnees to Ghana and the economic development of the country. While addressing an Emancipation Day crowd, Philip Moore, "the leader of the African-American Community in Ghana," made explicit the links between the politics of return, tourism, economic development, and Pan-African unity.[63] He asserted that the PANAFEST and Emancipation Day celebrations should be observed "as important spiritual exercises, aimed at strengthening the bonds of brotherhood between Africans and all the black people in the Diaspora...so that every visit we pay

---

[62] Many of the events occurred outside of Accra or in remote places; travel to such places would require a great deal of revenue for the average Ghanaian.

[63] Pan African News Agency, "Rawlings Calls For Unity of The Black Race" (opt. cit.)

to Africa will be a real home-coming and not a pleasure tour."[64] He went on to suggest that the Ministry of Tourism should focus on programs that would attract more African Americans to Ghana because "they have a lot to offer the country in all sectors of the economy."[65]

This response to Emancipation Day again points to the complex and changing relations between racial identifications, national affiliation, economics, and Pan-Africanism. In 1955, in a speech on the relationship between African American blacks and Africa, Du Bois lamented the fact that "American Negroes...are...doing little to help Africa in its hour of supreme need."[66] While Nkrumah fostered these connections around the political and cultural unity of black peoples, Rawlings has taken a more economically development-oriented approach. Echoing Nkrumah's call of nearly forty years earlier, President Rawlings in 1995 made a speech in Harlem in which he announced that peoples of African descent would be granted Ghanaian citizenship under the "Law of Return."[67] He encouraged African Americans with skills to come back to help the development of Ghana: "You must interact with our people more intensively and bring your talents and resources to Africa's march to progress and fulfillment... We must open our doors to you so that you and your children could feel in the very soul that Africa is indeed your mother country."[68]

However, while making the appeal along spiritual lines he made sure to reinforce the point that this was ultimately an economic proposition: "Do not come to the continent without the appropriate skills and resources because you will only be contributing to its poverty. Pool your savings together to invest in the economic and social future of Africa."[69] Some Ghanaians in the United States protested Rawlings's visit, pointing out that he was simply taking advantage of African Americans' historic connections to the history of Ghana for his personal and political gains.

Du Bois himself anticipated the contradictions that would be confronted by African liberation struggles in the face of economic necessity. In his address to the 1958 All Africa Peoples Conference in Accra, he called for African peoples to stand strong with their convictions in the face of

---

[64] Ibid.

[65] Ibid.

[66] *Seventh Son*, ed. Lester, 620.

[67] Ibid.

[68] Ibid.

[69] Ibid.

economic pressure during the complex moment of decolonization: "…You are not helpless. You are the buyers and to continue existence as sellers of capital, these great nations, former owners of the world, must sell or face bankruptcy. You are not compelled to buy all they offer now. You can wait. You can starve a while longer rather than sell your great heritage for a mess of Western capitalist pottage."[70] Du Bois realized that Africa needed financial investment but believed that the socialist and communist countries would eventually be able to supply that assistance without the prospect of reestablishing (neo)colonial economic relations, which Du Bois realized was a very real threat if any economic dependence was placed on the Western capitalist powers. As global socialist possibilities have faded, the stark predicament of Pan-Africanist liberation is confronting the dangers of its appropriation by global capitalism.

Again Du Bois foresaw the temptations and dangers of free-market capitalism in the particular form that arose in the 1980s and 1990s: "[The West] offers to let some of your smarter and less scrupulous leaders become fellow capitalists with the white exploiters if in turn they induce the nation's masses to pay the awful costs. This happened in the West Indies and in South America…. Strive against it with every fibre of your bodies and souls. A body of local private capitalists, even if they are black, can never free Africa; they will simply sell it into new slavery to old masters overseas…."[71]

In this light, what would Du Bois make of the contemporary legacy of his Pan-Africanism as manifest through private investment and commodified cultural forms in Ghana? What does Pan-Africanism, as we have described it above, mean in the context of the contemporary moment of capitalism and what possibilities does it still hold for a liberational politics around global racialized oppression? While Pan-Africanist ideologies are continually appropriated in the name of state politics, private investment, and the perpetuation of neocolonial frameworks of economic investment, we contend that they nevertheless foster concrete African/diaspora interaction and relationships. Such interactions reshape the cultural and political imaginaries of these two sets of communities as they continually structure "mutually transformative dialogues" with each other.[72] While dialogues

---

[70] Hisham Aidi, "Ghana's 'Law of Return,'"1999. Retrieved February 1, 2002 from http://www.africana.com/DailyArticles/index_20000523.htm.

[71] Ibid.

[72] Matory, "Afro-Atlantic Cultures," p. 50.

between peoples of the African continent and the diaspora have sometimes led to conflict over contradictory interests and purposes, we argue that Pan-Africanism and ideas of black solidarity continue to provide possibilities for alternate forms of political, intellectual, and cultural connections.

Conclusion

In this essay we have tried to show that interrogating the legacy of Du Bois's Pan-Africanism is crucial to understanding the complexities of post-independence African nationalism, decolonization, and, more broadly, the global sociohistorical production of racialized identities and their concomitant forms of inequality. The broader implications of this legacy remind us to examine the complex ways that contemporary Pan-Africanism affirms Du Bois's insights concerning the centrality of racialized inequality to global politics, economics, and social justice.

Contemporary Pan-Africanism, as a public political form from the 1980s, is not necessarily identified by *explicit* ideological, intellectual, or political treatises but rather through the practical and symbolic monuments, events, and practices that manifest the connections between Africa and its diaspora. In the Rawlings and current era, then, Pan-Africanist ideologies were appropriated in ambivalent ways; they offered both a way to reconnect critiques of neocolonialism, African political struggle, and global racial inequality while, at the same time, becoming part of the promotion of global tourism and the encouragement of private and international aid agency investment in Ghana. While attempting to realign global connections in terms of the history of racialized forms of oppression, these links were also appropriated as commodified forms of Pan-Africanist tradition by the capitalist free-market economy. In this way, shifting identifications concerning blackness, Africanity, and nationality have been rearticulated in terms of this new moment of capitalism and Pan-Africanism.

Works Cited

Ackah, William, 1999. Pan-Africanism: Exploring the Contradictions: Politics, Identity, and Development in Africa and the African Diaspora. Brookfield, VT: Ashgate.

Afari-Gyan, Kwadwo. "Kwame Nkrumah, George Padmore and W. E. B. Du Bois." *Institute of African Studies Research Review* 7/1-2 ([MONTH]1991): 1–21.

Agbeyebiawo, Daniel. *The Life and Works of W. E. B. Du Bois*. Accra: Stephil Printing Press, 1998.

Aido, Hisham. "Ghana's Law of Return." <http://www.africana.com/DailyArticles/index_20000523.htm>.

Appiah, Kwame A., 1998. "Pan-Africanism." In E. Craig (Ed.), *Routledge Encyclopedia of Philosophy*. London: Routledge. Retrieved September 28, 2006, from http://www.rep.routledge.com/article/Z018.

Appiah, Kwame, and Henry Gates, editors. *Africana: The Encyclopedia of the African and the African American Experience*. New York: Basic Vitas Books, 1999.

Boahen, A. Adu. *African Perspectives on Colonialism*. Baltimore MD: John Hopkins University Press, 1987.

Bourdieu, Pierre and Loic Wacquant. "On the Cunning of Imperialist Reason." *Theory, Culture & Society* 16/1 (February 1999): 41–58.

Campbell, Horace, 1994. "Pan-Africanism and African Liberation" in Sidney J. Lemelle and Robin D. G. Kelley, eds. *Imagining Home: Class, Culture, and Nationalism in the African Diaspora*. New York: Verso.

Drake, St.Clair, 1982. "Diaspora Studies and Pan-Africanism," in Joseph Harris, ed. *Global Dimensions of the African Diaspora*. Washington, D.C.: Howard University Press.

Du Bois, W. E. B. *The Negro*. 1915. Reprint, Oxford: Oxford University Press, 1970.

———. *Africa, Its Geography, People and Products*. Girard KS: Haldeman-Julius Publications, 1930.

———. *Africa—Its Place in Modern History*. Girad KS: Haldeman-Julius Publications, 1930.

———. *Black Folk: Then and Now*. New York: Henry Holt and Company, 1939.

———. *The World and Africa*. New York: Viking Press, 1947.

Eric Sundquist, editor. *The Oxford W. E. B. Du Bois Reader*. Oxford: Oxford University Press, 1996.

Edwards, Brent, 2001. "The Uses of Diaspora," *Social Text* 19 (1): 45-73

Esedebe, P. Olisanwuche. *Pan-Africanism: The Idea and the Movement, 1776–1991*. Washington DC: Howard University Press, 1994.

Harris, Joseph E., editor. *Global Dimensions of the African Diaspora*. Washington DC: Howard University Press, 1993.

Lemelle, Sidney, and Robin D. G. Kelley, editors. *Imagining Home: Class, Culture and Nationalism in the African Diaspora*. New York: Verso, 1994.

Lester, Julius, editor. *The Seventh Son: The Thought and Writings of W. E. B. Du Bois*, Vol. II. New York: Random House, 1971.

Lewis, David Levering. *W. E. B. Du Bois: The Fight For Equality and the American Century: 1919–1963*. New York: Henry Holt and Company, 2000.

Magubane, Bernard. *The Ties that Bind: African-American Consciousness of Africa*. Trenton NJ: Africa World Press, 1994.

Matory, J. Lorand, 1999. "Afro-Atlantic Culture: On the Live Dialogue Between Africa and the Americas" in Kwame A. Appiah and Henry L. Gates, eds, *Africana: The Encyclopedia of the African and African American Experience*. New York: Basic Civitas Books, pp. 36-44.

Nkrumah, Kwame, 1959. Opening address at the "All African Peoples Conference" in Accra, Ghana. In *All-African Peoples Conference Secretariat. News Bulletin Vol 1 (1-7) (Text of speeches, etc.)*. Accra.

Orgen, Kathy, 1994. "What Africa is to Me? African Strategies in the Harlem Renaissance" in Sidney J. Lemelle and Robin D. G. Kelley, eds. *Imagining Home: Class, Culture, and Nationalism in the African Diaspora*. New York: Verso.

Pan African News Agency (PANAPRESS) website: <http://www.panapress.com>.

Rawlings, Jerry John. *A Revolutionary Journey: Selected Speeches of Flt. Lt. J. J. Rawlings Chairman of the Provisional National Defence Council December 31, 1981–December 31, 1982, Volume One*. Accra: Information Services Department, Ghana Publishing Corporation.

Shepperson, George, 1965. "The African Abroad or the African Diaspora," in Terence O. Ranger, ed. *Emerging Themes of African History*. London: Heinemann Educational Books Ltd.

Walters, Ronald W. *Pan Africanism in the African Diaspora: An Analysis of Modern Afrocentric Political Movements*. Detroit: Wayne State University Press, 1993.

Rectificatory Justice and the Philosophy of W. E. B. Du Bois

Rodney C. Roberts
East Carolina University

William Edward Burghardt Du Bois was one of the most important American thinkers of his time. Born during the Reconstruction, on the eve of Andrew Johnson's impeachment,[1] Du Bois was a productive scholar and activist throughout most of his ninety-five years. By the time of his death in 1963, on the eve of the March on Washington DC, his corpus included twenty-one books and scores of other publications.[2] Although Du Bois was trained primarily as a historian, having received both is M.A.[3] and Ph.D. in history,[4] his undergraduate degree from Harvard was granted *cum laude* in philosophy. His aim was to study philosophy at Harvard and pursue philosophy for the rest of his life. Unfortunately for philosophy, Du Bois turned "back from the lovely but sterile land of philosophical speculation, to

---

[1] Du Bois tells us that "Thaddeus Stevens, the clearest-headed leader of this attempt at industrial democracy, made his last speech, impeaching Andrew Johnson on February 16, and on February 23 I was born." W. E. B. Du Bois, *The Autobiography of W. E. B. Du Bois: A Soliloquy on Viewing My Life from the Last Decade of Its First Century* (New York: International Publishers, 1968) 61. The resolution of impeachment was not passed by the House of Representatives until 24 February 1868 ("Johnson, Andrew," *Microsoft Encarta Encyclopedia 2000*).

[2] Herbert Aptheker, "A Selected Bibliography of the Published Writings of W. E. B. Du Bois," in Du Bois, *Autobiography*, 431–37.

[3] "I finished the first draft of my thesis and delivered an outline of it at the seminaries of American history and political economy December 7, 1891. I received my master's degree in the Spring." Du Bois, *Autobiography*, 149.

[4] Du Bois received his doctorate in history at Harvard in 1895 (*UMI ProQuest Digital Dissertations*, <http://wwwlib.umi.com/dissertations>).

the social sciences."[5] Fortunately the philosophical landscape in America is much different today, and it is not quite the "sterile land" of speculation that it was in the late-nineteenth century when Du Bois was a student. Indeed, it is not the sterile land it was in the 1950s when many of today's most senior philosophers were students. The American philosophical landscape now includes a relative abundance of normative theorizing in ethics as well as in social and political philosophy, and philosophical analyses dealing with issues concerning race, gender, class, and physical ability seem almost commonplace. Rectificatory justice is one area of the contemporary American philosophical landscape that is probably among the least sterile and that has gained increased attention recently. Surely Du Bois would be pleased to find that examining questions concerning injustice and the rectification of injustice is now a legitimate philosophical endeavor. In addition to a growing number of books addressing rectificatory concerns,[6] there is a growing movement in the United States for black reparations in particular.[7] Although the typical meaning of "reparations" is consistent with

---

[5] Du Bois, *Autobiography*, 148. Du Bois cites the influence of William James as instrumental to his move away from philosophy. For a discussion of James's influence on Du Bois, see James Campbell, "Du Bois and James," *Transactions of the Charles S. Peirce Society* 28/3 (1992) 569–81.

[6] Recent books in philosophy include: J. Angelo Corlett, *Race, Racism and Reparations* (Ithaca: Cornell University Press, 2003); Rodney C. Roberts, ed., *Injustice and Rectification* (New York: Peter Lang, 2002); and Janna Thompson, *Taking Responsibility for the Past: Reparation and Historical Justice* (Cambridge: Polity, 2002). See also Roy L. Brooks, ed., *When Sorry Isn't Enough: The Controversy over Apologies and Reparations for Human Injustice* (New York: New York University Press, 1999); Randall Robinson, *The Debt: What America Owes to Blacks* (New York: Plume, 2001); and Raymond A. Winbush, ed., *Should America Pay?: Slavery and the Raging Debate on Reparations* (New York: Amistad, 2003).

[7] A reparations march was held in Washington DC on 17 August 2002, inspired by the statement from the World Conference Against Racism (WCAR) that "strongly reaffirm[ed] as a pressing requirement of justice that victims of human rights violations resulting from racism, racial discrimination, xenophobia and related intolerance...should be assured of having access to justice, including [*inter alia*]...the right to seek just and adequate reparation." *Report of the World Conference Against Racism, Racial Discrimination, Xenophobia and Related Intolerance, Durban, South Africa, August 31–September 8, 2001*, U.N. Doc. A/CONF 189/12 (2002): 24 at <http://daccessdds.un.org/doc/UNDOC/GEN/N02/215/43/PDF/N0221543.pdf?OpenElement> (accessed 20 July 2006). Moreover, the Reparations Coordinating Committee, a group co-chaired by Harvard law professor Charles Ogletree, has moved forward with reparations litigation,

my idea of rectification, it is not likely to be identical with it. Since it is specifically with respect to concerns about injustice and rectification that I will be engaging Du Bois's thought, it will be helpful to give a brief account so that the idea is clear from the outset.

The moral conception of rectification is grounded in rectificatory justice. Rectificatory justice is that form of justice employed as a means of addressing those situations that arise when the requirements of a just system of distributive justice have broken down. Although the aim of rectificatory justice is clearly remedial, since it purports to remedy these situations, its specific aim is to take an unjust situation and set it right. Righting an injustice requires several things. First, restoration is required whenever possible. Restoration calls for the return of precisely that which has been lost as a result of injustice, as in the case of stolen property. Second, compensation may also be required. To provide compensation is to counterbalance an unjust loss with something else that is equivalent in value to that loss. Since providing compensation means providing something other than the exact thing that was lost, compensation is in this way distinguishable from restoration (typically "reparations" refers to some sort of rectificatory compensation). Finally, rectification calls for an apology. Since restoration and compensation can only address unjust losses, an apology is necessary in order to effect rectification because it is the apology that addresses the matter of righting the wrong of an injustice. What makes an injustice a *wrong* is the lack of respect shown when one's rights are violated. Hence the righting of the wrong is accomplished by way of an apology, i.e., an acknowledgment of wrongdoing that includes the reaffirmation that those who suffered the injustice have moral standing.[8]

The right to rectification, then, can only be legitimately ascribed when rights have been violated. Hence, the right to rectification is a "remedial

---

having "mounted a number of serious claims that have applications nationally and internationally." Charles J. Ogletree, Jr., "Reparations for the Children of Slaves: Litigating the Issues," *University of Memphis Law Review* 33/2 (2003): 259. See, e.g., Barbara Palmer, "Stanford alumnus seeks reparations for survivors of deadly 1921 Tulsa race riot," *Stanford Report*, 16 February 2005 at <http://news-service.stanford.edu/news/2005/february16/tulsa-021605.html> (accessed 31 October 2006).

[8] For a more thorough account of rectificatory justice, see Rodney C. Roberts, "Justice and Rectification: A Taxonomy of Justice," in *Injustice and Rectification*, ed. Roberts.

right" in the sense that it is "derived from the violation of other independently characterizable rights."[9] Since the right to rectification is grounded in rectificatory justice, it calls for addressing both the wrong of the injustice and any unjust losses resulting therefrom. Take a right that can be legitimately ascribed to all persons, such as the right not to be discriminated against unjustly. If this right is violated, if one is in fact discriminated against unjustly, this violation gives rise to a right to rectification and hence to all that rectificatory justice requires when the right to rectification applies. In the case of social groups, it is at least plausible to think that, in cases where it is impossible to spell out the content of the discrimination from which each individual in the group has a right to be free without referring to the group, the right not to be discriminated against unjustly can be legitimately thought of as a group right. If the group is in fact discriminated against unjustly, this violation gives rise to a right to rectification.

Forty Acres and a Mule

One rectificatory idea that has come to be "[s]ymbolic of reparations for [the] enslavement" of blacks in America, and that is "a recurring phrase in Black Culture and throughout the African American Experience since the Civil War,"[10] is the idea of "40 acres and a mule." It is this idea that prompted Representative John Conyers of Michigan to designate as HR 40 his Commission to Study Reparation Proposals for African-Americans Act. The act would "acknowledge the fundamental injustice, cruelty, brutality, and inhumanity of slavery in the U. S. and the 13 American colonies between 1619 and 1865" and "establish a commission to examine the institution of slavery, subsequent de jure and de facto racial and economic discrimination against African-Americans, and the impact of these forces on living African-Americans, to make recommendations to the Congress on appropriate remedies, and for other purposes."[11] Given the apparent

---

[9] Allen Buchanan, "Theories of Secession," *Philosophy and Public Affairs* 26/1, 1997): 39.

[10] Geneva Smitherman, *Black Talk: Words and Phrases from the Hood to the Amen Corner* (New York: Houghton Mifflin, 1994) 113.

[11] US Congress, HR 40 IH, 105th Cong., 1st sess., 7 January 1997. Rep. Conyers has been trying to get the Commission to Study Reparation Proposals for African-Americans

importance of 40 acres and a mule to the question of rectification for American blacks, and given that, like Du Bois's education, the idea came into existence during the Reconstruction, it is not surprising to find that Du Bois had something to say about it.

Several congressional bills put forth in 1864 were concerned with land for the former slaves who had been freed before the end of the war. However, all of these bills, including the one proposed by Senator Charles Sumner, merely call for leasing land to blacks, and none of them mention 40 acres.[12] Indeed, even the 1865 "Act to Establish a Bureau for the Relief of Freedmen and Refugees" only calls for temporary leasing, and makes no mention of 40 acres.[13] Hence, it seems likely that the idea arose earlier that year when Major General William Tecumseh Sherman issued his Special Field Orders, No. 15. Sherman ordered that "[t]he islands from Charleston, south, the abandoned rice fields along the rivers for thirty miles back from the sea, and the country bordering the St. Johns River, Florida, are reserved and set apart for the settlement of the Negroes now made free by the acts of war and the proclamation of the President of the United States."[14] Section 3 of the order provided that "each family shall have a plot of not more that (40) forty acres of tillable ground."[15] The idea of providing a mule along with the 40 acres is not mentioned in the order. This provision may have

---

Act out of committee and on to the House floor for debate since the bill was first introduced in 1989.

[12] US Congress, S. 63, 38th Cong., 1st sess., 18 January 1864; US Congress, S. 128, 38th Cong., 1st sess., 19 February 1864; US Congress, S. 227, 38th Cong., 1st sess., 12 April 1864; US Congress, HR 51, 38th Cong., 1st sess., 30 June 1864.

[13] US Congress, HR 698, 38th Cong., 2nd sess., 20 February 1865. Charles Sumner's proposal that year mentions 40 acres, but only insofar as it quotes Sherman's order in an effort to "warrant and confirm the land titles of grantees" under that order. US Congress, S. 19, 39th Cong., 1st sess., 11 December 1865. Du Bois seems to have thought that the idea of 40 acres preceded Sherman's order. According to Du Bois, the seized lands under the control of the Freedmen's Bureau "was the nucleus of the proposal to furnish forty acres to each emancipated slave family. The scheme was further advanced when Sherman, embarrassed by the number of Negroes who followed him from Atlanta to the sea and gathered around him in Savannah and South Carolina, as a war measure settled them upon the abandoned Sea Islands and the adjacent coast." W. E. B. Du Bois, *Black Reconstruction in America 1860-1880* (New York: The Free Press, 1998) 601.

[14]. Major General William T. Sherman, "Special Field Orders, No. 15, January 16, 1865," sec. 1, in *Should America Pay?* ed. Winbush, 331.

[15]. Ibid. 332.

come to be added to complete the phrase "40 acres and a mule" because of the view that "Sherman also encouraged the army to lend the families army mules for plowing."[16]

It almost goes without saying that Du Bois thought that the newly freed slaves were justified in their demand for a reasonable portion of the land upon which they had labored. Specifically, he argued that "for 250 years the Negroes had worked on this land, and by every analogy in history, when they were emancipated the land ought to have belonged in large part to the workers."[17] According to Du Bois, the Negro had

> but one clear economic ideal and that was his demand for land, his demand that the great plantations be subdivided and given to him as his right. This was a perfectly fair and natural demand and ought to have been an integral part of Emancipation. To emancipate four million laborers whose labor had been owned, and separate them from the land upon which they had worked for nearly two and a half centuries, was an operation such as no modern country had for a moment attempted or contemplated. The German and English and French serf, the Italian and Russian serf, were, on emancipation, given definite rights in the land. Only the American Negro slave was emancipated without such rights and in the end this spelled for him the continuation of slavery.[18]

But even if Du Bois's argument goes through (and I think that it does) it is not an argument grounded in rectificatory justice—it does not call for providing land to the newly freed slaves because of a requirement in justice to rectify the injustices perpetrated against them.

The belief that 40 acres and a mule is a rectificatory idea rests on the mistaken assumption that its aim was to aid blacks in their transition from slavery *and* compensate them for the injustices that resulted from that "peculiar institution."[19] But even if newly freed black families had been granted 40 acres and a mule, it clearly would not have constituted rectification for the injustices perpetrated against blacks in America through

---

[16]. Noralee Frankel, "Breaking the Chains: 1860–1880," in Robin D.G. Kelley and Earl Lewis, ed., *To Make Our World Anew: A History of African Americans* (New York: Oxford University Press, 2000) 239.

[17] Du Bois, *Black Reconstruction*, 368.

[18] Ibid., 611.

[19]. Geneva Smitherman (e.g.) thinks that the legislation that would have provided the 40 acres "was designed to make [the former slaves] self-sufficient and to compensate for 246 years of free labor" (Geneva Smitherman, *Black Talk*, 114).

1865—it fails by virtue of the lack of an apology alone. Moreover, in no way was the idea to make up for the injustice of slavery; rather, it was the strictly forward-looking notion of helping newly freed blacks in their transition from slavery to freedom.[20] This is underscored by the legislative proposals in 1866 by the 39th Congress. First, like the Freedmen's Bureau Act itself, these proposals did not only concern newly freed slaves, but whites as well. They concerned both freedmen *and* "loyal refugees." Second, the "parcels not exceeding (40) forty acres each" were to be rented, with the possibility of purchasing them in the future.[21] Even Congressman Thaddeus Stevens, who, along with Charles Sumner was at the vanguard of the Congressional struggle for aiding the newly freed slaves, offered a bill devoid of the idea that the 40-acre parcels were meant to be compensation for the injustice of slavery. Steven's proposal was clearly the most "radical." It called for the forfeiture of "all the public lands belonging to the ten States of the Confederacy," and the distribution of 40-acre parcels to the freedmen. These parcels were to be held in fee simple and "inalienable" for ten years, after which "absolute title" to the property was to be granted.[22] However, Stevens's rationale for the proposal did not include providing rectificatory compensation to the freedmen for the injustices perpetrated against them by the institution of slavery. His "Bill Relative to damages done to loyal men, and for other purposes," while "due to justice," was meant "as an example," and to inflict "proper punishment" on those who constituted the Confederacy for their declaration of an "unjust war against the United States for the purpose of destroying republican liberty and permanently establishing slavery...and also to compel them to make some compensation for the damages and expenditures caused by said war."[23]

Hence, "40 acres and a mule" does not even amount to rectificatory compensation—it was never intended to, nor would it, counterbalance the unjust losses sustained by blacks as a result of their enslavement. Moreover,

---

[20]. As historian John David Smith observes, "proponents of land distribution never defined their plans as reparations to former slaves for their centuries of servitude and unrequited labor." John David Smith, "The Enduring Myth of 'Forty Acres and a Mule,'" *Chronicle of Higher Education*, 21 February 2003, B11.

[21] US Congress, HR 87, 39th Cong., 1st sess., 18 January 1866; US Congress, S. 60, 39th Cong., 1st sess., 7 February 1866; US Congress, HR 330, 39th Cong., 1st sess., 26 February 1866; US Congress, HR 359, 39th Cong., 1st sess., 7 March 1866.

[22] US Congress, HR 29, 40th Cong., 1st sess., 11 March 1867, sec. 1, sec. 4.

[23] Ibid. sec. 1.

since there is no acknowledgment or remembrance of the injustice, or any show of respect for the newly-emancipated Americans of African decent, "40 acres and a mule" fails even as rectificatory symbolism. It is by way of an apology, coupled necessarily with at least some manner and substantive degree of compensation, that the wrongdoing of the injustice is acknowledged, and the moral standing of those upon whom the injustice was perpetrated is reaffirmed.

Of course, even if "40 acres and a mule" had counted as rectificatory compensation, the proposal was never fulfilled. Although Du Bois saw "the vision of 'forty acres and a mule'" as something that "the nation had all but categorically promised the freedmen,"[24] "[Andrew] Johnson's proclamation and orders of 1865 provided for the early restoration of all property except property in slaves and such of the Port Royal lands as had been sold for taxes…. [B]y Federal force, Negroes were compelled to leave most of the lands and to make contracts as common laborers."[25]

Outside the context of 40 acres and a mule, Queen Mother Audley Moore, "renowned as the mother of the reparations movement," spoke to Du Bois regarding the fight for reparations and found that he "did not accept reparations at first but began to 'come around' prior to his death."[26] But Du Bois had expressed concern for rectificatory matters long before his death. Following World War I he suggested that "[i]t would be the least that Europe could do in return and some *faint reparation* for the terrible world history between 1441 and 1861 to see that a great free central African state is erected out of German East Africa and the Belgian Congo."[27] Moreover, an important part of what explained the prosperity of the British empire for Du Bois was that it had been built "on lands and materials which had been *seized without compensation* by the British throughout the world."[28] Finally, on the legitimacy of Africa's due, Du Bois said: "Of the *debt* which the white

[24]. W. E. B. Du Bois, *The Souls of Black Folk* (New York: Vintage Books, 1990) 8–9.

[25] Du Bois, *Black Reconstruction*, 386.

[26] Vincene Verdun, "If the Shoe Fits, Wear It: An Analysis of Reparations to African Americans," *Tulane Law Review* 67/3 (1993): 605, 605n23, citing Interview with Queen Mother Audley Moore, 17 June 1991 (transcripts on file in the Ohio State University Law Library).

[27] W.E.B. Du Bois, "The Negro's Fatherland," *Survey* 39 (1917), in David Levering Lewis, ed., *Du Bois: A Reader* (New York: Henry Holt, 1995) 654.

[28] Du Bois, *Autobiography*, 15, emphasis added.

world owes Africa, there can be no doubt."[29] But these statements do not tell us much about how we ought to think about injustice or its rectification. What light, then, might Du Bois be able to shed on rectificatory justice theory?

In the remainder of this essay I will bring Du Bois's thinking to bear on a particular aspect of rectificatory justice theory: the moral psychology of rectification. Although what I have had to say about this subject finds some support from Du Bois,[30] reflection on some of Du Bois's ideas, especially his notion of double-consciousness, suggests an account of a sense of justice that will add substantively to my present view while helping to explain the apparent paradox that arises when we consider Japanese American rectification vis-à-vis African American rectification: why have rectificatory efforts been constrained in the case of African Americans but not in the case of Japanese-American World War II internees? This is an important consideration because it sheds light on an apparent paradox in the moral psychology of rectification, and in so doing underscores the explanatory power of the account.

Du Bois and the Moral Psychology of Rectification

Clearly, the prevailing rectificatory sentiment during Reconstruction toward the 4 million newly freed black folk was overwhelmingly negative. "Against any plan [like that of 40 acres and a mule] was the settled determination of the planter South to keep the bulk of Negroes as landless laborers and the deep repugnance on the part of Northerners to confiscating individual property."[31] Moreover, the United States was disinclined "to add to its huge debt by undertaking any large and costly social adjustments after the war. To give land to free citizens smacked of 'paternalism;' it came directly in opposition to the American assumption that any American could be rich if he wanted to, or at least well-to-do; and it stubbornly ignored the

---

[29] W. E. B. Du Bois, "Whites in Africa After Negro Autonomy," in *Du Bois: A Reader*, ed. Lewis, 685, emphasis added.

[30] Cf. my discussion of how Japanese Americans may be perceived based on perceptions of Japan with Du Bois's discussion of pre-WWI Japan. See Rodney C. Roberts, "Why Have the Injustices Perpetrated Against Blacks in America Not Been Rectified?," *Journal of Social Philosophy* 32/3 (2001): 364–65, and W. E. B. Du Bois, "The African Roots of the War," in *Du Bois: A Reader*, ed. Lewis, 645–46.

[31] Du Bois, *Black Reconstruction*, 601.

exceptional position of a freed slave."[32] Unfortunately, the rectificatory sentiment toward blacks in the US today is not much better. While most blacks seem to be in favor of rectificatory measures, most whites seem to be opposed to them.[33]

Concerned with the lack of even an attempt to rectify the injustices perpetrated against blacks in America, I sought to shed some light on this matter by offering an account of rectificatory action. The account arises from my analysis of the case of blacks in America vis-à-vis the only attempt at rectification by the United States for injustice perpetrated against a nonterritorial ethnic minority: the attempt at rectification in favor of the Japanese Americans interned during World War II.[34] The Civil Liberties Act of 1988 (HR 442) declares that:

> (1) a grave injustice was done to citizens and permanent resident aliens of Japanese ancestry by the evacuation, relocation, and internment of civilians during World War II; (2) these actions were without security reasons and without any acts of espionage or sabotage documented by the Commission on Wartime Relocation and Internment of Civilians, and were motivated by racial prejudice, wartime hysteria, and a failure of political leadership; (3) the excluded individuals suffered enormous damages for which appropriate compensation has not been made; and (4) the Congress apologizes on behalf of the Nation.[35]

---

[32] Ibid., 601–602.

[33] In a CNN/USA Today/Gallup poll, "[n]ine out of 10 white respondents said the government should not make cash payments to slave descendants," 62% of white respondents said corporations that profited from slavery should not apologize for having done so, and 61% of white respondents were opposed to having companies that profited from slavery set up scholarship funds for slave descendants. Peter Viles, "Suit seeks billions in slave reparations," CNN.com/LAWCENTER, 27 March 2002, at <http://archives.cnn.com/2002/LAW/03/26/slavery.reparations/index.html> (accessed 27 November 2006).

[34] I borrow the phrase "nonterrritorial ethnic minority" to refer to those ethnic minorities without territories. James Nickel, "Group Agency and Group Rights," in *NOMOS XXXIX: Ethnicity and Group Rights*, ed. Ian Shapiro and Will Kymlicka (New York: New York University Press, 1997) 236.

[35] US Congress, HR 442, 100th Cong., 2nd sess., 10 August 1988 (from conference report filed in House, H. Rept. 100-785, 26 July 1988). Interestingly, President Roosevelt's order never specifically mentions people of Japanese decent. As a means of ensuring "every possible protection against espionage and against sabotage to national defense material, ...premises and...utilities," he "authorized and direct[ed] the Secretary

The act gave Japanese-American survivors of the World War II internment camps an apology and $20,000 in compensation for damages. The government paid 82,210 former internees a total of more than $1.6 billion. I argue that the lack of even an attempt at rectification in favor of African Americans in light of the efforts put forth in favor of the internees could be explained by way of a prima facie inferior status (one that is not necessarily racist) being ascribed to African Americans by whites.[36]

Rectificatory action in favor of blacks is constrained because the desert criterion of what I call the Rectificatory Status Thesis (RST) has not been met. The RST provides criteria by which the status of a group is such that, at the very least, it is likely that an attempt will be made to rectify the injustice(s) done to that group. There are two necessary conditions for a positive rectificatory status: (1) there must be a prevailing sense of injustice by the dominant group towards the group in question, and (2) the dominant group's conception of the group in question must be such that the group is believed to be deserving of rectification (or, at the very least, rectificatory symbolism).[37] The task now is to develop an account of a sense of justice that will provide an appropriate sense of injustice for use in the first criterion.

---

of War, and the Military Commanders whom he may from time to time designate, whenever he or any designated Commander deem such action necessary or desirable to prescribe military areas in such places and of such extent as he or the appropriate Military Commander may determine, from which... the right of any person to enter, remain in, or leave shall be subject to whatever restriction the Secretary of War or the appropriate Military Commander may impose in his discretion" (Exec. Order No. 9066 [1942] at <http://bss.sfsu.edu/internment/executiorder9066.html> [accessed 6 October 2006]).

[36] For a more thorough account of my present theory of rectificatory action, see Rodney C. Roberts "Why Have the Injustices Perpetrated Against Blacks in America Not Been Rectified?," *Journal of Social Philosophy* 32/3 (2001): 357–73, and Rodney C. Roberts "Toward a Moral Psychology of Rectification: A Reply to Thomas and Boxill," *Journal of Social Philosophy* 33/2 (2002): 339–43.

[37] The rectificatory efforts advanced in favor of the internees give an example of rectificatory symbolism. As Jeremy Waldron rightly notes: "The point was to mark—with something that counts in the United States—a clear public recognition that this injustice did happen, that it was the American people and their government that inflicted it, and that these people were among its victims. The payments give an earnest of good faith and sincerity to that acknowledgment.... It is no objection to this that the payments are purely symbolic." Jeremy Waldron, "Superseding Historic Injustice," *Ethics* 103/1 (1992): 7

The genus of morality we call justice has only two species: distributive justice and rectificatory justice. To have a sense of justice, therefore, is to have a sense of right and wrong, both when the concern is with the just distribution of rights and duties to members of society (distributive justice) and when the concern is with addressing situations in which the requirements of a just system of distributive justice have broken down and where justice requires that the unjust situation be set right (rectificatory justice). Moreover, as David Gauthier points out, the sense of justice "manifests itself both affectively in evaluation and conatively or practically in deliberation and action."[38] A sense of justice "leads one to demand one's own due as well as to recognize what is due others. It leads one to seek justice and not to acquiesce in injustice whether toward oneself or one's fellows."[39] So when a person has a *sense of justice*, we can say that person (1) gives consideration to claims in justice, both distributive and rectificatory, and (2) is generally moved to just action when faced with sound reasoning in support of any such claim.[40]

Now consider Du Bois's well-known idea of double-consciousness. As Robert Williams describes it: "This insight is indispensable for articulating the totality of the American—and the black—experience in the New World. Such a view is relevant and necessary to any viable program in American philosophy. For an analysis of consciousness—of an epoch, a nation, or a people—is one reliable means of carrying out the task of philosophy. An analysis of American consciousness that excludes black consciousness is flawed."[41] The idea is articulated by Du Bois in his classic work *The Souls of Black Folk*:

> ...the Negro is...born with a veil, and gifted with second-sight in this American world,—a world which yields him no true self-consciousness,

---

[38] David Gauthier, "Value, Reasons, and the Sense of Justice," in *Value, Welfare, and Morality*, ed. R. G. Frey and Christopher W. Morris (Cambridge: Cambridge University Press, 1993) 183.

[39] Ibid., 200.

[40] John Rawls recognized rectificatory concerns when he included in his sense of justice "the inclination to make good the loss to others (reparation) and to admit what one has done and to apologize." John Rawls, "The Sense of Justice," *Philosophical Review* 72/3 (1963): 289.

[41] Robert C. Williams, "W. E. B. Du Bois: Afro-American Philosopher of Social Reality," in *Philosophy Born of Struggle: Anthology of Afro-American Philosophy From 1917*, ed. Leonard Harris (Dubuque IA: Kendall/Hunt, 1983) 17.

but only lets him see himself through the revelation of the other world. It is a peculiar sensation, this double-consciousness, this sense of always looking at one's self through the eyes of others, of measuring one's soul by the tape of a world that looks on in amused contempt and pity. One ever feels his two-ness,—an American, a Negro; two souls, two thoughts, two unreconciled strivings; two warring ideals in one dark body, whose dogged strength alone keeps it from being torn asunder.

The history of the American Negro is the history of this strife,—this longing to attain self-conscious manhood, to merge his double self into a better and truer self…. He simply wishes to make it possible for a man to be both a Negro and an American, without being cursed and spit upon by his fellows, without having the doors of Opportunity closed roughly in his face.[42]

Since rectificatory action is largely dependent upon the dominant group, we need to consider what double-consciousness might suggest about its members. First, Du Bois's view of black consciousness implies that, in contrast to blacks, whites *have* a true self-consciousness; they have a consciousness unfettered by a "second-sight" and uncluttered by a "veil" from birth. Second, the view also implies that, unlike blacks, whites only see themselves *as* the world. White consciousness is a one-ness. In single-consciousness there is no dependency for self in the relation to some other world, there is no other world—there is only *my* world. This being the case, it must therefore be true that there are a fair number of things I expect in life. Certainly in the world of single-consciousness "any of my expectations can gain normative force in being met." When my expectations are frequently met, they "may come to form the map of the world that I depend on and take as stable."[43] This is in sharp contrast to the shifting and unstable geography found in a map of the "other" world, the world of two-ness. In the world of one-ness, "positive expectations create a negative perceptual space of what is unnoticed, ignored, excluded, or dismissed as unimportant in ways that are themselves missed because only the encoding of

[42] W. E. B. Du Bois, "Of Our Spiritual Strivings," chap. 1 of *Souls*, 8–9.

[43] Sue Campbell, "Dominant Identities and Settled Expectations," in *Racism and Philosophy*, ed. Susan E. Babbitt and Sue Campbell (Ithaca NY: Cornell University Press, 1999) 223. Cf. Thomas Pogge's idea of legitimate expectations in Thomas W. Pogge, "Group Rights and Ethnicity," in *Ethnicity and Group Rights*, ed. Shapiro and Kymlicka, 209, 218n24, 220n26.

expectations as norms is being attended to."[44] As Sue Campbell notes: "Those with dominant identities have considerable power to order environments through what they attend to; thus their environments do not impinge on them or change them."[45] This is important to rectificatory justice, and to the moral psychology of rectification in particular, because it is likely that in such cases "the parameters of appropriate remedies are not dictated by the scope of the injury to the subjugated, but by the extent of the infringement on settled expectations of whites."[46] Consider Du Bois's account of British expectations in the late 1950s:

> I came therefore to Europe in 1958, to try to learn if possible how far the lessons of the past were guiding the future, and what the hope of that future was. I came to the conclusion that the people of Britain were determined to proceed on the whole along the same paths which they had followed in the past—that they were determined to maintain their comforts and civilization by using cheap labor and raw materials, seized without rightful compensation, and to change their treatment of other people only if this required no essential yielding of comfort or even luxury.[47]

In this case, even expectations of luxury remain intact and, moreover, must continue to be met, even in the face of the injustice upon which these expectations are grounded.

Where injustice is concerned, the sense of justice still includes that "special kind of anger"[48] we feel when we are denied our due, empathy when injustice is experienced by others, and the "feeling that some action should be taken to correct the injustice that has taken place."[49] The problem is that, as it stands, the sense of injustice does not entail rectification; it is not a sense the possession of which will ensure that the agent actually engages in

---

[44] Campbell, "Dominant Identities," in *Racism and Philosophy*, ed. Babbitt and Campbell, 225.

[45] Ibid., 229. Cf. David Gauthier's discussion of expectations in "Value, Reasons," in *Value, Welfare, Morality*, ed. Frey and Morris, 194.

[46] Cheryl I. Harris, "Whiteness As Property," *Harvard Law Review* 106/8 (1993): 1768.

[47] Du Bois, *Autobiography*, 15.

[48] Judith N. Shklar, *The Faces of Injustice* (New Haven: Yale University Press, 1990) 83.

[49] K. Sue Jewell, *From Mammy to Miss America and Beyond: Cultural Images and the Shaping of U.S. Social Policy* (London & New York: Routledge, 1993) x.

rectificatory action.[50] Put another way, fulfillment of both the sense of injustice criterion and the desert criterion of the RST does not entail the feeling that the action that should be taken toward a person or group deserving of rectification should actually be taken *by me*. Moreover, we have no connection between rectificatory action and my self-interest such that we help to ensure a just outcome even when that outcome is perceived to be injurious to dominant interests. What is needed is an account that covers cases where the requirements of justice fly in the face of dominant group expectations. Let us say, then, that when one possesses a strong sense of justice, one has a sense of justice in the fullest moral sense. On this view, one who has a *strong sense of justice* (1) gives serious, thoughtful consideration to claims in justice, both distributive and rectificatory, and (2) has a sense of urgency with respect to seeing justice done and is almost always moved to just action when faced with sound reasoning in support of any such claim, even when fulfilling a particular claim entails enormous loss to oneself or to a group to which one belongs. Persons having a strong sense of justice are almost always prone to act justly.

Compared to the actions of those who posses merely a sense of justice, the actions of those who possess a strong sense of justice seem almost supererogatory. Acting from a strong sense of justice is not, of course, to act beyond the requirements of duty. However, acting from a strong sense of justice shares at least one aspect with supererogatory acts. Consider the paradigmatic characterization of acting "with total disregard for one's own safety." What makes this kind of action supererogatory is precisely that it is so other-regarding. In such cases one observes that "X needs to be done to save Y and Z," and one proceeds to do X, period, even if it is at the risk of one's own life. It is this wholly other-regarding approach, this absolute selflessness in the face of total loss, that gives this kind of act the high moral worth we associate with supererogation. Like supererogatory acts, acting from a strong sense of justice demands action even in the face of enormous loss. In short, it entails the ability to act justly precisely at those times when it is the most difficult to do so. Positing this notion of a strong sense of

---

[50] Cf. David Gauthier's claim that "it is possible to ascertain what is just without thereby committing oneself to any positive or favorable evaluation of what is just, and without being in any way disposed to bring about or support what is just in one's actions." Gauthier, "Value, Reasons," in *Value, Welfare, Morality*, ed. Frey and Morris, 185.

justice recognizes the importance of a non-dominant group perspective. From this perspective there is a natural concern regarding the extent to which a sense of justice can be expected to prevail in the face of the most serious injustices. John Rawls, for example, only requires that the level of desire to act that accompanies his sense of justice exist "at least to a certain minimum degree."[51] This minimal requirement will hardly suffice in overcoming the significant threat to dominant group interests that rectification of the most serious injustices is likely to include.

There are several other advantages to this account of a sense of justice. First, it can explain the failure of the United States to rectify the injustices perpetrated against indigenous peoples, including those in North America and Hawai'i. Even if rectification did not mean the dissolution of the country as we now know it, white Americans are far from prepared to relinquish the spoils of conquest. Even when land redistribution would not directly affect the continental US, sincere rectificatory effort has not been forthcoming. The US "apologized" to the native people of Hawai'i' over a decade ago for the unjust overthrow of their islands.[52] However, no sincere rectificatory efforts have been advanced in their favor.

Second, this account can help explain why rectificatory efforts in favor of African Americans have been constrained but were not constrained in the case of Japanese Americans. Although absent the necessary connection to land that is universal in rectificatory concerns involving indigenous peoples, the loss white America perceives as being entailed in any substantive efforts toward the rectification of the injustices perpetrated against blacks in America is nevertheless far too high. The lack of a strong sense of justice helps to explain why rectificatory efforts in favor of African Americans continue to be constrained in the face of rectificatory efforts in favor of the Japanese-American World War II internees. At least insofar as rectificatory symbolism was advanced in favor of the internees, in the end, America may have acted justly. However, there was no appreciable loss associated with these efforts. Indeed, the financial expenditure might be viewed as an offset to the war reparations paid by Japan following World War II. Moreover, positing a strong sense of justice allows for the presence of a plausible sense of justice in the face of this kind of disparity in treatment. In other words,

---

[51] John Rawls, *A Theory of Justice* (Cambridge: Belknap Press, 1971) 505.

[52] 107 Stat. 1510 Public Law 103–150, 23 Nov. 1993, on the 100th anniversary of the overthrow of the Hawaiian kingdom.

we can make plausible the idea that the US is a "just" nation, even in the face of its treatment of blacks and indigenous peoples.

Another advantage of this account is its consistency with the evolution of Du Bois's conception of persons. As a young man, Du Bois clearly had a Socratic perspective on persons. Reflecting on the year 1896 when he was at the University of Pennsylvania, Du Bois recalled that in his mind the "Negro problem" was "a matter of systematic investigation and intelligent understanding. The world was thinking wrong about race, because it did not know. The ultimate evil was stupidity. The cure for it was knowledge based on scientific investigation."[53] Nearly a half-century later, his conception had changed. In a discussion of the latest version of his program of emancipation for black folk in 1944, Du Bois said that his plan "realizes that the majority of men do not usually act in accord with reason, but follow social pressures, inherited customs and long-established, often sub-conscious, patterns of action. Consequently, race prejudice in America will linger long and may even increase."[54] Hence for Du Bois, inherited customs and long-established patterns of action constrain just behavior in the majority of people. One way of accounting for this constraint is by recognizing the distinction between having a strong sense of justice and merely having a sense of justice.

Objections

Some may object to my proposal because they find that it places too much emphasis on the need to protect nondominant groups from rectificatory constraint. It may be thought that the analysis exaggerates the problem of rectifying injustice. This objection suggests that there is a greater prevalence of just action on the part of dominant groups in the face of substantial loss than my discussion seems to allow. Holders of this objection are likely to

---

[53] Du Bois, *Autobiography*, 197.

[54] W. E. B. Du Bois, "My Evolving Program for Negro Freedom," in *Du Bois: A Reader*, ed. Lewis, 618. Howard McGary confirms the hint in this quotation regarding Du Bois and the question of the permanence of racism. According to McGary, "In the present debate over the significance of race and the permanence of racism, Du Bois clearly sides with those who believe that race is significant, but that racism can be overcome." Howard McGary, "Du Bois, the New Conservatism, and the Critique of African-American Leadership," chap. 11 of *Race and Social Justice* (Malden: Blackwell, 1999) 187. Cf. Derrick Bell, *Faces at the Bottom of the Well: The Permanence of Racism* (New York: Basic Books, 1992).

invoke the example of Germany's rectificatory efforts in favor of the Jews as paradigmatic. Unfortunately, this objection fails to recognize the extent of injustice in the world and rests on a mistaken conception of German rectificatory efforts. It fails to recognize the extent of injustice toward nondominant groups because it ignores the extant unjust states of affairs throughout the world. The actions of the United States toward the native peoples it has affected since its inception are alone sufficient to demonstrate the lack of understanding that accompanies this objection. Since it was not moral suasion that prompted Germany to compensate Jews for the injustices perpetrated under Hitler, the objection also rests on a mistaken conception of German rectificatory efforts. The prompting for German compensation began when they lost World War II and were made to pay war reparations. Contrary to the conception of US rectificatory posture suggested by this objection (where the US is indeed exhibiting a strong sense of justice) the example of Germany may exacerbate the concern over the lack of US rectificatory efforts. Manfred Henningsen tells us that:

> Germans were not allowed to master their past according to rules…followed by almost all societies in the twentieth century, including the U.S. and the other victors of World War II. As a result of the growing pressure from outside, and, later, inside Germany to recognize and process the memory of evil, Germany concluded the twentieth century by establishing a compensation fund for the surviving forced laborers from Nazi occupied countries and deciding to build a memorial near Berlin's Brandenburg Gate commemorating the six million victims of the Jewish Holocaust. Although these political decisions by the German government and parliament in 1999 were accompanied by public pressure, including pressure coming from American politicians, journalist, and intellectuals, they are supported by majorities in German society.[55]

But even with the eventual majority support for substantive rectificatory efforts by the German people, if Henningsen is correct, "[f]ighting the 'Good War' against the evil empire of the Holocaust has replaced the conquest of the West as a core narrative of American

---

[55] Manfred Henningsen, "The Place of the Holocaust in the American Economy of Evil," in *The German-American Encounter: Conflict and Cooperation between Two Cultures, 1800–2000*, ed. Frank Trommler and Elliott Shore (New York: Berghahn Books, 2001) 198.

mythology. Overcoming slavery and its aftermath of Jim Crow-Apartheid never made it to the theme reservoir of American self-interpretation."[56] Hence the example of Germany may exacerbate the concern over the lack of US rectificatory efforts, since a fuller understanding of US attitudes in this case reveals the obvious hypocrisy of US injustice toward indigenous peoples and African Americans and its pressure on Germany to take rectificatory measures in favor of the Jews.

Perhaps one of the most serious objections that might be pressed against the view I have proposed is that it implies a moral failing on Du Bois's part. Since a strong sense of justice calls for serious and thoughtful consideration of claims in justice, and since Du Bois appears to agree with North American conquest and hence with the injustices perpetrated against Native Americans, he therefore lacked a strong sense of justice. Fortunately, this objection is merely specious. Like many youngsters then and since, Du Bois innocently played "Indians" as a child (a game that is perhaps more commonly referred to today as "cowboys and Indians").[57] However, there is evidence to support the contention that he regularly overlooked the unjust foundation of the US, and hence the injustices perpetrated against the indigenous peoples of North America. Du Bois said of the US that it "arose 200 years ago as a free-thinking democracy, with *limitless land and resources*...."[58] Moreover, "red" is not included among the colors of those who own the land and its resources. According to Du Bois, "It would be shame and cowardice to surrender this glorious land and its opportunities for civilization and humanity to the thugs and lynchers, the mobs and profiteers, the monopolists and gamblers who today choke its soul and steal its resources. The oil and sulphur; the coal and iron; the cotton and corn; the lumber and cattle belong to you the workers, *black and white*, and not to the thieves who hold them and use them to enslave you."[59] For purposes of economic success, Du Bois encouraged American blacks to acquire land. Moreover, he seemed to think that blacks possessed "native" rights to do so. In his statement expressing what he took to be "the legitimate aims and needs of the peoples of Negro descent" at the Fourth Pan-African Congress

---

[56] Ibid., 206.

[57] Du Bois, *Autobiography*, 85.

[58] Ibid., 16, emphasis added.

[59] W.E.B. Du Bois, "Behold the Land," in *Du Bois: A Reader*, ed. Lewis, 549, emphasis added.

in New York in August 1927, Du Bois said that "Negroes everywhere need...*Native rights to the land* and its natural resources."[60] Regarding Negroes in the US in particular, Du Bois writes: "The economic situation of American Negroes is still precarious. We believe that along with their entry into industry as skilled and semi-skilled workers and their *growing ownership of land* and homes they should especially organize as consumers and from co-operative effort seek to bring to bear upon investors and producers the coercive power which co-operative consumption has already attained in certain parts of Europe and of America.[61] Finally, Du Bois describes the "American Negro" as "the most intelligent and effective group of colored people fighting *white civilization* face to face and *on its own ground*, on the face of the earth."[62] Since Du Bois implicitly supports the legitimacy of North American conquest, he can support the legitimacy of African Americans acquiring stolen Native-American lands from whites. Hence, Du Bois appears to agree with North American conquest and the injustices perpetrated against Native Americans.

Putting aside any possible tension between the advancement of black Americans and land redistribution in favor of Native Americans, I do not think this objection succeeds. First, the theft of land was clearly fundamental to Du Bois's concerns regarding Africa. He notes that: "The methods by which this *continent has been stolen* have been contemptible and dishonest beyond expression. Lying treaties, rivers of rum, murder, assassination, mutilation, rape, and torture have marked the progress of Englishman, German, Frenchman and Belgian on the dark continent."[63] Second, even when his concern extends beyond Africa, he seems to acknowledge the misappropriation of indigenous lands outside of the United States. He writes: "Thereupon with no guidance from the past the nation marched on with officers strutting, bands playing and flags flying to secure colonial

---

[60] W. E. B. Du Bois, "The Pan-African Congresses: The Story of a Growing Movement," in *Du Bois: A Reader*, ed. Lewis, 672, emphasis added.

[61] Ibid., 672 emphasis added. For a discussion of a dilemma concerning land ownership for non-indigenous peoples, see Rodney C. Roberts, "The Morality of a Moral Statute of Limitations on Injustice," *Journal of Ethics* 7/1 (2003): 129–31.

[62] W. E. B. Du Bois, "The Negro and Communism," in *Du Bois: A Reader*, ed. Lewis, 588, emphasis added.

[63] W. E. B. Du Bois, *Africa—Its Place in Modern History*, in W. E. B. Du Bois, *Africa, Its Geography, People and Products, and Africa—Its Place in Modern History* (1930; repr., Millwood NY: KTO Press, 1977) 42, emphasis added.

empire and new cheap slave labor and *land monopoly* in Asia, Africa and the islands of the seas."[64]

Finally, there is no question that as a young man Du Bois recognized the character of America's relationship with the indigenous peoples of North America. In 1890, while speaking on Jefferson Davis at his bachelor's degree commencement at Harvard, Du Bois noted that the foundation of a Davisonian civilization "is the idea of the strong man—Individualism coupled with the rule of might—and it is this idea that has made the logic of even modern history, the cool logic of the Club. It made a naturally brave and generous man, Jefferson Davis: now advancing civilization by *murdering Indians....*"[65] Moreover, like Frederick Douglass before him, Du Bois had an *emancipatory imperative*. Like Douglass's fight for freedom from slavery, much of Du Bois's life included the struggle against the overt racial oppression of black codes, burning, lynching, Jim Crow, etc. As Bernard Boxill reminds us, the human rights of blacks were "denied some years ago" by "white experts" who "managed to hold their own, and create uncertainty in the public mind, for a considerable period;" it is only fairly recently that the controversy has been over "what these rights involve or require, and how they can be compensated when they are violated."[66] Hence, when we add the emancipatory imperative and Du Bois's life in devotion to it, it makes sense to think that the extent to which Du Bois appears to agree with the conquest of the indigenous people of North America is of no serious consequence, and that he did indeed have a strong sense of justice. What Du Bois's scholarship suggests, I think, is a reminder. A reminder that even those who are at the vanguard of the struggle for justice can sometimes overlook injustice and the need to rectify it.[67]

---

[64] W. E. B. Du Bois, "The Lie of History as it is Taught Today," in *The Seventh Son: The Thought and Writings of W. E. B. Du Bois*, vol. 2, ed. Julius Lester (New York: Random House, 1971) 669, emphasis added.

[65] Du Bois, *Autobiography*, 146, emphasis added.

[66]. Bernard R. Boxill, "Washington, Du Bois and *Plessy v. Ferguson*," *Law and Philosophy* 16/3 (1997): 316.

[67] For comments on earlier versions of this essay, I wish to thank Mary Keller, the audience at Forty Acres and a Mule: The Case for Black Reparations, A Research Conference, Columbia University, November 2002, and the audience at the 30th Annual National Conference on the Black Family in America, The Black Family and the 3R's: Reparations, Restitution and Restoration, Louisville, Kentucky, March 2003. I also wish to thank Lewis Gordon for his comments on the penultimate version.

Works Cited

Babbitt, Susan E., and Sue Campbell, editors. *Racism and Philosophy*. Ithaca NY: Cornell University Press, 1999.

Balfour, Lawrie. "Unconstructed Democracy: W. E. B. Du Bois and the Case for Reparations." *American Political Science Review* 97/1 (2003): 33–44.

Bell, Bernard W., Emily Grosholz, and James B. Stewart, editors. *W.E.B. DuBois on Race and Culture: Philosophy, Politics, and Poetics*. New York/London: Routledge, 1996.

Bell, Derrick. *Faces at the Bottom of the Well: The Permanence of Racism*. New York: Basic Books, 1992.

Boxill, Bernard R. "Washington, Du Bois and *Plessy v. Ferguson*." *Law and Philosophy* 16/3 (1997): 299–330.

Brooks, Roy L. editor. *When Sorry Isn't Enough: The Controversy over Apologies and Reparations for Human Injustice*. New York: New York University Press, 1999.

Buchanan, Allen. "Theories of Secession." *Philosophy and Public Affairs* 26/1 (1997): 31–61.

Campbell, James. "Du Bois and James." *Transactions of the Charles S. Peirce Society* 28/3 (1992): 569–81.

Corlett, J. Angelo. *Race, Racism and Reparations*. Ithaca: Cornell University Press, 2003.

Du Bois, W.E.B. Black Reconstruction in America 1860-1880. New York: The Free Press, 1998.

Du Bois, W. E. B. *The Souls of Black Folk*. New York: Vintage Books, 1990.

———. *Africa, Its Geography, People and Products, and Africa—Its Place in Modern History*. Millwood NY: KTO Press, 1977.

———. *The Autobiography of W. E. B. Du Bois: A Soliloquy on Viewing My Life from the Last Decade of Its First Century*. New York: International Publishers, 1968.

Frey, R. G., and Christopher W. Morris, editors. *Value, Welfare, and Morality*. Cambridge: Cambridge University Press, 1993.

Harris, Cheryl I. "Whiteness As Property." *Harvard Law Review* 106/8 (1993): 1707–91.

Harris, Leonard, editor. *Philosophy Born of Struggle: Anthology of Afro-American Philosophy From 1917*. Dubuque IA: Kendall/Hunt, 1983.

Horne, Gerald, and Mary Young editors. *W.E.B. Du Bois: An Encyclopedia*. Westport CT: Greenwood Press, 2001.

Jewell, K. Sue. *From Mammy to Miss America and Beyond: Cultural Images and the Shaping of U.S. Social Policy*. London/New York: Routledge, 1993.

Kelley, Robin D. G., and Earl Lewis, editors. *To Make Our World Anew: A History of African Americans*. New York: Oxford University Press, 2000.

Lester, Julius, editor. *The Seventh Son: The Thought and Writings of W. E. B. Du Bois*. Volume 2. New York: Random House, 1971.

Lewis, David Levering, editor. *W. E. B. Du Bois: A Reader*. New York: Henry Holt, 1995.

McGary, Howard. *Race and Social Justice*. Malden: Blackwell, 1999.

Ogletree, Charles J., Jr. "Reparations for the Children of Slaves: Litigating the Issues." *University of Memphis Law Review* 33/2 (2003): 245–64.

Palmer, Barbara. "Stanford alumnus seeks reparations for survivors of deadly 1921 Tulsa race riot." *Stanford Report*. 16 February 2005, <http://news-service.stanford.edu/news/2005/february16/tulsa-021605.html>.

Rawls, John. "The Sense of Justice." *Philosophical Review* 72/3 (1963): 281–305.

———. *A Theory of Justice*. Cambridge: Belknap Press, 1971.

Report of the World Conference Against Racism, Racial Discrimination, Xenophobia and Related Intolerance, Durban, South Africa, August 31–September 8, 2001, U.N. Doc. A/CONF 189/12 (2002): 24 at <http://daccessdds.un.org/doc/UNDOC/GEN/N02/215/43/PDF/N022154 3.pdf?OpenElement> (accessed 20 July 2006).

Roberts, Rodney C. "The Morality of a Moral Statute of Limitations on Injustice." *Journal of Ethics* 7/1 (2003): 115-138.

------. "Toward a Moral Psychology of Rectification: A Reply to Thomas and Boxill." *Journal of Social Philosophy* 33/2 (2002): 339-343.

------, editor. *Injustice and Rectification*. New York: Peter Lang, 2002.

------. "Why Have the Injustices Perpetrated Against Blacks in America Not Been Rectified?" *Journal of Social Philosophy* 32, no. 3 (2001): 357-373.

Robinson, Randall. *The Debt: What America Owes to Blacks*. New York: Plume, 2001.

Shapiro, Ian, and Will Kymlicka, editors. *NOMOS XXXIX: Ethnicity and Group Rights*. New York: New York University Press, 1997.

Sher, George. *Approximate Justice: Studies in Non-Ideal Theory*. Landham MD: Rowman & Littlefield, 1997.

Shklar, Judith N. *The Faces of Injustice*. New Haven: Yale University Press, 1990.

Smith, John David. "The Enduring Myth of 'Forty Acres and a Mule,'" *Chronicle of Higher Education*, 21 February 2003, B11.

Smitherman, Geneva. *Black Talk: Words and Phrases from the Hood to the Amen Corner*. New York: Houghton Mifflin, 1994.

Thompson, Janna. *Taking Responsibility for the Past: Reparation and Historical Justice*. Cambridge: Polity, 2002.

Trommler, Frank, and Elliott Shore, editors. *The German-American Encounter: Conflict and Cooperation between Two Cltures, 1800–2000*. New York: Berghahn Books, 2001.

Verdun, Vincene. "If the Shoe Fits, Wear It: An Analysis of Reparations to African Americans." *Tulane Law Review* 67/3 (1993): 597–668.

Waldron, Jeremy. "Superseding Historic Injustice." *Ethics* 103/1 (1992): 4–28.

Winbush, Raymond A., editor. *Should America Pay?: Slavery and the Raging Debate on Reparations*. New York: Amistad, 2003.

Challenging Liberal Justice:
The Talented Tenth Revisited

Carole Lynn Stewart

The Souls of Black Folk has often been read as offering a paradigmatic model of modernist African-American selfhood and its correspondent leaders, the black bourgeoisie. Du Bois's early ideas about "talent," freedom, and a paradoxically "aristocratic" form of democracy have been critically assessed within the context of his later Marxist and somewhat misleading assessments of the elitism implicit in his early ideas. According to Cornel West, the Harvard- and Berlin-educated Du Bois was apparently horrified by the backward "masses" just emerging from chattel slavery, which the later Marxist Du Bois wisely recognized.[1] As a result of recent critical attacks on the elitist model of leadership and selfhood, and the postmodern intellectuals' problematic continuation of the Du Boisian elitist legacy, Joy James has written *Transcending the Talented Tenth*. As a cautionary tale, she "recalls" the example of Du Bois's early aristocratic and intellectualist ideas and his later sensible "denunciation" of them. Still, her recuperation and democratization of his ideas does not necessarily surpass the model of freedom and leadership offered in *The Souls of Black Folk*. Du Bois's democratization of his own concepts began much earlier, after the "age of miracles," which is at about the time he composed *Souls*.[2] The

---

[1] See Cornel West, *The American Evasion of Philosophy: A Geneology of Pragmatism* (Madison: University of Wisconsin Press, 1989).

[2] Along with others, James makes it appear as if Du Bois's statements about his shift in critical outlook, away from a hierarchical notion of leadership, occurs very late in his life. This is misleading since Du Bois claims in *Darkwater* that the "age of miracles" in his life "began with Fisk and ended with Germany." Further, the often referred to statement "I was blithely European and imperialist in outlook; democratic as democracy as conceived in America" is quite clearly a remark about his 1888 graduation speech on

democratization can be understood within the context of Du Bois's dialogue with the promising moment of secularization in the formation of American democracy that proposed a loss of absolutism and hierarchical thinking and potentially opened the way for cross-cultural exchanges. This promise, however, was eclipsed by the advent of white American Protestantism, its twin doctrines of self-determination and work ethic as forms of democratic "freedom," and the problematic existence of the American exceptional self.

Without claiming that Du Bois was ever a champion of the masses, particularly since he was critical of the "tyranny of public opinion," I want to remember that Du Bois never suggested the mass of "black folk" had no value in themselves. To interpret Du Bois's "talented tenth" as a cultured and educated elite, who guide the uneducated and "primitive" masses into acquiring the "tools of civilization," would be to conflate Du Bois's concept of the constitution of civilization as cross-cultural with his mentor Alexander Crummell's normative and hierarchical concept of "civilization," which I dispute. I argue that his concept of a talented tenth is implicitly democratic; the model of leadership is not the singular privilege of the bourgeois professional class—anyone could potentially be talented. The notion of a potential talented tenth is also similar to Du Bois's insistence that democracy exists only as an idea and not as a reality.[3] On another level, the term is radically democratic since it appeals to and reformulates a concept of freedom and interactive selfhood that challenges the very way in which the nation conceives of its "secular" and "democratic" identity and its history. Instead of constructing an aristocracy, Du Bois opposes the legislation of natural and biological ideas about separation and privacy, and the correlative understanding of democracy that assumes the protection of these private or pluralistic rights will be enough to constitute freedom. A "rule of

---

Bismark delivered at Fisk (W. E. B. Du Bois, *Dusk of Dawn: An Essay Toward an Autobiography of a Race Concept*, in *W. E. B. Du Bois: Writings* [New York: Library of America, 1986] 577). Manning Marable also notes that Du Bois's shift in theoretical and political outlook, his own democratization of his concepts about selfhood, was evident in *Souls of Black Folk*.

[3] See, for instance *Dusk of Dawn*, 654, where Du Bois describes racialization and the imprisonment within these categories as an "inner spiritual slavery"; he also claims that until these categories are broken, nothing like "democracy," "the grand equality," can exist.

inequality,"[4] by which he means difference and not hierarchy, exists that liberal individualism constantly wants to deny.

Throughout his life Du Bois was concerned with a viable and creative life for African Americans; this concern should not overshadow the fact that he was simultaneously concerned with the nature and possibilities of radical democratic institutions as forms of human life and exchange in the modern world. He did not champion the cause of African Americans so they would simply assume the forms of American culture and join the mainstream. While he showed an interest in Africa and African peoples, it was not a romanticism or essentializing of the continent and its peoples. He was, rather, interested in a critical reassessment of world history and the role of Africans within it, especially in the formation of the Atlantic world and the United States and the possibilities this world opened for radical democratic institutions. As a historian, he knew that nothing came into being *ex nihilo*. Thus in his assessment of the American situation he undertook a critical revision of the American religious traditions, the political philosophy of the American Revolutionary Republic, and the complex meanings that have emerged from the enslavement of African peoples in the "democratic republic"; he mines these traditions as a basis for his discussion of the future of a viable humane secular world. In this respect, he is quite different from African American popular and/or intellectual leaders who are either interested in African Americans joining the mainstream under the aegis of an ideology of progress, on the one hand, and those who would romanticize and essentialize African or African American as the basis for *sui generis* meanings, offering an inverse notion of superiority.

The Promise of Heterogeneity in Secularization: Missed Opportunities for Cross-Cultural Understanding

The idea of an innate equality is Christian in origin since all human beings were created by God. This freedom gave dignity to the person but for most of the existence of Christianity it took on an inward locus in relationship to society. The Protestant Reformations in Europe and the forms brought to America openly opposed hierarchy and thus implied a new place for the expression of freedom as a form of social order. Du Bois understood that the

---

[4] W. E. B. Du Bois, *The Souls of Black Folk*, 1st Signet Classic ed. (New York: Penguin Books, 1995) 116.

Protestant conversions, awakenings, and revivals were pivotal in the movement toward freedom for the slave population, with their promise of a democratization of religious experience, consistent with what I intend by secularization. Once the slave population was imbued with the knowledge of divine freedom for every soul, the attempt to continue chattel slavery would seem to be sacrilegious and unchristian. As Du Bois would write elsewhere, the revivalists recognized that "either they must stop teaching or these people are going to be men, not serfs or slaves."[5] The fear of slave insurrection, however, with the examples of leaders Gabriel Vesey and Nat Turner, led to the prohibition of the religious gatherings—the promising moments of democratization and secularization—and, according to Du Bois, to the "adjustment of religion and ethics" so that racial and biological difference was legislated in the name of Christianity.[6] This fear of violence, although logical given the brutality of slavery, was also supplemented by the fear of a loss of an exclusionary and homogeneous identity. Only the "exceptional" self could transcend race or be regarded as equal, and equality here entails being seen as an honorary white.[7] The idea of being an exception to one's race is not the same as the ideas of distinction and racial "talent" Du Bois will develop and question throughout his writings.

Complexities arise where race and slavery become conflated with moralisms, since both the dominant Christianity and science would establish a form of social Darwinism and racial hierarchy that was to be achieved in the name of an ultimate societal "good." Du Bois recognized that redemption and freedom were legislated as natural rights and required metaphysical similarity, or natural "equality," before the law. When secularization was understood as a matter of separation of church and state and privatization of belief, rather than a hollowing out of traditional moral and legal hierarchies, the public nature of religion was lost and American democracy advanced the separation of religious worship "along the color line."[8] Enslavement was naturally legislated through racial difference and American civil-religious "divine" laws of individual liberty and social normativity. The futuristic ideal of salvation and freedom led not only to a

[5] W. E. B. Du Bois, "Religion in the South," in *The Negro in the South: His Economic Progess in Relation to His Moral and Religious Development*, William Levi Bull Lectures, 1907 (New York: Citadel Press, 1970) 123–91.

[6] Ibid., 168.

[7] Ibid., 169.

[8] Du Bois, *Souls*, 173.

whitening process, but also to the transcendence of the moral ambiguity and heterogeneity of passive "souls" in slavery. These souls seemed to lack the self-determining power and privatized notion of freedom that was encouraged by the American secularization process. This is also why the study of slavery was connected to an understanding of racialization for Du Bois.

Du Bois interprets this desire for similarity in the national identity as co-extensive with the American imperialistic outlook of endless expansion to eventually achieve the ideal and homogeneous "promised land." The crusade for democracy ushers in an impossible future of correspondence-based notions of truth, which Du Bois also regards as clearly a hubristic impossibility, fed by the American Protestant work ethic and the accumulative desire. He implies that the process of endless expansion promises a false and absolute cure from the condition of being human and fragile, or of being in need of recognizing each other's ordinary and partial "truths." This theme—the flight from suffering and uncertainty to impossible perfection—will become central in *Darkwater*. And in "The Souls of White Folk," Du Bois accuses white pride of creating a condition of fleeing our need, dependence, or one might say enslavement to one another. Du Bois will argue in a plea for the ordinary, the "more mundane matters of honor and fairness," that white Christianity has been incapable of "acknowledg[ing]" "human frailty" and "scoffs endlessly at our shortcomings."[9] Since those who suffer and are excluded from the law had not been seen as self-sufficient selves, the desire to overcome slavery also fed into a form of American individualism that loathed the passive and dependent. The experience of being bound to others coalesced with the experience of being black and enslaved. Private freedom, as opposed to the public freedom Du Bois subtly unveils, emerges from the overcoming of moral ambiguity and the condition of the passive and meek.

Whereas Du Bois has been criticized for portraying the slaves as exceptional for their "humility" and "meekness," related to his racial exceptionalist vision of Christ-like passivity, i.e. the martyrdom of the Uncle Tom,[10] his praise for humility can be understood within the context of the moral ambiguities and possibilities for communal interactions that were eclipsed in American secularization. Humility speaks to human frailty and

---

[9] Ibid., 36.
[10] Ibid., 53.

moral uncertainty; he obviously does not support the experience of slavery. Du Bois's particular values, however, need not be considered as "slave" values. Rather, the values are both "African" and "Calvinist," the mergers of which are connected to a "hard theology" for Du Bois and survive *in spite of* and alongside slavery rather than, necessarily, as a consequence of it. Thus, from the opening of *Souls*, Du Bois stresses ancient African virtues and later, in the chapter "Of the Faith of Our Fathers," the argument emphasizes the distortion of African virtues by white Christianity. According to Du Bois, "courtesy became humility, moral strength degenerated into submission, and the exquisite native appreciation of the beautiful became an infinite capacity for dumb suffering."[11] It is therefore not necessary to suggest with West that a "'germ theory' [of racial development] had its political analogue in his doctrine of the Talented Tenth." West contends that Du Bois "promoted both [conditions of elitism and passivity] simultaneously" and offered different roles for the former slaves. As West continues: "While the Afro-American masses are busy giving the world its meekness, humility, and joviality, the Talented Tenth are providing leadership and guidance for these spiritual masses."[12] West assumes that meekness is a separate phase of development and this assumption also corresponds to Wilson Moses's argument that Du Bois carries on the tradition of the Uncle Tom with his beliefs in black nationalism and exceptionalism.[13]

However, Du Bois's point seems to be that the white race suffers from an ideology based upon metaphysical moral perfection or an impossible notion of redemption, which leads it to distort the nature of others' "gifts" of spiritual values that are formed from ordinary structures of community. These "gifts" were at the locus of the "American" experience. In Du Bois's famous words from *The Souls of Black Folk*: "Your country? How came it yours? Before the Pilgrims landed we were here. Here we have brought our three gifts and mingled them with yours: a gift of story and song—soft, stirring melody in an ill-harmonized and unmelodious land." The slaves gave "story and song," "sweat and brawn," and "the Spirit." To be sure, Du Bois points out, "we have woven ourselves with the very warp and woof of

---

[11] Du Bois, *Souls*, 219.

[12] Cornel West, *Prophesy Deliverance! An Afro-American Revolutionary Christianity* (Philadelphia: Westminster Press, 1982) 76.

[13] Wilson J. Moses, *Black Messiahs and Uncle Toms: Social and Literary Movements of a Religious Myth* (University Park/London: Pennsylvania State University Press, 1982) 113.

this nation, —we have fought their battles, shared their sorrow, mingled our blood with theirs."[14] He claims that the founding of America was authentic and collective, requiring the active gifts and the willingness of slaves, which would only later be misunderstood as foreordained victimhood by a "headstrong and "careless people"[15] who had confused the dignity of gift-giving and sacrifice with nonwhite passivity.

Du Bois is not simply "essentializing" or romanticizing race and positing a hierarchy intrinsic in the development of the "black messiah." His "talented tenth" never advance from the position of passivity and dependence—a necessary quality for the public actor who acknowledges moral ambiguity and heterogeneity. It might seem that Du Bois's leaders transcend passivity because he seems to condescend to slave religion at times. But Du Bois's critique of revivalism, "the Preacher, the Music, and the Frenzy,"[16] is not based on the "backwardness" of the former slaves but rather on the sometimes fatalistic and compensatory quality of slave religion under the dominion of white Christianity. When Du Bois's criticisms of slave religion occur, they imply that the revivals developed into private narratives of consent to legalism and normativity rather than maintaining the cross-cultural and interpretative aspects they initially posed. Rather than accusing Du Bois of making Eurocentric remarks about the "heathen," which is often done, one could trace the emergence of his own "theology" in *Souls*, which disrupts and mediates in between various experiences of moral redemption and absolute belief formation. In *The Negro*, an early book on Africanisms, he will comment on "fetishism," which he claims is not "mere senseless degradation" but rather "a philosophy of life."[17] The "pluralistic universe" he depicts here recurs in *Souls* and has influenced the creation of "American democracy."[18] Du Bois is nowhere simply dismissing

---

[14] Du Bois, *Souls*, 275.

[15] Ibid., 276.

[16] Ibid., 211.

[17] W. E. B. Du Bois, *The Negro* (London/New York: Oxford University Press, 1970) 74.

[18] Richard Cullen Rath, "Echo and Narcissus: The Afrocentric Pragmatism of W. E. B. Du Bois," *Journal of American History* 84/2 (September 1997): 461–95, discusses the use of "fetish" in *Souls* and he also emphasizes that Du Bois himself, when reviewing his own book, referred to *Souls* as an "African" book. If this is true, it is also the case, however, that an ostensible purpose of the book is to articulate America's debt to the slaves, and to Africa, thus leading to an Africanization of American democracy.

"primitivism" but rather seriously considering the merit of various historical developments in religious interaction. He would criticize the "pythian madness" of spirit possession or Obi worship but he would not oppose ancestor worship, or fetishism articulated in manner that resembles a philosophy of responsible selfhood—a way, he writes, of "accounting"[19] for good and evil in the world.

In *Souls*, it is the initial promising moment of meeting, rupture, cross-cultural interaction, and "contact"[20] between different groups and value systems Du Bois harks back to, a difficult and fleeting historical moment of possibility and certainly not indicative of a lost Edenic and static truth of the African or American forebears. As he will write much later, "Americanization has never yet meant a synthesis of what Africa, Europe, and Asia had to contribute to the new and vigorous republic of the West; it meant largely the attempt to achieve a dead level of uniformity, intolerant of all variation."[21] The desire to achieve uniformity can be understood as a corollary to the Christian assimilative aspect of eventual consent and conformism. The early invocation in *The Souls of Black Folk* for leaders to "foster and develop the traits and talents of the negro, not in opposition to or contempt for other races, but rather in large conformity to the greater ideals of the American Republic"[22] is not necessarily conformist even though one "conforms" or acknowledges these great ideals of Republicanism. The moral content—the ideals of the Republic—is so vague in substance that it can be interpreted as an idea of public freedom and communicative or interactive justice. The ideal of America exists as a fragile possibility for heterogeneous, democratic freedom through the cross-cultural interaction of various nations or diverse interpretations of the moral laws.

The moral absolutism and values that other theorists will stress as American "exceptionalist" are absent here; a notion of divine and innate equality consists of stable, similar rational truths and laws *in potentia* if not in actuality. For Du Bois, the innate self is so radically anarchical that it almost causes him to lose faith in his own life goals.[23] As a consequence of his

---

[19] Du Bois, *Negro*, 75.

[20] Du Bois, *Souls*, 121.

[21] W. E. B. Du Bois, *Color and Democracy: Colonies and Peace* (New York: Harcourt Brace, 1945) 72.

[22] Du Bois, *Souls*, 52.

[23] In *Darkwater* Du Bois discusses his experience of almost succumbing to cynicism and doubt about his own abilities because he realized that his rise to a position of

continual pragmatic commitment to being "courageous" and responsible for
a world that he most certainly did not create, Du Bois is quite willing to live
through this moral uncertainty.[24] His early depiction of himself as an
"exception" has already, by his own profession, been complicated by the
recognition that his success was largely a matter of "chance," and he began
conceptualizing his (hundred-year) scientific plan of "explor[ing] and
measur[ing] the scope of chance and unreason in human action."[25] Du Bois
does not mention ultimately eliminating chance and unreason in a chaotic
world that seems to function by an anarchic force rather than a grand
narrative of moral absolutes. The early concept of "strivings" and "talent" in
Souls is clearly plural and "when ripe for speech, [is] spoken in various
languages."[26] Du Boisian "talent" can be understood by considering the
mixture in the seemingly incongruous traditions that informed his
"philosophy of life." He praises his "partial Puritanism" for "never ma[king]
him afraid of life"[27] and therefore stresses the courageous aspect of his
public self. But if he depicts his "partial" Puritanism here, which is surely
connected to his own beloved New England town meeting, we should also
keep in mind that he will equally praise the sound African tribal democracies
and theological outlooks that indirectly shape his character. As a
consequence of that philosophical mixture, his life begins to reveal its value
as the central "problem," not only of racism but of the related failed
experiment in participatory and public freedom manifested in local forms of

---

intellectual prominence was largely a matter of chance. Critics often imply that this was a
moment in which he would have dismissed his early idea of "genius," or a "talented
tenth," but what I suggest here is that Du Bois learned how to live that skepticism, not
"overcome" it in the way that he describes his mentor Crummell did. In effect, Du Bois
decides that "genius" is a concept that can be located anywhere; the problem will be in
"eliminating chance" so that the population can find their distinct possibilities through
public discussion. Du Bois, *Dusk of Dawn*, 792.

[24] Although David Levering Lewis humorously titles one of his chapters "The Age of
Miracles: At but Not of Harvard" to echo the "Puritan" ideal of being in the world but not
of it, Du Bois's understanding of his "partial Puritanism" is anarchical in terms of moral
normativity and does not reach toward an otherworldly telos. He praises his background
for offering the "courage" to "live[] completely, testing every normal appetite, feasting
on sunset, sea and hill, and enjoying wine, women, and song." Du Bois, *Dusk of Dawn*,
792.

[25] Ibid., 558.

[26] Du Bois, *Souls*, 103.

[27] Du Bois, *Dusk of Dawn*, 791.

council democracy. Du Bois suggests that participatory democracy or public talent entered the modern world through Africa. In *Dusk of Dawn*, he writes, "I place black iron-welding and village democracy, and yellow printing and state building, side by side with white representative government and the steam engine, and unhesitatingly give the palm to the first."[28] Du Bois implies that through cross-cultural contact, a new ideal of secular, participatory—rather than representative—democracy is possible.

Possibilities for public exchanges reemerge for Du Bois in the period of the Reconstruction. Critics who charge Du Bois with elitism overlook the difference between a public concept of freedom, inserting one's voice into the public process of decision-making, and a concept of private liberty, also necessary but concerning only the protection of basic human rights and formal equality. Du Bois will hint at the necessity for these public forums by seeing the "splendid failure" of the missed moment of freedom in the Reconstruction period. These interactive spaces span from the educational and religious to municipalities and local self-government, which the New England crusade aided in the emergence of by attempting to provide a "friend,"[29] a form of friendship that signifies the engaged philosophical form of immediate recognition of the "strivings in the souls of black folk" for which he will persistently demand "generous acknowledgment."[30] Du Bois

---

[28] Ibid., 659.

[29] Du Bois, *Souls*, 131.

[30] The concept of acknowledgment, which needs to be explored at greater length, can be thought to consist of "sympathy" and political recognition (and not the "amused pity" and contempt of the white world). This acknowledgment and celebration of each other is demanded throughout Du Bois's work, particularly in the case of the former slaves, whom he writes "deserved not only the pity of the world but the gratitude of both the South and the North." W. E. B. Du Bois, *Black Reconstruction: An Essay Toward a History of the Part which Black Folk Played in the Attempt to Reconstruct Democracy in America: 1860–1880* (Philadelphia: Harcourt Brace, 1935) 188. Robert Gooding-Williams also discusses acknowledgment in his paper "Du Bois's Counter-Sublime" and with "knowledge," it is regarded as an undercurrent to "sympathy." This implies that sympathy is the goal and the other two virtues essential to it. Robert Gooding-Williams, "Du Bois's Counter-Sublime," *Massachusetts Review* 35 (Summer 1994): 209. However, Du Bois does not seem to be entirely consistent with his designation of concepts, which makes it a bit unruly to attempt to extrapolate them as such. For a good discussion of sympathy, see Susan Mizruchi, "Neighbors, Strangers, Corpses: Death and Sympathy in the Early Writings of W. E. B. Du Bois," in *Centuries' End, Narrative Means*, ed. Robert D. Newman (Stanford: Stanford University Press, 1996): 191–211.

suggests that the most overwhelming fear characteristic of modernity and secularization is the discovery of a lack of absolutes and the necessary human effort required for the birth of a fragile public space based on revisable truths. Du Bois will write much later in *Black Reconstruction* that, indeed, during Reconstruction the actual success of the former slaves frightened those in power more than the fear of their failure: "The attempt to make black men American citizens was in a certain sense a failure, but a splendid failure. It did not fail where it was expected to fail."[31] He further points out that "In a thousand schools of the South after the war were brought together the most eager of the emancipated blacks and that part of the North which believed in democracy, and that social contact of human beings became a matter of course. The results were of all sorts.... On the whole, the most astonishing successes in the new and sudden human contacts."[32] Local and radical democracy was not an impossible dream but rather fully within the realm of human possibility, so much so that the newly freed were well on the way to establishing public spaces of freedom.

We notice that Du Bois's opposition to the submissive and assimilative stance demands that the first necessity for black people is "political power" and then "insistence on civil rights."[33] His concepts of power and freedom derive much from the Revolutionary tradition; one could compare Du Bois's demand for "the freedom of life and limb, the freedom to work and think, the freedom to love and aspire"[34] with the famous idea of "distinction" stressed by Hannah Arendt. She salvages John Adams's "passion for distinction," or "emulation," as an attraction to the public world, to "the desire to be heard, talked of, approved and respected."[35] Du Bois will also use the expression a "finer type of courage"[36] to articulate this example of freedom and genius in the slave population. The achievement of this courage requires that public spaces must be constructed for blacks and whites to appear to each other, to make decisions together, and to build a new Republic.

Du Bois's plural "strivings" cannot be conflated with the Protestant work ethic or self-made exceptionalism that became normative in light of

[31] Du Bois, *Black Reconstruction*, 708.
[32] Ibid., 190.
[33] Du Bois, *Souls*, 87.
[34] Ibid., 52.
[35] Hannah Arendt, *On Revolution* (New York: Viking Press, 1963) 116.
[36] Du Bois, *Black Reconstruction*, 104.

the eclipse of cross-cultural exchange and the privatization of religious experience. The work ethic is performed in isolation from one another and is stressed by Booker T. Washington. In contrast to Washington, who worked for eventual "equality," or assimilation, Du Bois was firmly committed to the need for democratic institutions and to the need for a public sphere that would guarantee formal and social equality to whites while at the same time allowing them to strive for a form of selfhood and public freedom that formal equality alone could not provide.

Booker T. Washington's American Work Ethic and the Sacralization of Progress

In a speech delivered before the Cotton States International Exposition in 1895, Booker T. Washington (the Tuskegee "genius") had effectively nullified the need for public spaces—spaces of contact among and between the races. His metaphor of the hand unified in mutual progress with the races as separate as the fingers provides for no precise space for either the deliberation that could define the meaning of progress or the intent of work, its integration, or its practice. We are thus left with a "work ethic" as one "eternal striving" rather than the strivings of plural souls united in a common endeavor.

Washington's Atlanta Compromise address represented an attitude of "adjustment and submission."[37] His famous speech was an effort to achieve racial cooperation in the South. Washington had announced that he would accept the restriction on black enfranchisement and make no further demands for social and political equality if efforts were made to control lynching. He seemed to suggest a sense of mutual public decision-making in the latter part of his speech, in which he claims that the races could be "separate but equal," "'one as the hand in all things essential to mutual progress.'"[38] Although Washington did not merely endorse the outcome of *Plessy v. Ferguson*, which had affirmed the constitutionality of segregation, he did, in Du Bois's opinion, make the transition to a new form of industrial slavery much easier for the white Southerners. Indeed, for Du Bois, the

---

[37] Du Bois, *Souls*, 87.
[38] Du Bois, *Souls*, 80.

South was thinking, "'If that is all your race asks, take it.'"[39] Washington was, therefore, "essentially the leader not of one race but of two."[40]

Du Bois claimed that "Washington's programme" entailed a gospel of Work and Money to such an extent as apparently almost completely to [have] overshadow[ed] the higher aims of life"[41] Washington imbued the "American assumption" (the notion that wealth is a result of one's effort, which in America was given a particularly divine hue when coupled with the "protestant work ethic") so thoroughly that he had become a "race man." Du Bois felt that whether or not Washington had more dignified political ideals in mind for the future, the latter's leadership was based upon lies, "cajoling" to white power with "indiscriminate flattery." Du Bois, in contrast, argued that "straightforward honesty" and a "firm adherence to their higher ideals and aspirations [would] ever keep those ideals within the realm of possibility."[42] The latter was convinced that "the way for a people to gain their reasonable right is not by voluntary throwing them away."[43] Washington, a former slave, had written in his autobiography *Up from Slavery* that "teaching or preaching [was] an easy way to make a living," and "culture" to him was simply an example of laziness by which the useless "would be free from most of the hardships of the world, and, at any rate, could live without manual labour."[44] Certainly, one of "the saddest thing[s]" he witnessed in the South was the poor "young man...sitting down in a one-room cabin, with grease on his clothing, filth all around him, and weeds in the yard and garden, engaged in studying French grammar."[45] Du Bois, without arguing that one should disregard or look down upon manual labor, "wonder[ed] what Socrates and St. Francis of Assisi would say to this"[46] speechless, unreflective, and inarticulate American work ethic.

While Washington criticizes the religion and culture of the former slaves as indicative of laziness, he uses the ideals of the white Christian work ethic and self-made exceptionalism—the American assumption. The

---

[39] Ibid., 82.

[40] Ibid., 86.

[41] Ibid., 87.

[42] Ibid., 90.

[43] Ibid.

[44] Booker T. Washinton, *Up From Slavery: An Autobiography*. New York: Doubleday, Page & Co., 1902. 81.

[45] Washington, 122.

[46] Du Bois, *Souls*, 81.

"eternal striving" defers the realization of freedom in a public space of conversation and cultural exchange and instead propounds a limitless ideal of self-improvement. Washington praises the civilizing capacity of Christianity and judges his own "rise" to success by virtue of his capacity to "use the good things of the earth, not as an end, but as a means toward promoting its own moral and religious growth and the prosperity and happiness of the world."[47] Civilization would come to mean, for Washington, the "moral and religious growth" for growth's sake, for the sole purpose of "want[ing] more wants"[48] and thus needing to strive endlessly.

A degree of "thrift" is recommended by Du Bois, which may seem Puritanical, and Du Bois will also criticize "indifference, or shiftlessness, or reckless bravado,"[49] a cynicism and indifference to striving that may result from a history of slavery and subsequent witnessing of endless compromises to achieve freedom. However, Du Bois does not base a moral and religious system upon instrumentalization and the utilitarian anxiety over the security of wealth as a foundational tenet of the possibility for freedom. It was also this courage that he sensed in slave culture, despite the obscurity of the talents in a climate of laissez-faire selfhood and the doctrine of the work ethic. Du Bois displays a regard for the slave culture and its chosen actors, the "Preacher and Teacher," whom Washington, most recently portrayed as more in touch with the masses, could only imagine as expressions of laziness. For Du Bois, the "Preacher and Teacher" "embodied once the ideal of this people—the strife for another and a juster world, the vague dream of righteousness, the mystery of knowing"; they lived a "simple beauty and weird inspiration" that was replaced by "a quest for cash and a lust for gold."[50] In contrast to Washington, Du Bois does not criticize the moral degeneration or backwardness of the former slaves, although he does draw attention to the tendency to succumb to resignation or "doubt" in a world that valued little the ordinary and communal achievements that public space could promise.

---

[47] Washington, "The Economic Development of the Race Since its Emancipation" in *the Negro in the South: His Economic Progress in Relation to His Moral and Religious Development*, William Levi Bull Lectures 1907 (New York: Citadel Press, 1970) 43-75.

[48] Ibid., 56.

[49] Du Bois, *Souls,* 103.

[50] Du Bois, *Souls*, 114.

Ironically, the puritan and "elitist" Du Bois considered the phenomenon of "laziness" at some length, not always in a critical mode, because a more relaxed pace of "human doing"[51] could only represent resistance to the white work ethic; yet it could also present another more local and epistemological orientation toward work. He looked at laziness in terms of a total situation of slavery, thus in a critical but not a criticizing mode. Du Bois implies that the lingering mode of work evoked the possibility for a "black work ethic," an ethic that epitomized the communal exchange that may have been possible. In *The Souls of Black Folk*, Du Bois begins to reflect on what is considered to be "laziness" as he considers the stereotypical "shiftlessness" of the former slaves: "Shiftless? Yes, the personification of shiftlessness. And yet follow those boys: they are not lazy; to-morrow morning they'll be up with the sun; they work hard when they do work, and they work willingly. They have no sordid, selfish, money-getting ways, but rather a fine disdain for mere cash."[52]

This acknowledgment of the dignified relation to work will develop into a more sustained commentary on the so-called "primitives" of Africa who are not impressed with the imperialistic human beings of the West. As Du Bois remarks in *Dusk of Dawn*, "I began to learn: primitive men are not following us far, frantically waving and seeking our goals: primitive men are not behind us in some swift foot-race. Primitive men have already arrived."[53] Even if Du Bois does not directly articulate this vision in *The Souls of Black Folk*, he begins to express this conviction particularly because it is in this book that he alludes to and plays on the double meanings of time, progress, and space. "These folk have the leisure of true aristocracy—leisure for thought and courtesy, leisure for sleep and laughter,"[54] Du Bois remarks. That "aristocratic" spirit parallels the "simple beauty and weird inspiration" that Du Bois argues in *The Gift of Black Folk* "brought to modern manual labor a renewed valuation of life"[55] and "certain spiritual values not yet fully realized."

However, when the "renewed valuation of life" and everyday exchange turned into an impossible metaphysic of salvation and American progress,

---

[51] Du Bois, *Souls*, 275.

[52] Du Bois, *Souls*, 179.

[53] Du Bois, *Dusk of Dawn*, 323.

[54] Du Bois, *Dusk of Dawn*, 647.

[55] W. E. B. Du Bois, *The Gift of Black Folk: The Negroes in the Making of America* (Boston: Stratford Co., 1924) 54, 53.

the former slaves, Du Bois comments, faced the temptation of succumbing to resignation, fatalism, and doubt. Du Bois therefore chides American Protestantism for having prepared the slaves to anticipate an absolute end of days or an apocalypse that would come with legal emancipation. He claims that "Away back in the days of bondage they thought to see in one divine event the end of all doubt and disappointment: few men ever worshipped Freedom with half such unquestioning faith as did the American Negro for two centuries."[56] Although Du Bois praises the "worship" of freedom, it can become meaningless and fatal without a public space. This new faith in freedom and salvation that equated progress with Providence led some to believe that "when Emancipation finally came," it was "a literal Coming of the Lord."[57] Evidently this did not seem to be the case, but for Du Bois, as I have implied, perhaps the best possibility for salvation did momentarily occur in the foundation of public space.

Yet in order to achieve the grand ideal of "progress" and privatized freedom, Washington had shifted the burden of slavery onto the shoulders of black folk, primarily because he followed the "American assumption," an assumption that could not be applied to the history of chattel slaves. The issue of moral degeneration or incapacity is applied to the slaves as an innate quality, while Du Bois repeatedly remarks that the possibility for freedom for the slaves and their success at it must be a "burden [that] belong to the nation, and the hands of none of us are clean if we bend not our energies to righting these great wrongs."[58] The newly freedmen's attempt to found freedom in the "transition from slavery to freedom"[59] must not "simply [be] seconded, but rather aroused and encouraged, by the initiative of the richer and wiser environing group."[60] For Du Bois, the fate of the nation depended upon this sharing of the "burden." Considering the situation and success of those who were in chains for 300 years through the lenses of the American assumption would be misguided not only because of an unequal starting point but also because the individualist way of measuring freedom was false. If the surrounding group seems "wiser," as Du Bois pointed out, it does not "require any fine-spun theories of racial differences to prove the necessity of

---

[56] Du Bois, *Souls*, 46.

[57] Ibid., 220.

[58] Ibid., 94.

[59] Ibid., 125

[60] Ibid., 93.

such group training after the brains of the race have been knocked out by two hundred and fifty years of assiduous education in submission, carelessness, and stealing."[61] And yet, there was more dignity in slave culture for Du Bois than he sometimes implies. The "new birthright" promised in the transition from slavery to freedom required that the freedmen's novel ways of being in the world, and their novel expressions of truth and beauty, would be heard.

Washington's program of moral improvement insinuated that black people would eventually integrate into the individualist structure of Americanism and its instrumentalist ideology of progress. Du Bois, on the other hand, redefines the "meaning of progress" throughout his work, most specifically in his chapter "Of the Meaning of Progress" in *The Souls of Black Folk*. For Du Bois, the slaves manifested the negative truth of the meaning of progress, and, to be sure, invoked fear in the hearts of those who had so deeply imbibed theories of racial hierarchies that coincided with a white exceptionalist work ethic. According to him, when the Reconstruction "failed" and the former slaves failed to prove themselves human, or equivalent to the "American self" based on the work ethic as it was, the elucidating cry rang out: "Be content to be servants, and nothing more; what need of higher culture for half-men? Away with the black man's ballot, by force or fraud, —and behold the suicide of a race! Nevertheless, out of the evil came something of good." This "good" was the "sobering realization of the meaning of progress."[62] This meaning for Du Bois is "necessarily ugly,"[63] and the form of self it epitomized had little to do with the "souls" of the nation, which elicit an ordinary, though heterogeneous meaning of American democracy. Du Bois uses a "deflationary strategy"[64] to play with and redefine the meaning of progress outside of the futuristic parameters of instrumentalism. The revised meaning of progress for Du Bois can be

---

[61] Ibid., 191.

[62] Du Bois, *Souls*, 51.

[63] Ibid., 105.

[64] I have borrowed the term "deflationary strategy" from Gooding-Williams, "Counter-Sublime," 217, although I intend a slightly different meaning. The sense of deflation that Gooding-Williams attributes to Du Bois's building up of Crummell, only to subvert the image, fits remarkably well with an awakening to novelty and plurality; Du Bois uses this strategy of writing throughout *Souls*, often using the language of manifest destiny, Americanism, and progress only to deflate such terms and make their meanings contingent upon establishing participatory democracy.

understood as an awareness of the "'swift' and 'slow' in human doing, and the limits of human perfectibility."[65]

The particular danger for Du Bois is that this black work ethic, which is aware of the need for communal reflection of the methods of "advancement" and progress, will lose sight of the sacredness in such human discussion. As a result of conquest by an American assumption that "is the arrogance of peoples irreverent toward Time, and ignorant toward the deeds of men,"[66] the descendants of slaves might succumb to a sense of resignation, purposelessness, "indifference, or shiftlessness, or reckless bravado."[67] At this point, Du Bois is fairly genuine about his sense of betrayal in the "missed opportunity" to realize what was promising in American democracy and the everyday "progress" that could be acknowledged in reverence toward time, the time of the former slaves' "new birthright"[68] of freedom.

While Washington's position and policies were almost diametrically opposed to Du Bois's vision, sentiment, and intellect, Alexander Crummell's life and thought presented a great temptation for him. For Washington, the tools of civilization were acquired through the practice of the Protestant work ethic in manual labor; he promoted a progressivist movement on economic levels complemented by a benign Christianity that monitors substantial sins, ensuring that the "eternal striving" was the way to salvation. In contrast, Crummell espoused a merger of civilization and Christianity that engaged the highest "talents" of the Negro. He attempted to cleanse Christianity of its racism and prepare Africans and those of African descent in America for an authentic role in the history of scripture and history. It was from Crummell that Du Bois derived the term "talented tenth." Crummell shared Du Bois's enthusiasm for an intellectual meaning of black culture. It was from Crummell that Du Bois derived the notion of "talent" as a critical and positive meaning of race leadership.

---

[65] Du Bois, *Souls*, 275.

[66] Ibid., 274.

[67] Ibid., 103.

[68] Ibid., 62.

The Civilizing Mission of Alexander Crummell

Although Du Bois honored Crummell in *The Souls of Black Folk* more than any other figure, in his chapter "Of Alexander Crummell," we should keep in mind that Du Bois fundamentally disagreed with the plans for African colonization, or the colonizing mindset. He would also later criticize those who seemed to think of themselves as "American" with no link to a more "primitive" and uncivilized "Africa." As he later notes, the older, liberal members of the NAACP "felt themselves Americans, not Africans. They resented and feared any coupling with Africa."[69] Though Crummell never feared Africa, to be sure, he had little regard for the uncivilized. Crummell was the founder of the American Negro Academy at the turn of the twentieth century who coined the term "talented tenth" in opposition to Washington's accomodationist policies. In this respect, the idea of a black nationalist elite was created by those who were fully aware of the negative implications of the Protestant work ethic when that ethic no longer possessed its higher ideals or gave human dignity to work. Crummell was also one of the founders of the African Methodist Church and supported the foundation of Liberia and Sierra Leone, non-slave colonies to which Abolitionists carried "civilization." Du Bois would understand the desire to leave America on a civilizing mission to Africa to retrieve and construct particular race spirit as more admirable than following Washington, but he viewed it as another compromise, a compromise on the issues of moral ambiguity and democratic possibility. For Du Bois, "'primitive men have already arrived'"; he had an understanding of humanity as that which pre-exists an introduction to Christianity or what goes under the banner of civilization.[70]

In at least one respect, as Sundquist notes, Crummell and Washington were alike: "Crummell shared the view with Washington that civil rights activism was secondary to acquisition of the tools of civilization."[71] Washington had demeaned the souls, according to Du Bois, and had eliminated the necessity to acknowledge the totality of the human character, not simply the body used for labor but the mind and its reflective capacities.

---

[69] Du Bois, *Dusk of Dawn*, 755.

[70] Du Bois, *Dusk of Dawn*, 647.

[71] Sundquist, *To Wake the Nations: Race in the Making of American Literature* (Cambridge: Belknap Press, 1993) 515.

In *The Souls of Black Folk*, Du Bois applauds Crummell's determination. Crummell was "not admitted to the seminary" because of his race, but he did not succumb to the "temptation of Despair."[72] Crummell believed that the achievement of a racially pure black spirit and nationalism would usher in the salvation—the former slaves' manifest destiny. Du Bois admired this planned program of racial pride and uplift, but he did not share Crummell's verve for "civilization," or rather, he did not understand civilization in a normative sense, whereby the "primitives" become human when they acquire the prescriptive morality and laws associated with Christianity.

In his inaugural address to the American Negro Academy, Crummell claimed that the "special undertaking" for African American leaders was "the civilization of the Negro race in the United States, by the scientific processes of literature, art, and philosophy, through the agency of cultured men of this same Negro race." Crummell saw the "special race problem" as a result of a lack of "civilization." In marked contrast to Du Bois, Crummell proclaimed that as anyone could see, "as a race in this land, we have no art; we have no science; we have no philosophy; we have no scholarship." There may be exceptional "individuals," but on the whole, descendants of slaves had not "attain[ed] the role of civilization." While Washington thought it was necessary to acquire "money," Crummell argued that "man cannot live by bread alone but by every word that proceedeth out of the mouth of God." And civilization, rather than having to do with acquiring the "machinery" of "material things," was the "ability to grasp the grand general conceptions of being." Without the idealist grasp of the universals of "lofty civilization," "men are sure to remain low, debased and groveling."[73] Du Bois also used Crummell's rhetoric in *The Souls of Black Folk*; he writes: "The function of the university is not simply to teach bread-winning, or to furnish teachers for the public schools or to be the centre of polite society; it is above all, to be the organ of that fine adjustment between real life and the growing knowledge of life, and adjustment which forms the secret of civilization."[74] The attitude of "adjustment" between "real life and the growing knowledge of life" offers the reader another understanding of civilization as an arena for

---

[72] Du Bois, *Souls*, 236–37.

[73] Quoted in John Cromwell, *The Negro in American History: Men and Women Eminent in the Evolution of the American of African Descent* (1914; repr., New York: Johnson Reprint Corporation, 1968) 134–35.

[74] Du Bois, *Souls*, 117.

exchange rather than as a process of acquisition by which one escapes sub-human "groveling."

Du Bois understood and sympathized with Crummell's religion, and he described his meeting Crummell as a moment in which he "began to feel the fineness of his character, —his calm courtesy, the sweetness of his strength." "Instinctively I bowed before this man," Du Bois wrote, "as one bows before the prophets of the world."[75] Coupled with universalist beliefs about civilization, Crummell thought of the races as separate but pure "families." According to Wilson Moses, Crummell used "Christian," "mystical, teleological rhetoric" and was a representative of an Ethiopianism that prophesied a "Rising Africa" and the apocalyptical "impending doom of Western civilization."[76] This "impending doom," nonetheless, was in store because civilization had been "hypocritical" and had failed to achieve the moral and cultured ideals it prophesied; Crummell was not challenging the normative concept of "civilization." Many critics follow Moses in tying Du Bois closely to Crummell, particularly given his own use of this rhetoric. Yet, while Du Bois sympathized with and even at times supported the need for a positive recovery of the meaning of racial identity, he would interpret schemes of romanticizing Africa as another form of cynicism; likewise he felt sympathy for "the black man who is tired of begging for justice and recognition from folk who seem to him to have no intention of being just and do not propose to recognize Negroes as men."[77]

Given Du Bois's own criticism of leadership, he paints Crummell's "pilgrimage" in *The Souls of Black Folk* with a profound sense of pride that borders on vanity: "A voice and vision called him to be a priest, —a seer to lead the uncalled out of the house of bondage."[78] This sense of "leading" the "uncalled" into the virtues of Ethiopianism sits uncomfortably next to Du Bois's own criticisms of the "civilizing" mission: "Depravity, Sin, Redemption, Heaven, Hell, and Damnation are preached twice a Sunday after the crops are laid by; and few indeed of the community have the hardihood to withstand conversion."[79] Here, Du Bois understands the type of "conversion" usually offered to the former slaves as a critique of moral

[75] Du Bois, *Souls*, 234.
[76] Moses, "The Poetics of Ethiopianism: W. E. B. Du Bois and Literary Black Nationalism." 94.
[77] Du Bois, *Dusk of Dawn*, 697.
[78] Du Bois, *Souls*, 237.
[79] Ibid., 214.

and substantial sins and an effort at purification and indoctrination. More to the point, "[w]ar, murder, slavery, extermination, and debauchery, —this has again and again been the result of carrying civilization and the blessed gospel to the isles of the sea and the heathen without the law."[80] As with Washington, Crummell yielded to the "temptation" of thinking that he held the destiny of other humans in his hands. In this pride and vanity, he formed a meaning of manifest destiny for his own clan while opposing similar meanings for others.

Du Bois had no major argument with Crummell.[81] However, Crummell, according to Du Bois, had to face "three temptations": "the temptation of Hate," "the temptation of Despair," and "the temptation of Doubt,"[82] and although Du Bois honored Crummell by ending the chapter with a resounding "'Well done!'" as the "morning stars s[i]t singing" at Crummell's life's work, he implies that Crummell fell prey to doubt.[83] One of the greatest temptations for Du Bois seems to have been the "temptation of doubt": "Doubt struck the deepest."[84] This "doubt" can lead to a misunderstanding of the plural and morally ambiguous nature of democratic "striving." The temptation of doubt in one's life mission occurs for Du Bois because he, like Crummell, could sometimes succumb to expecting an ultimate moral truth as the end of "striving." However, Du Bois recognizes that the doubt expressed toward the former slaves' capacity toward "advancement" might be misdirected –the very meaning of advancement had to be questioned so that the burden of slavery would not be shifted onto the victims. Crummell's focus is uniquely and singularly on the "moral" advancement of the race. In Du Bois's words, "deep down below the slavery and servitude of the Negro people he saw their fatal weaknesses, which long years of mistreatment had emphasized. The dearth of strong moral character, of unbending righteousness he felt, was their great shortcoming, and here he would begin."[85] But, as Gooding-Williams comments, Crummell doubts when he shifts "from a preoccupation with slave suffering to an emphasis on negro moral deficiency."[86] Gooding-Williams also points

---

[80] Ibid., 187.

[81] Sundquist, *Wake the Nations*, 515.

[82] Du Bois, *Souls*, 233.

[83] Du Bois, *Souls*, 234.

[84] Ibid., 239.

[85] Ibid., 238.

[86] Gooding-Williams, "Counter-Sublime," 213.

out that Du Bois's thought is "essentially rooted in the experience of slavery."[87] By situating the character of freedom already apparent in a position of captivity, Du Bois does not mean to value the private consciousness excluded from public discussion or to romanticize chattel slavery. Rather, he locates another world and community marked by the knowledge of a Limit, thus suggesting a communal form of soul that is not bound up with the fear of slavery that came to shape the post-revolutionary, individualist American self.

Du Bois stressed the plural and "unlovely" condition of humanity, and he would note in *Black Reconstruction* that "we rule by junta; we turn Fascist, because we do not believe in men; yet the basis of fact in this belief is incredibly narrow."[88] The post-Reconstruction South had shown that "it still did not believe in intelligence," save as an "exception."[89] At the time Crummell was pursuing his life mission, however, all that was being asked was the recognition of the probability of black intelligence, and Washington sacrificed even that minimum goal. Du Bois admires Crummell because Crummell fought for the recognition of black intelligence, not in deference to white power but for itself. Nonetheless, Du Bois's revolutionary sensibility differed from Crummell's. On the one hand, to be sure, he fought for this recognition, be it on "exceptionalist" terms; however, Du Bois will note that one "becomes provincial and centered upon the problems of a particular group, a 'race' man." In this sense, there is a particular "'group imprisonment within a group'" that can be fed by "unreasoning resentment and even hatred, deep disbelief in them and refusal to conceive honesty and rational thought on their part."[90] Race as a metaphysic returns one to the stifling ambiguity of the prison-house: the "entity" of a "group" is a "metaphysical hypothesis that had its uses in reasoning but could not be regarded as corresponding to exact truth. No such group over-soul has been proven to exist"[91] What was needed, rather than "belief" as a singular and solitary act, was a "knowledge of one's ignorance" that could only come through interactions and ordinary, daily confrontations with the "folk." Du Bois experienced this "knowledge of [his] ignorance" in former slave

---

[87] Ibid., 203.

[88] Du Bois, *Black Reconstruction*, 382.

[89] Ibid., 697.

[90] Ibid., 651.

[91] Du Bois, *Dusk of Dawn*, 679.

communities in the South — a knowledge of a limited capacity for absolute certainty for the meaning or goals of any democratic communities.

Crummell's teachings offer a plan of righteousness and moral improvement that also echoes the reasons his fellow bishops offered when they excluded him from the seminary. As Du Bois writes of Crummell's fellow bishops, "They were not wicked men, —the problem of life is not the problem of the wicked, —they were calm, good, Bishops of the Apostolic Church of God, and strove toward righteousness."[92] He implies that their striving for righteousness is essential to their "problem" and their exclusion of Crummell. Later in the chapter, Du Bois writes about Crummell in a plea to honor and remember his story: "herein lies the tragedy of the age: not that men are poor, —all men know something of poverty; not that men are wicked, —who is good? not that men are ignorant, —what is Truth? Nay, but that men know so little of men" (243). The lack of space for exchanges and listening to each other to advance understanding is the tragedy for Du Bois. The questions "what is Truth?" and "who is good?" one imagines are not questions Crummell shared with Du Bois.

The program of moral works and "civilization" coincides with the futuristic ideology that is part of the problem with America's rhetoric of manifest destiny. The focus on the future when freedom will be achieved has increased the sense of resignation, held off only by the powerful who by "dogged" strength alone do not capitulate to doubt. Du Bois writes: "What can it expect but crime and listlessness, offset here and there by the dogged struggles of the fortunate and more determined who are themselves buoyed by the hope that in due time the country will come to its senses."[93] The possibilities for redemption have been placed within an absolute teleology; this longing for perfection would contribute to an ideology of victimization and apathy, or to a sense of resignation and indifference, or to violent retaliation and the construction of exclusionary identities that, to be sure, could not succeed in mediating between worlds.

The cross-cultural meetings that occurred during the slave trade and the "discovery" of different worlds promise a form of religion, a form of Christianity that "would undergo characteristic change[s] when [it] entered the mouth of the slave."[94] It was also, Du Bois later notes in *The Negro*,

---

[92] Du Bois, *Souls,* 236–37.

[93] Du Bois, *Souls*, 202.

[94] Ibid., 273.

"through Africa that Christianity became the religion of the world."[95] Du Bois's true ideal of freedom is a fragile possibility produced through minglings, "contacts," and the conglomerate interaction of plural cultural orientations.

One way of thinking about cross-cultural exchanges and the type of public self Du Bois salvaged in the promise of "America" is through the experience of Protestant awakenings, as noted at the opening of this essay. Because the Christian space was the only public forum allowed to the slaves, it is also the realm that allows us to sense the African-American slave agency that Du Bois sees at work in the creation and possible salvation of the nation. According to Mechal Sobel, the early interaction between the slaves and Christian forms of religious experience, of awakening and conversion, used rhetoric of the apocalypse or an ultimate end to achieve its purpose of conversion, allowing the slaves population to inflect their own West-African traditions and concepts of religious experience into the Christian narratives. West African forms of rebirth were, however, somewhat different from the Protestant emphasis on absolute change or its idea of a break with the past through an absolute mastery of self and the subsequent creation of an absolutely new self, which gave rise to a perfectionist and individualist framework.[96] Through the appeal to what Du Bois characterizes as the African gifts to the Republic during early attempts at secularization, Du Bois challenges the structure of democratic freedom in America. Du Bois will continue to imply and then forcefully stress at the end of the book that throughout the history of enslavement, African Americans nevertheless actively inserted their voices into the cultural fabric of the nation, giving it its story, its labor, and its music. America's dependence upon the slaves for its survival and culture makes the former slaves the ones who are capable of correcting the American misconstrual of their "message."

The experience of novelty, rebirth, and talent is cross-cultural and indicative of the new song or the fragile novelty produced by coming together, for which Du Bois longs in the final chapter of *Souls*. The stress on

---

[95] Du Bois, *Negro*, 77.

[96] For a discussion of the differences between African and European conceptions of time, see Mechal Sobel, *The World They Made Together: Black and White Values in Eighteenth-Century Virginia* (Princeton: Princeton University Press, 1976). She also discusses the development of the Afro-Baptist faith through this cross-cultural interaction as well as various Africanisms in this tradition in her book *Trabelin' On: The Slave Journey to an Afro-Baptist Faith* (London: Greenwood Press, 1979).

the spiritual "My Soul wants something that's new"[97] is the "wail of the wanderer," and he will continue this repetitive echoing for the experience of freedom and novelty, a difference and distinctness that is produced through public dialogue, rather than referring to a static racial essence, as late as the writing of *Black Reconstruction*. In the later work we encounter a "great song" and a "new song" that is not derivative of Africa nor of America but "swelled and blossomed like incense, improvised and born anew out of an age long past, and weaving into its texture the old and new melodies in word and in thought." This song is the same song in *Souls*, with the same echo and "message" the "white Southerners" could not understand and to which the "white Northerners listened without ears"[98] In this promise for revolutionary public space and freedom, new voices and stories can continually be reinserted into a great new song, forming a space for plural beginnings rather than ultimate endings or conformist sacrifice.

Rather than being an authentic African product, the spirituals are for Du Bois a specific example of the type of public space, the aesthetic and performative space, he has in mind as the "truth" of American Democracy.[99] The genuine experience of novelty can only be located in the verbal experience of every person coming forth to recount his or her story. Suffice it to say that the structure of the spirituals needs to be considered in more detail, without simply making a few generalizations about improvisation. The presence of musical form, however, does demand the acknowledgment of an ineffable relation to the human voice, so that new voices must continually be added in order for the song to be understood—that we need each other's help here. Du Bois is often not given enough credit, however, for his consideration of musical form; even in a recent analysis of jazz improvisation, Du Bois's musicological reflections are limited to intending the "idea of two warring ideals" or an "irresolvable conflict."[100] Du Bois's

---

[97] Du Bois, *Souls*, 271.

[98] Du Bois, *Black Reconstruction*, 124.

[99] See Dena Epstein's discussion of the cross-cultural and conglomerate nature of the spirituals, particularly the chapter "Conversion to Christianity," in *Sinful Tunes and Spirituals: Black Folk Music to the Civil War* (Chicago: University of Illinois Press, 1977) 100, in which she comments that "one can hardly overstate the importance of conversion to Christianity in the acculturation of blacks in the New World. It was an essential precondition for the emergence of the Negro spiritual."

[100] Ingrid Monson, *Saying Something: Jazz Improvisation and Interaction* (Chicago/London: University of Chicago Press, 1996) 105.

presentation of the conflictual nature of cross-cultural experience is not at all irresolvable conflict, but it does present a hiatus or a gap where language and musical form end and the demand for constructing those face-to-face physical spaces begins. The African forms of music to which Du Bois refers have very little sense of harmony and use part-singing instead. Du Bois's recurrent stress on the lack of harmonizing implies that the form of talent he suggests is negotiated through a reflective and relational self and not simply through imitation or consent. The everyday work of freedom, which requires that everyone come forth to add his or her voice and judgment to the story, requires that public spaces are maintained and founded for interaction so that small ends and achievement are performed, not the establishment of a homogeneous Zion.

In a recurrent motif, Du Bois ends *Souls* with the plea that "in Thy good time may infinite reason turn the tangle straight, and these crooked marks on a fragile leaf be not indeed THE END."[101] Du Bois understood the fragility of freedom, the striving for the next self, so that the notion of an ultimate END in capital letters would also be the end to freedom—the continual desire for "another juster world,"[102] which the addition of more voices or selves to the Republic promotes. In the famous last words of Du Bois, read by Kwame Nkrumah—"'Time is Long'"[103]—we glimpse the vision of the eternal and the necessity of adding one's interpretive voice to history. This echo is certainly not indicative of a manifest chauvinism, nor of passivity or resignation, but rather of a common theme for Du Bois—that America's flight from this everyday relation to time—to the "swift," "slow," and morally ambiguous work required to give birth to democratic "souls"—is the tragedy of our age.

Although Du Bois supported the idea of independent African states and the recognition of racialized identity, it decontextualizes and belittles his thought to assume that he was uncritical of the form of nation to develop, or the continued existence of nations and races as categories of thought. He recognized risks on both sides of the racial divide, assimilation or essentialism, but until African Americans and Africans were acknowledged as human beings there would be no talk of an end to racialized thinking.

---

[101] Du Bois, *Souls*, 278.

[102] Ibid., 114.

[103] Quoted in Arnold Rampersad, *The Art and Imagination of W. E. B. Du Bois* (Cambridge: Harvard University Press, 1976) 291.

Familiar with his mentor Crummell's singular hopes in African colonization, in *Dusk of Dawn* he writes, "American Negroes have always feared with perfect fear the eventual expulsion from America. They have been willing to submit to caste rather than face this. The reasons have varied but today they are clear: Negroes have no Zion."[104] He repeated as much in *Souls* thirty-seven years earlier, and yet possibly the best articulation of this message, the "meaning of the swift and slow in human doing, and the limits of human perfectibility,"[105] is heard in the conversive, communally-progressive relation to Zion in the African turn of the Bible phrase "Weep, O captive daughter of Zion" into "Zion, weep-a-low.... As in olden time."[106]

Works Cited

Arendt, Hannah. *On Revolution*. New York: Viking Press, 1963.

Cromwell, John. *The Negro in American History: Men and Women Eminent in the Evolution of the American of African Descent*. 1914; reprint, New York: Johnson Reprint Corporation, 1968.

Du Bois, W. E. B. *Black Reconstruction: An Essay Toward a History of the Part which Black Folk Played in the Attempt to Reconstruct Democracy in America: 1860–1880*. Philadelphia: Harcourt Brace, 1935.

———. *Color and Democracy: Colonies and Peace*. New York: Harcourt Brace, 1945.

———. *Darkwater: Voices From Within the Veil*. New York: Harcourt Brace, 1920.

———. *Dusk of Dawn: An Essay Toward an Autobiography of a Race Concept*. In *W. E. B.Du Bois: Writings*. N. Huggins, ed. New York: Library of America, 1986.

———. *The Gift of Black Folk: The Negroes in the Making of America*. Boston: Stratford Co., 1924.

———. *The Negro*. London/New York: Oxford University Press, 1970.

———. "Religion in the South." In *The Negro in the South: His Economic Progress in Relation to His Moral and Religious Development*, William Levi Bull Lectures, 1907 (New York: Citadel Press, 1970) 123–91.

---

[104] Du Bois, *Dusk of Dawn*, 777.
[105] Du Bois, *Souls*, 275.
[106] Du Bois, *Souls,* 273.

———. *The Souls of Black Folk.* First Signet Classic edition. New York: Penguin Books, 1995.

Epstein, Dena J. *Sinful Tunes and Spirituals: Black Folk Music to the Civil War.* Chicago: University of Illinois Press, 1977.

Gooding-Williams, Robert. "Du Bois's Counter-Sublime." *Massachusetts Review* 35 (summer 1994): 202–24.

James, Joy. *Transcending the Talented Tenth: Black Leaders and American Intellectuals.* New York and London: Routledge, 1997.

Lewis, David Levering. *W. E. B. Du Bois: A Biography of a Race: 1868–1919.* New York: Henry Holt and Company, 1993.

Marable, Manning. *W. E. B. Du Bois: Black Radical Democrat.* Boston: Twayne Publishers, 1986.

Mizruchi, Susan, "Neighbors, Strangers, Corpses: Death and Sympathy in the Early Writings of W. E. B. Du Bois." In *Centuries' End, Narrative Means,* edited by Robert D. Newman (Stanford: Stanford University Press, 1996) 191–211.

Monson, Ingrid. *Saying Something: Jazz Improvisation and Interaction.* Chicago and London: University of Chicago Press, 1996.

Moses, Wilson J. *Black Messiahs and Uncle Toms: Social and Literary Manipulations of a Religious Myth.* University Park/London: Pennsylvania State University Press, 1982.

———. "'The Conservation of Races' and its Context: Idealism, Conservatism and Hero Worship," *Massachusetts Review* 35 (Summer 1993): 275–94.

———. "The Poetics of Ethiopianism: W. E. B. Du Bois and Literary Black Nationalism." In *Critical Essays on W. E. B. Du Bois,* edited by William L. Andrews (Boston: G. K Hall, 1985): 92–105.

Rampersad, Arnold. *The Art and Imagination of W. E. B. Du Bois.* Cambridge: Harvard University Press, 1976.

Rath, Richard Cullen. "Echo and Narcissus: The Afrocentric Pragmatism of W. E. B. Du Bois." *Journal of American History* 84/2 (September 1997): 461–95.

Sobel, Mechal. *The World They Made Together: Black and White Values in Eighteenth-Century Virginia.* Princeton: Princeton University Press, 1987.

———. *Trabelin' On: The Slave Journey to an Afro-Baptist Faith.* London: Greenwood Press, 1979.

Sundquist, Eric. *To Wake the Nations: Race in the Making of American Literature*. Cambridge: Belknap Press, 1993.

Washington, Booker T. *Up From Slavery: An Autobiography*. New York: Doubleday, Page & Co., 1902.

———."The Economic Development of the Negro Race Since Its Emancipation." In *The Negro in the South: His Economic Progress in Relation to His Moral and Religious Development*, William Levi Bull Lectures 1907 (New York: Citadel Press, 1970): 43–75.

West, Cornel. *The American Evasion of Philosophy: A Genealogy of Pragmatism*. Madison: University of Wisconsin Press, 1989.

———. *Prophesy Deliverance! An Afro-American Revolutionary Christianity*. Philadelphia: Westminster Press, 1982.

Toward a Synaesthetics of Soul: W. E. B. Du Bois and the Teleology of Race[1]

Steve Andrews
Grinnell College

The Souls of Black Folk has always been a difficult text to teach. Not the least of this difficulty stems from W. E. B. Du Bois's strategic use of music throughout the book. Indeed, the fourteenth chapter, "Of the Sorrow Songs," is not only a veritable archive, spongy as it is with black folk music; it is also one of the few written arguments that risks ending in musical notation. In this chapter, Du Bois utilizes the figure of synaesthesia (from the Greek "to feel or perceive together"[2]) in order to merge his vision of black folks' place within what he calls the "warp and woof"[3] of the text of America with his ongoing, often implicit revision of William James and G. W. F. Hegel, philosophical influences which are by now canonical in Du Boisean scholarship. (Recent critical interventions by Ross Posnock and

---

[1] A version of this paper was delivered at the *W. E. B. Du Bois and Frantz Fanon: Postcolonial Linkages and Transatlantic Receptions Conference* at the University of Stirling, Scotland, UK, 15–17 March 2002. I would like to thank the conference organizers for the opportunity to present these ideas, and I gratefully acknowledge the criticisms and suggestions of various conferees as well as comments from the editors of this collection, Chester Fontenot and Mary Keller, and the anonymous reader(s). Such exchanges are always helpful. Portions of this paper appear, in a radically different context in my unpublished dissertation, "Salvaging Virginia: Transitivity, Race and the Problem of Consent," University of Washington, 1998.

[2] Jack Myers and Michael Simms, eds., *The Longman Dictionary of Poetic Terms* (New York: Longman, Inc., 1989).

[3] W. E. B. Du Bois, *The Souls of Black Folk* (New York: Penguin Books, 1989) 215.

Shamoon Zamir, for instance, draw the clearest lines of influence, resistance, and revision between these major thinkers.) In concluding with nearly a full page of musical notation, Du Bois claims for black music the privileged typographic space usually reserved for the teleological finesses of the written word. By that point, having taken his readers through thirteen chapters of a masterful mix of expository and narrative technique, Du Bois has elaborated plenty of good reasons for making such a claim.

In the following pages, I make a strong link between James and Du Bois on what I take to be a crucial but critically unattended issue in *Souls*—Du Bois's aesthetic figuration of the fluid nexus of felt relations that James calls "transitivity." Defining and situating transitivity in the Jamesean context and suggesting ways in which Du Bois turns or tropes it constitutes the first two sections of this essay. Then, after a brief transitional discussion in the third section of some of the Hegelian implications for Du Bois relative to music as a source and index for feeling, I conclude with a discussion of some of the problems of reading Du Bois's synaesthetic interweave of music and linear text. In doing so, I return the reader to those years when Du Bois was a student under the tutelage of James during a period when scientific curiosity about synaesthesia was nearing its peak. Coined in 1892 by the Frenchman Jules Millet,[4] the term synaesthesia refers to "the translation of a physical sensation from one sense into another," as, for example, "images simultaneously experienced as sound and texture or sight and smell."[5] As John Harrison reminds us, though, the usual condition is one in which a "visual sensation" is "caused by auditory stimulation."[6] Examined from the perspective of Du Bois's strategic use of synaesthesia, the "problem" of reading the fourteenth chapter, with its heightened auditory implications, becomes a masterful performative manipulation of the "visual sensation" implied by the color line—of the "problem," that is, "of being a Negro" with which Du Bois began thirteen chapters before. To better engage both "problems," this paper will take advantage of internet technology unavailable to Du Bois in order to link the reader with a web

---

[4] See Nicholas Cook, *Analysing Musical Multimedia* (Oxford: Clarendon Press, 1998) 25.

[5] *Longman Dictionary*, ed. Myers and Simms. They too mention that the term "first appears" in Jules Millet's *Audition Coloree*.

[6] John Harrison, *Synaesthesia: The Strangest Thing* (Oxford: University Press, 2001) 3.

page specifically designed to allow the reader multimedia interaction with the synaesthetic moves Du Bois makes within the final pages of *Souls*.[7]

I.

In *The Marrow of Tradition*, Charles Chesnutt, one of Du Bois's favorite writers, likened the ongoing social problem of race to a "serial story which we are all reading, and which grows in vital interest with each successive installment."[8] A keen observer of the prevailing social practice of his time, Chesnutt views race as a kind of text reliant on fixed notions of semantic value and proper syntactic placement, all tending toward a teleology of "vital

---

[7] For purposes of engaging more fully the premises of this essay, it will be helpful to log on to the Internet and connect to the following URL: <http://web.grinnell.edu/cts/dubois/>. While this web site was conceptualized by the author of this essay, he would like to take this opportunity to thank Munindra Khaund, who designed the web site; David Berk and Todd Coleman, who digitally captured the music; Ralph Russell, for performing and arranging the music; and the Young, Gifted and Black Choir of Grinnell College for singing Prof. Russell's interpretations of various songs, especially "Let Us Cheer the Weary Traveler." Thanks also to Associate Dean Helen Scott and the Mellon Foundation for organizing and funding the "Teaching with Technology in the Liberal Arts" workshop in the summer of 2001, which was taught by David Berk, Munindra Khaund, Wayne Twitchell, and Alex Wirth-Cauchon, and to Mike Conner for all of his recent help in maintaining it.

This web site started out as a project for that workshop. The site will soon be updated to the point where most of the music—in notation or implied by lyric or title—will be available. For purposes of this paper, however, the reader need only access "Do Bana" (5) and "Let Us Cheer the Weary Traveler" (15). QuickTime is required to access these songs. I shall situate the reader parenthetically by reference to this website, followed by the appropriate page number as occasion requires. Follow the prompt on each web page for maximum effect.

[8] See Charles Chesnutt, *The Marrow of Tradition* (Ann Arbor: University of Michigan Press, 1990) 51. On Du Bois's "favorite" writers, see David Levering Lewis, *W. E. B. Du Bois: Biography of a Race, 1868–1919* (New York: Henry Holt and Company, 1993) 282. Prior to the publication of *Souls,* Du Bois makes fairly frequent reference to Chesnutt's excellence, especially in lists of great African-American cultural leaders, as in his October 1900 article for *Church Review* entitled "The Present Outlook for the Dark Races of Mankind"; his review of Booker T. Washington's *Up from Slavery* (1901); and, shortly after publication of *Souls,* his article for *Booklover's Magazine*, "Possibilities of the Negro; The Advance Guard of the Race" (June 1903).

interest." Such conventions—the codes of Jim Crow, for instance—police
and reinforce strict protocols of reading, citing, and reception, the better to
ensure a conclusion amenable, even in its surprises, to the majority white
readership. According to Robert Scholes, "we need protocols of reading for
the same reason that we need other codes and customs—because we desire a
framework in which to negotiate our differences."[9] But what if, as in the case
of the serial story of "race," the frameworks that shape desire and difference
are the problem? "Reading," as Jacques Derrida has written (simultaneously
acknowledging and undercutting the idea of protocols), "is transformational.
I believe that this would be confirmed by certain of Althusser's propositions.
But this transformation cannot be executed however one wishes. It requires
protocols of reading. Why not say it bluntly: I have not yet found any that
satisfy me."[10] Du Bois likewise acknowledges protocols or "governing
codes," if only to expose their inadequacies in the transformative process, as
Louis Althusser describes it, of "laying bare," "of peeling" and "refining"
entrenched notions of what constitute *differences* worth negotiating.[11] *Souls*
thus begins its "Forethought" with an invitation to, and immediate occlusion
of, the reader's eye—"herein lie buried many things"[12]—and ends in an
"Afterthought" whose primary plea—"hear my cry"[13]— has been pitched to
the reader's ear in graphic representations of song that the reading eye
cannot liquidate. As we shall see and hear, the disruptions of the governing
codes of text and sense can easily be amplified to expose what was, in 1903,
the ongoing political problem of whiteness imagined as the teleological
vanishing point of history.

I'd like to return for a moment to the example of Chesnutt in order to
underscore what kind of protocols early-twentieth-century readers of race

---

[9] Robert Scholes, *Protocols of Reading* (New Haven: Yale University Press, 1989)
51.

[10] Jacques Derrida, *Positions*, trans. Alan Bass (Chicago: University of Chicago
Press, 1981) 63. This passage, with the reference to Althusser elided, is cited and
critiqued by Scholes, who insists that Derrida's bemoaning the inadequacy of existing
protocols is something of an alibi for Derrida's own reliance on "rigor" (74). Rigor, for
Scholes, implies a "govern[ing]" "code" (78).

[11] So Althusser tropes the process of reading in "Lenin Before Hegel." See Louis
Althusser, *Lenin and Philosophy*, trans. Ben Brewster (New York: Monthly Review
Press, 1971) 114–16. This is the passage referred to by Derrida and elided by Scholes.

[12] Du Bois, *Souls*, 1.

[13] Ibid., 217.

might or might not have found adequate. When Dr. Will Miller, the fictional black protagonist of *The Marrow of Tradition*, occupies a vacancy in the "whites only" train car at the behest of his socially progressive mentor, Dr. Burns, he is deemed to be out of place relative to the governing codes of Jim Crow. Miller is subsequently reminded, as was the historical Homer Plessy, of the proper syntax of race relations when the conductor ushers him away. As Du Bois shrewdly reminds his readers in *Dusk of Dawn*, amidst all the permutations of skin color between light and dark that are possible for "black" folk, we identify who is black by virtue of the fact that "the black man is a person who must ride 'Jim Crow' in Georgia."[14] The enforced separation of colleagues by virtue of race initiates for Chesnutt the process of peeling away what Justice John Marshall Harlan, in his dissent in *Plessy v. Ferguson*, called "the thin disguise of equal accommodations."[15] By way of an historical turn masked as biographical update, Chesnutt's narrator had previously traced Miller's trajectory from New York (to buy accommodations for his hospital) to North Carolina (where it is needed) and from medical school in Philadelphia, Paris, and Vienna to the restrictive color-codings of Jim Crow.[16] The movement *from* this more progressive, cosmopolitan past *to* the clearly regressive present tense of the story is thus Chesnutt's way of critiquing nineteenth-century narratives ("frameworks," one might say) of historical progress that rather too consistently make the essentialist presumption that blacks are temporally lagging and are therefore "primitive." This "lag" was too often used to justify the enforcement of situational protocols that placed whites over blacks, thereby provoking creative animosity in writers such as Chesnutt, Pauline Hopkins, and Du Bois, among others.

Readers of Chesnutt can, along with Dr. Will Miller, infer both temporal lag and hierarchical inflection in the following sentence uttered by

---

[14] Du Bois, *Dusk of Dawn: An Essay Toward an Autobiography of a Race Concept* (New Brunswick: Transaction Publishers, 1983) 153. Unlike the historical Homer Plessy, Dr. Miller is, as Chesnutt pointedly indicates, discernibly "black, or, more correctly speaking, brown." That late-nineteenth-century America's practice of race is, for the most part, essentialist, I take for granted. Within the governing codes of Jim Crow, the Homer Plessys of the world are exceptions that prove the rule. Appearance notwithstanding, nineteenth-century readers would "read" the very "white-appearing" Plessy as "black," as Du Bois intimates, because of his syntactic placement in the Jim Crow car.

[15] *Plessy v. Ferguson*, 163 US 562 (1896).

[16] Chesnutt, *Marrow of Tradition*, 50, 51.

Dr. Burns, the white Northerner who initially invokes the serial text of race. "It is not only your problem," he says, "but ours. Your race must come up or drag ours down." Being beneath is thus apposite to being behind, as Miller's response makes clear: "We shall come up.... If our race had made as much progress everywhere as they have made in Wellington, the problem would be well on the way toward solution."[17] Here, Miller's invocation of "progress" signals the teleology toward which the prepositions "ahead" and "above" move us. And, to use a turn of phrase, it clearly *is* an uphill struggle, as the assumption of white superiority is underwritten by no less an authority than Hegel.

"The Negro," according to Hegel, "exhibits the natural man in his completely wild and untamed state." From this primal exhibitionism another, perhaps even more damning, exhibition follows: Africa "is no historical part of the World; it has no movement or development to exhibit."[18] In the Hegelian worldview, Africa and Africans, ostensibly mired in the embodied muck of primal desires, are outside the telos of Universal History as exemplified in the rational "movement" and "development" of cultural artifacts such as Hegel's own textual exposition of "the" philosophy of history. Exhibiting too much nature, Africa and Africans are thereby assigned an ahistorical or "fixed" place as exhibits that index—positively, to be sure—the curator's role in managing the flow of history proper.[19] As

---

[17] Ibid., 51. Of course, most readers of the novel would be aware of the ironic implications of "progress" in such close proximity to "Wellington," as Wellington is a thinly disguised pseudonym for Wilmington, North Carolina, where "race riots," or, as Eric Sundquist more accurately defines the white reaction to black political power, a "white political coup," broke out in 1898, just three years prior to the publication of Chesnutt's novel. See Eric Sundquist, *To Wake the Nations: Race in the Making of American Literature* (Cambridge: Belknap Press, 1993) 13.

[18] G. W. F. Hegel, *Lectures on the Philosophy of History*, trans. J. Sibree (London: Henry G. Bohn, 1856) 97, 103.

[19] The layout of Chicago's Columbian Exhibition in 1893 is an excellent example of the kind of placement, exhibition, and significance I am discussing. According to Thomas J. Schlereth, African Americans, along with "several other nonwhite cultures," were "the exhibited, rather than exhibitors...kept 'in their place'; that is, they were located by the fair's white-controlled Department of Ethology in miniature villages, compounds, and reservations on the fair's midway.... The village displays reinforced American racial prejudices and ethnic stereotypes. The exhibits, often depicting people as curiosities (the Javanese) or trophies (the Sioux) were staged on what one contemporary called a 'sliding scale of humanity.' Nearest the White City were the Teutonic and Celtic races,

such, they embody the ostensibly "static" difference whence the signification or value of the linear progression of European civilization can be measured against where it is not. Time, then, is an arrow tethered to Africa, but, as Hegel makes clear, it makes its point elsewhere: "America is...the land of the future, where, in the ages that lie before us, the burden of the World's History shall reveal itself."[20] Not surprisingly, in the latter half of the nineteenth century Americans returned the favor, finding in Hegel ample "support," according to Zamir, for rationalizing post-Civil War "American nationalism" in conjunction with its antebellum vision of "manifest destiny."[21] In fact, in Chicago in 1893 (just up the road from St. Louis, the gateway of American Hegelianism), arguably the most famous and enduring intellectual product to come out of the Columbian Exposition was Frederick Jackson Turner's implicitly Hegelian thesis on "The Significance of the Frontier in American History." Likening the United States to "a huge page in the history of society," Turner approvingly cites the Italian economist Achille Loria's notion that "the land that has no history reveals luminously the course of universal history."[22] Unfortunately, the hard facts of lynching, Western reservations, the lack of suffrage for women, and appalling living conditions in urban tenements were too often swallowed up by the glare of a Gilded Age in love with its own luminosity. To the dismay of Native Americans, black folk, and other victims of the onslaught of "universal" history, the teleology of American time and space had become a little *too* Hegelian. Within this sociopolitical framework, then, what is ultimately progressive in the exchange between Drs. Burns and Miller is that black folk are not, as in the case of Hegel, an icon for the trope of permanent or essential cultural belatedness but merely *temporarily* lagging.

---

represented by the two German and two Irish enclaves; the midway's middle contained the Muhammadan and Asian worlds; then, continued the observer, 'we descend to the savage races, the African of Dahomey and the North American Indian, each of which has its place' at the remotest end of the midway." See Schlereth, "Columbia, Columbus, and Columbianism," *Journal of American History* 79/3 (December 1992): 964.

[20] Hegel, *Philosophy of History*, 90; also cited by Shamoon Zamir in *Dark Voices: W. E. B. Du Bois and American Thought, 1888–1903* (Chicago: University of Chicago Press, 1995) 124 and Ross Posnock, *Color and Culture: Black Writers and the Making of the Modern Intellectual* (Cambridge: Harvard University Press, 1998) 119.

[21] Zamir, *Dark Voices*, 13.

[22] Frederick Jackson Turner, *The Significance of the Frontier in American History*, ed. Harold Simonson (New York: Frederick Ungar Publishing Co., 1963) 34.

For Du Bois, however, "catching up" is less at issue than exposing existing cultural value suppressed by what Richard Poirier, in reference to James's student Gertrude Stein, calls the "cultural imposition" inherent in syntactic formations. From the Jamesean point of view Poirier is concerned to elaborate (and on which I shall have more to say a bit later), "the customary structure of sentences give precedence to substantives, while transitives, including prepositions, conjunctions, and adverbs, merely speed the way toward nouns, *more or less expending themselves in the process.*"[23] Within the protocols of precedence Poirier outlines, readers of Hegel, Chesnutt, and Du Bois—indeed, Western readers in general—enact in their movement from left to right the expectation of a linear progression toward clarification of meaning from one substantive to another, all under the aegis of an ostensibly supervisory eye. Du Bois, however, by way of his graphic imposition of musical notation, betrays such expectations by offering something in the way of a visual scandal or stumbling block.

America's social vision at the turn of the twentieth century, as played out against the backdrop of lynching and the color line, was clearly antidemocratic and thus in need of a corrective. But the corrective to social myopia and racial megalomania, the affect of which is implied in Du Bois's famous line "I sit with Shakespeare and he winces not,"[24] is not a stronger lens but a synaesthetic shift to another sense with the attendant hope of ultimately embodying a different sensibility. By imposing musical notations that disrupt protocols of citation and reception, Du Bois calls into question the oppositional hierarchies of various binaries—linearity over circularity, written over oral history, knowing over feeling, white over black, to name a few—that can be subsumed under the master sensory pairing of vision over aurality. Rather than reinscribe the terms of binary opposition by overturning the hierarchical inflections—ear *over* eye, black *over* white, for instance—Du Bois leaves the reader to ponder instead the problem of synaesthesia, of how to "feel together" a world in which sound and sight, music and writing, "Negro" and "American," and even "James" and "Hegel" are no longer reduced to and by the anesthetic logic of disjunction but are instead dislocated from fixed protocols of sense, genre, and caste. The hope was that such sensory dislocation would better facilitate a response on the

---

[23] Richard Poirier, *Poetry and Pragmatism* (Cambridge: Harvard University Press, 1992) 40, emphasis added.
[24] Du Bois, *Souls*, 90.

part of readers toward recognizing simultaneous, omni-sensual cultural interactivity by blacks and whites. One such respondent was Du Bois's Harvard mentor and "guide to clear thinking," William James.[25]

In a June 1903 letter gently chiding his brother's plan to travel in order to come into "contact" with "new material," William James nonetheless encouraged Henry by offering something tangible in the way of the experience he sought: "I am sending you a decidedly moving book by a mulatto ex-student of mine, Du Bois," he responded. The elder James then goes on to recommend "Chapters VII to XI for local color, etc."[26] Written some two months after the publication of *The Souls of Black Folk*, that comment by James must now stand as the earliest and most trenchant acknowledgment of his former student's troping of sources that James could clearly identify. Shifting the inflection from emotion to motion, *The Souls of Black Folk*—"the only 'Southern' book of any distinction published for many a year," according to Henry James in *The American Scene*—is a decidedly *moving* book.[27]

Although much recent criticism seems comfortable with the idea of William James as an influence on W. E. B. Du Bois, most of that criticism has focused, in varying degrees and from differing points of view, on the issue of double-consciousness.[28] While that focus is hardly misplaced, I would nonetheless like to shift attention to the *motion* implied in James's phrase. I believe that key components of *Souls* "turn" on James's own project of reinstating the transitivity that constitutes an unexamined or "omitted"

---

[25] Du Bois, *Dusk of Dawn*, 38.

[26] William James to Henry James, in *Letters of William James,* 2 vols., ed. Henry James III (Boston: Little Brown, 1926) 2:195–96. This letter is cited in Lewis's *Biography of a Race*, 294.

[27] Henry James, *The American Scene*, ed. with an intro. by W. H. Auden (New York: Charles Scribner's Sons, 1946) chap. 12, 418. For Henry, this effort by "that most accomplished of members of the negro race, W. E. B. Du Bois," is pitched as a negative query about how far "everything" can "have so gone" as to leave *Souls*, as accomplished as it might be, as the South's best effort.

[28] See, for instance, Priscilla Wald, *Constituting Americans* (Durham NC: Duke University Press, 1993); Charles Lemert, "A Classic from the Other Side of the Veil: Du Bois's *Souls of Black Folk*," *Sociological Quarterly* 35/3 (August, 1994): 383–96; Dickson D. Bruce, Jr., "W. E. B. Du Bois and the Idea of Double Consciousness," *American Literature* 64/2 (June 1992) 299–309; and Cynthia D. Schrager, "Both Sides of the Veil: Race, Science, and Mysticism in W. E. B. Du Bois," *American Quarterly* 48/4 (December 1996): 551–86.

part of our consciousness,[29] an appreciation of which Du Bois suggests "lie[s] buried" in the text of *Souls of Black Folk*. Between "Forethought" and "Afterthought," Du Bois performs a stellar turn on this aspect of James, more so than has hitherto been credited. In light of this, I take James's statement in two ways: *Souls* is *affective*; and its affect is, in part, a function of its unique strategic engagement with issues of motion, stasis, and liquidity. From the larger movements and fixtures of local, national, and global politics to the inner motivations of thought and language as manifested in the textual relationship between writer and reader, Du Bois attempts to "translate" the "*finer* feelings" of being a problem.[30]

Admittedly "extremely emotional on the race problem" while at Harvard, Du Bois turned early to "the philosophy of William James" for much needed "direct[ion]."[31] From James he would have learned that "[f]ree will pragmatically means *novelties in the world*, the right to expect that in its deepest elements as well as in its surface phenomena, the future may not identically repeat and imitate the past."[32] As James had argued in "The Dilemma of Determinism" (1884), free will was a function of chance,[33] and

---

[29] "The Stream of Thought" chapter was derived from an earlier article, "On Some Omissions of Introspective Psychology," published in *Mind* 33 (January 1881)[**:PAGE#**]. See William James, *The Principles of Psychology*, 2 vols. (New York: Dover Publications, 1950) 1:224

[30] W.E.B. Du Bois, *Book Reviews by W.E.B. Du Bois,* in *Collected Published Works of W.E.B Du Bois,* compiled and edited by Herbert Aptheker (Millwood, New York: KTO Press, 1977) p. 9, emphasis added. The review was originally published in *The Independent*, v. 57 (November 17, 1904) p. 1152

[31] W. E. B. Du Bois, letter to Ben F. Rogers, Jr., 20 December 1939, in *Selections, 1934–1944*, vol. 2 of *The Correspondence of W. E. B. Du Bois*, ed. Herbert Aptheker (Amherst: University of Massachussetts Press, 1976) 2:204.

[32] William James, *Pragmatism and the Meaning of Truth* (Cambridge: Harvard University Press, 1978) 60.

[33] The lectures from 1906 and 1907 that were collected to form *Pragmatism* certainly would not have been available to Du Bois in 1903, but James lectured on free will and determinism throughout the period Du Bois took courses from him. The sentiments James expresses in *Pragmatism* cited here, for instance, are presaged in "The Dilemma of Determinism." There, arguing on behalf of a "pluralistic, restless universe, in which no single point of view can ever take in the whole scene," James insistently champions a world in which chance, "even if the chance never come to pass, is better than a world with no such chance at all. That 'chance' whose very notion I am exhorted and conjured [by determinism] to banish from my view of the future as the suicide of reason

in a world saturated with contingency we are entitled, he wrote in *Pragmatism*, to a sort of "promise"—perhaps nothing more than a working hope—that "improvement [is] at least possible."[34] Allowing for the possibility of agency in the world made the following statements in lesson 7 of James's course in Philosophy (1888) that much more pertinent. At one point Du Bois wrote down, "force was 'nothing more or less than will.'" He concluded from this that since "souls were forces," "*all* forces had wills."[35] *The Souls of Black Folk*, as the embodiment of will as aesthetic force or desire, would, if rightly read, become what James in reference to free will had called a "doctrine of relief."[36] Du Bois would insist on such "relief" for all Americans by holding the egalitarian premises of the New World to the promise of its own novelty—that the future *would not repeat and imitate the past* and that *improvement is possible.*

Belief in the promise of novelty allowed Du Bois to acknowledge as fact both racism *and* beauty, as articulated in the following passage from *Darkwater* (1920):

> Pessimism is cowardice. The man who cannot frankly acknowledge the 'Jim-Crow' car as a fact and yet live and hope is simply afraid either of himself or of the world. There is not in the world a more disgraceful denial of human brotherhood than the 'Jim-Crow' car of the southern United States; but, too, just as true, there is nothing more beautiful in the universe than sunset and moonlight on Montego Bay in far Jamaica. And

---

concerning it, that 'chance' is—what? Just this—the chance that in moral respects *the future may be other and better than the past has been.*" *The Will to Believe and Other Essays in Popular Philosophy,* eds. Frederick H. Burkhardt, Fredson Bowers, and Ignas K. Skrupskelis (Cambridge, Massachusetts: Harvard University Press, 1979) 136, 137, emphasis added.

[34] James, *Pragmatism*, 61.

[35] Richard Cullen Rath, "Echo and Narcissus: The Afrocentric Pragmatism of W. E. B. Du Bois," *Journal of American History* 84/2 (September 1997) 473–74. While Rath cites lesson 7, I think it important to note too that at the end of lesson 6 Du Bois writes: "Of Force: this means nothing more or less than Desire—a causes b" therefore "a <u>desires</u> b. Cause in philosophical discussions is nothing more than desire." See *The Papers of W. E. B. Du Bois* (Sanford, N.C.: Microfilming Corporation of America, 1980-81), reel 88, "Philosophy Notes," frames 204-205. Rath also underscores Du Bois's Jamesean mediation of Hegel and notes that Du Bois "stunningly employed James's conviction that relations, although invisible, were powerfully real" (463).

[36] Du Bois, *Souls*, 61.

both things are true and both belong to this world, and neither can be denied.[37]

Enacting the complicated commotions of a "simple wish" to "make it possible for a man to be both a Negro and an American," *The Souls of Black Folk* will conjoin "double words" with "double ideals" in order to reinstate the idea, and reconstruct the possibility, of a conjunctive America.[38] This turn from "extreme emotion" toward the ameliorative promise of what Ross Posnock calls "philosophical pragmatism" was, as Du Bois remarks in *Dusk of Dawn*, a Jamesian legacy: "the turning was due to William James."[39] But what, exactly, is Du Bois turning? To find out, we must ourselves turn to James's *Principles of Psychology* (1890).

In that monumental work, James divides the "stream of thought" into "resting-places" and "places of flight." *"Let us call these resting-places the 'substantive parts,' and the places of flight the 'transitive parts,' of the stream of thought."*[40] He goes on to say that the "main end" of thinking is the movement *to* one substantive *from* another substantive. Since "we" are rhetorically figured as being "dislodged" from the previous substantive, the "main use" of the transitive parts is to "lead us" to new lodgings. The migration toward "ends," "attainments," and "conclusions" is effected by the labor use-value of the transitive.[41] Since the transitive places seem to defy

---

[37] Du Bois, "Of Beauty and Death," in *Darkwater: Voices from Within the Veil* (New York: Dover Publications, 1999) 135.

[38] Du Bois, *Souls*, 5, 165.

[39] Du Bois, *Dusk*, 39; cited by Posnock in *Color and Culture*, 114. Here, as elsewhere, Posnock has most consistently moved Du Bois's writing toward a Jamesian aesthetics of the "vague," which, by definition, implies the transitivity (or, as Posnock phrases it, the "predilection for the mobility of troping" [114]) that I shall explore in the next few pages. "Philosophical pragmatism"—the "esteem for experimental action" and a "commitment to simultaneous and multiple forms of inquiry"—is a term Posnock employs to counter the "colloquial pragmatism" of Booker T. Washington with its "accommodation and compromise" but also its singleness of vision that was dogmatic and often repressive, the "virtual antithesis" of philosophical pragmatism (36–37). Such a distinction performs a necessary distancing within the space of the single, complex signifier "pragmatism." Posnock's "philosophical/colloquial" distinction contains as dramatic a sense of difference within a continuum as the modifiers "liberal" and "manual" when attached to the single substantive term "art"—especially when applied to the Du Boisean project, both in its particulars and in its general disposition.

[40] James, *Principles*, 1:243, emphasis original.

[41] Ibid.

analysis—stopping them on the way to the substantive "annihilates" them, while waiting till the conclusion of the thought "swallows" them[42]—James turns to the way we use language for an example of how our *feelings* of transitivity are "eclipsed" by our tendency to privilege the substantive. "If there be such things as feelings at all," James writes, "*then so surely as relations between objects exist in rerum natura, so surely, and more surely, do feelings exist to which these relations are known.*"[43] Locating transitivity in "conjunctions," "prepositions," "adverbial phrases," "syntactic form," and "inflection of voice," James suggests that we "ought," then, "to say a feeling of *and*, a feeling of *if*, a feeling of *but*, and a feeling of *by*, quite as readily as we say a feeling of *blue* or a feeling of *cold*."[44] What prevents us from expressing our *blue* selves in this way is our "inveterate" "habit" of "recognizing" the substantive parts "alone."[45] "It is, in short," says James, "the reinstatement of the vague to its proper place in our mental life which I am so anxious to press on the attention."[46]

Turning once again to the figure of a stream to emphasize his point, James suggests that the "traditional psychology" can only imagine the stream of consciousness substantively, as "moulded forms of water," "pails and buckets"—while everywhere "between" these moulded forms the "free water would continue to flow":

> Every definite image in the mind is steeped and dyed in the free water that flows round it. With it goes the sense of its relations, near and remote, the dying echo of whence it came to us, the dawning sense of whither it is to lead. The significance, the value, of the image is all in this halo or penumbra that surrounds and escorts it, —rather that is fused into one with it and has become bone of its bone and flesh of its flesh; leaving it, it is true, an image of the same *thing* it was before, but making it an image of that thing newly taken and freshly understood.[47]

This "free water that psychologists overlook" is what James is concerned to reinstate, and it is the tropic force of this passage (with its "penumbra," its reference to the biblical text of Genesis, and its wandering

---

[42] Ibid.

[43] James, *Principles*, vol.1 245, emphasis original.

[44] Ibid., 245–46.

[45] Ibid., 246.

[46] Ibid., 254.

[47] Ibid., 255.

between "dying echo" and "dawning sense") that Du Bois clearly applies to the *relation* between "Forethought" and "Of Our Spiritual Strivings" and then out to other key passages in *Souls*.

II.

David Levering Lewis, Du Bois's biographer, is skeptical about the "extent" to which James's "insights" in the *Principles of Psychology* are the "source of Du Bois's own special insights" into "the double nature of the African-American psyche."[48] Nevertheless, Lewis does situate Du Bois squarely within the texts and contexts produced by his mentor: "Du Bois probably did hear James expound on the neurological and epiphenomenal nature of mind; [and] certainly he would have read his favorite professor's groundbreaking book soon after publication."[49] In a self-review written for *The Independent* in November of 1904, Du Bois leaves little doubt that he, like Gertrude Stein, had learned much from his mentor:

> A clear central message it has conveyed to most readers, I think, but around this center there has lain a penumbra of vagueness and half-veiled allusion which has made these and others especially impatient. How far this fault is in me and how far it is in the nature of the message I am not sure. It is difficult, to translate the finer feelings of men into words. The Thing itself seems fearfully uncouth and inchoate. Nevertheless, as the feeling is deep the greater the impelling force to seek to express it. And here the feeling is deep.[50]

Posnock has recently suggested that Du Bois's use here of the phrase "penumbra of vagueness" reads "as if" Du Bois were "proud" of "heeding James's plea for a 'reinstatement of the vague.'"[51] I think he is right to see the connection to James, but it is not pride of heeding a call so much as an insistence on the part of the author to his audience that there are "buried" clues yet to be unraveled. *Vagueness* was one such clue; however, it is Du

---

[48] Lewis, *Biography of a Race*, 96.

[49] Ibid.

[50] Aptheker, *Book Reviews by W.E.B. Du Bois*, 9.

[51] Ross Posnock, "The Distinction of Du Bois: Aesthetics, Pragmatism, Politics," *American Literary History*, 7/3, (Fall 1995) p. 507 [pp. 500-524]; see also Posnock, *Color and Culture*, 104–106. While I am much indebted to both the content and the tendencies of this article, I will try to show an even stronger influence *from* James, and hence a more persistent troping *of* James.

Bois's use of *penumbra* to substantiate "vagueness" (so to speak) that clearly argues for a more active, insistent troping of the Jamesian call for reinstatement. While "vague" was to remain one of Du Bois's favorite relational descriptions (his novels *The Quest of the Silver Fleece* and *Dark Princess* are replete with its strategic uses), the more rare "penumbra" suggests that Du Bois is flagging, for readers of the self-review, a direct connection to the passage cited from James's *Principles of Psychology*.

In the Jamesean context, *penumbra* isn't just a "halo"; it also connotes "*psychic overtone, suffusion*, or *fringe*."[52] James goes on to say that "[r]elation…is constantly felt in the fringe, and particularly the relation of harmony or discord."[53] By the next page, what is "felt in the fringe" is transformed into the "fringe of felt affinity or discord."[54] While I have taken the trouble of tracking the progression of "penumbra" from *halo* to *fringe of felt affinity* in order to add one more possibility to the layering of sources for Du Bois's metaphor of the "Veil,"[55] I would also point out that the words "psychic overtone," "harmony," and "discord" all have musical as well as affective connotations.

In suggesting that a "penumbra of vagueness" surrounded an otherwise "clear central message" that admittedly left some readers "impatient," Du Bois is nudging the reader of his review to recall the first line of *Souls*: "Herein lie buried many things which if read with *patience* may show the strange meaning of being black here in the dawning of the Twentieth

---

[52] James, *Principles*, 258, emphasis original. According to the *Oxford English Dictionary*, a penumbra is "the partially shaded region around the shadow of an opaque body, where only a part of the light from the luminous body is cut off; the partial shadow, as distinguished from the total shadow or *umbra*; esp. that surrounding the total shadow of the moon, or of the earth, in an eclipse, producing respectively a partial (or annular) eclipse of the sun, or a fainter obscuration bordering the full shadow on the disk of the moon." I do not wish to give the impression that neither James nor Du Bois would have known the "dictionary" definition of this word. Indeed, if the refusal of his visiting card by the white girl in "Of Our Spiritual Strivings" is to be taken as a point of origin for the modernist project that becomes *The Souls of Black Folk*, that project begins with a self-conscious awareness of the "*shades* of the prison-house clos[ing] round about" him (Du Bois, *Souls*, 5, emphasis added).

[53] James, *Principles*, 259.

[54] Ibid., 260.

[55] For other possible sources from the Biblical book of *Esther* to Hawthorne and Jefferson, see Wald, *Constituting Americans*, 182–90. For a link to Hegel by way of Exodus, Hebrews, and Matthew, see Zamir, *Dark Voices*, 135.

Century."[56] The *impatient* reader is thus the reader who adheres to the standard protocol of privileging substantives (the "center") at the expense of Du Bois's own aesthetic attempt to "translate the finer *feelings* of men into words."[57] That too had been James's concern—to have his audience acknowledge those transitive "feelings of tendency, often so vague that we are unable to name them at all."[58] While such feelings may remain nameless, "namelessness," for James, is nonetheless "compatible with existence."[59] By dint of his reference to "penumbra of vagueness," Du Bois is suggesting that his project is also, in part, an attempt at the difficult task of translating namelessness into words. "*Penumbra* of vagueness" is a doubled sign, then, of a new take offered to the reader and of the authorial struggle to keep it fresh.

Any doubts about the extent of Du Bois's involvement with Jamesian transitivity should dissolve upon perusal of the relationship he sets up between "Forethought" and "Of Our Spiritual Strivings." In the concluding paragraph to the forethought, Du Bois makes two claims. Both, in some significant way, also claim him. First he points out the supplemented "bar" of "Sorrow Songs" that precedes the prose in each chapter, "some echo of haunting melody from the only American music which welled up from black souls in the dark past."[60] Since it "wells up" from souls, the bar of sorrow song that stands before each chapter must be figured as a "bar" of water or liquidity. Thus barred, the reader must somehow negotiate that water in order to get to the more familiar, *substantive* comforts of prose. Placed in front of—above —the bar of music from "Nobody knows the trouble I've seen" is the following passage from Arthur Symons's "The Crying of Water":

> O water, voice of my heart, crying in the sand,
> All night long crying with a mournful cry,
> As I lie and listen, and cannot understand
> The voice of my heart in my side or the voice of the sea,
> O water, crying for rest, is it I, is it I?

---

[56] Du Bois, *Souls*, 1, emphasis added.

[57] Aptheker, *Book Reviews by W.E.B. Du Bois*, 9.

[58] James, *Principles*, 254.

[59] Ibid., 254.

[60] Du Bois, *Souls*, 2.

All night long the water is crying to me.

Unresting water, there shall never be rest
Till the last moon droop and the last tide fail,
And the fire of the end begin to burn in the west;
And the heart shall be weary and wonder and cry like the sea,
All life long crying without avail,
As the water all night long is crying to me.[61]

What makes these lines so apposite, standing before the bar of the
sorrow song, is that they introduce the figure of the sorrow songs as the
liquid voice of the "soul" while also serving as an index to the Jamesian
figuration of transitivity as "free water." The "unresting" nature of the water
recalls James's sense of the incessant flow of the "continuous," "unbroken"

---

[61] The poem appears in vol. 2 of Arthur Symons, *Poems* (1901; repr., New York:
Dodd, Mead and Company, 1929). The content of the poem clearly underscores what I
take to be Du Bois's commitment to the aesthetic possibilities inherent in Jamesean
transitivity, a commitment that places Du Bois's project within the modernist milieu of
others such as Gertrude Stein, who self-consciously appropriate James's "stream of
thought." If, as Lewis suggests, the pairing of Euro-American poetry with African-
American music was intended to "advance the then-unprecedented notion of the creative
parity and complementarity of white folk and black folk alike" (278) then Du Bois's
choice of Symons establishes his critical authority to make such claims. For Symons,
remembered chiefly for his 1899 work *The Symbolist Movement in Literature* (London:
William Heineman), would have to be considered a cutting-edge critic who had
influenced the likes of Joyce, Yeats, and Eliot, and whom Yeats called "the greatest critic
of his generation" (see Karl Beckson, *Arthur Symons: A Life* [Oxford: Clarendon Press,
1987] 1). How much familiarity Du Bois had with the work of Symons is difficult to
ascertain. Did he read the chapter on Rimbaud, where he would have encountered
"Voyelles," Rimbaud's sonnet to synaesthesia? Even if Du Bois had only read the
introduction to the book on the Symbolists, he would have encountered, and I think
appreciated, the stress on both souls and literature in the following: "Here, then, is the
revolt against exteriority, against rhetoric, against a materialistic tradition; in this
endeavor to disengage the ultimate essence, the soul, of whatever exists and can be
realized by the consciousness; in this dutiful waiting upon every symbol by which the
soul of things can be made visible; literature, bowed down by so many burdens, may at
last attain liberty, and its authentic speech. In attaining this liberty, it accepts a heavier
burden; for in speaking to us intimately, so solemnly, as only religion had hitherto spoken
to us, it becomes itself a kind of religion, with all the duties and responsibilities of the
sacred ritual" (Symons, *Symbolist Movement*, 10).

stream of thought.[62] However, in deploying it to carry the sorrow of
"troubles" unknown, Du Bois exposes the *racialization* of the consciousness
of American history, thus performing, in part, the goal he set out for himself
of "applying 'philosophy to an historical interpretation of race relations.'"[63]
We can see that the application at work here as "unresting water"
relationally implies the substantive "resting-places" James says transitives
lead to but cannot occupy. Further elaborating the tropes of home and
homelessness as metaphors for the provisionality of truth in a "tramp and
vagrant world," James would write in *Pragmatism* that all "homes are in
finite experience. Finite experience, as such, is homeless."[64] In Du Bois's
opening maneuver, then, the longing for "home" on terms resistant to the
institutional effects of slavery but open to the promise of renewal offered by
his pragmatistic critique is very strong indeed.

   To further appreciate the aesthetic use-value of the trope of "free
water" to Du Bois's project, we should recall Booker T. Washington's
strategic use of water in his Atlanta Exposition address. In that speech,
which we have come to know as the Atlanta Compromise, Washington
famously reassured his white audience "that in all things purely social we can
be as separate as the fingers, yet one as the hand in all things essential to
mutual progress."[65] But more importantly, for our purposes, Washington
underscores the strategic value of manual labor as well as political and social
subordination by spinning out a narrative (with more than a faint echo of
Luke 5:1–10) of a "ship lost at sea":

   A ship lost at sea for many days suddenly sighted a friendly vessel.
   From the mast of the unfortunate vessel was seen a signal, "Water, water;
   we die of thirst!" The answer from the friendly vessel at once came back,
   "Cast down your bucket where you are." A second time the signal,
   "Water, water; send us water!" ran up from the distressed vessel, and was
   answered, "Cast down your bucket where you are." And a third and
   fourth signal for water was answered, "Cast down your bucket where you
   are." The captain of the distressed vessel, at last heeding the injunction,
   cast down his bucket, and it came up full of fresh, sparkling water from
   the mouth of the Amazon River. To those of my race who depend on
   bettering their condition in a foreign land or who under-estimate the

---

[62] James, *Principles*, 240, 248.

[63] From the *Autobiography*, as cited by Rath, "Echo and Narcissus," 467.

[64] James, *Pragmatism*, 125.

[65] Booker T. Washington, *Up from Slavery* (New York: Signet, 2000) 154.

importance of cultivating friendly relations with the Southern white man, who is their next-door neighbor, I would say: "Cast down your bucket where you are"—cast it down in making friends in every manly way of the people of all races by whom we are surrounded.[66]

As we know, Du Bois was initially enthusiastic about Washington's speech. There are times, after all, when a bucket of water is exactly what one needs. But just as there is more than one kind of fishing, there are other kinds of thirst. By the time he reviewed Washington's autobiography, *Up from Slavery*, for *The Dial* in 1901, Du Bois numbered himself among the many who had "deep suspicions" about the Hampton-Tuskegee project. He favored instead "the higher education of Fisk and Atlanta Universities" where a belief in "self-assertion" and "the right of suffrage for blacks on the same terms with whites" was not a thing of the past.[67] In 1902, as Du Bois re-encountered the words of the Atlanta Exposition address while revising the review into chapter 3 of *Souls*, one can imagine him recalling his favorite professor's insistence that "traditional psychology" can only imagine the stream of thought substantively, as "moulded forms of water"—"pails and buckets"—while everywhere between these moulded forms the "free water would continue to flow." Du Bois would do to Washington's traditional programme—"the old attitude of adjustment"[68]—what James had done to "traditional psychology." Both would insist on reinstating the continuous, liberating flow of free water to the dominant, restrictive discourse of pails and buckets.

In "Of the Training of Black Men," Du Bois offers a counter-narrative of ships and water and race: "From the shimmering swirl of waters where many, many thoughts ago the slave-ship first saw the square tower of Jamestown, have flowed down to our day three streams of thinking."[69] These three "vast and partially contradictory streams of thought" can be glossed as the pursuit of happiness or desire within commodity exchange, the invention of race by way of chattel slavery, and a "boastful" New World whose democratic flux is contaminated by the first two streams. They are to be reconciled, as Du Bois "vaguely" says, by the "panacea" of education

---

[66] Ibid, 152–53.

[67] Aptheker, *Book Reviews by W.E.B. Du Bois*, 5.

[68] Ibid.

[69] Du Bois, *Souls*, 74.

whereby all, black and white, can be "wed with truth" above the often humiliating pathos of the Veil.[70]

Before addressing the significance of that famous matrimonial trope, I want to return to the second of the two claims made in the "Forethought." After pointing out the bar of the sorrow song, Du Bois claims something by way of an addition that is figured as going without saying: "Need I add that I who speak here am bone of the bone and flesh of the flesh of them that live within the Veil"[71]? Pitching this declaration of racial identity as a rhetorical question complicates the proceedings. Does he "need" to add it? If so, what is he adding? As you know, I want to suggest that the "veil" is, among other things, what James had called "a fringe of felt affinity and discord." It makes sense, I think, to read Du Bois's revision of the adamic passage as a "twice-told tale" of cultural and racial solidarity that performatively anticipates the very double-consciousness that Du Bois will famously declare in the opening chapter of *Souls* and that he will so sharply delineate in "Of the Faith of the Fathers."

In implying his theoretical affiliation with James's attempt to acknowledge the affective significance of transitive relationships in our lived experience, Du Bois, in his self-review, admitted that "in giving up the usual impersonal and judicial attitude of the traditional author [he] lost in authority but gained in vividness."[72] By declaring his racial solidarity, his *relatedness*, Du Bois recuperates that loss (for one imagines the "Forethought" as something written after the fact of the fourteen chapters). According to Hazel Carby, the use of the biblical reference "grants" Du Bois "the authority to evoke a convincing portrayal of the black folk" by "mark[ing] his own body as an essential part of that wider community his text imagines."[73] In that sense, Du Bois becomes, as Carby suggests, "representative," but not without the gendered political ramifications that underwrite his textual strategy to ameliorate the "moral hesitancy" of American Negro faith caught in the dominant "current" of the nineteenth century while "yet" struggling with the peculiar "eddies" of the fifteenth

---

[70] Du Bois, *Souls,* 90.

[71] Du Bois, *Souls*, 2.

[72] Aptheker, *Book Reviews by W.E.B. Du Bois*, 9.

[73] Hazel Carby, *Race Men: The W. E. B. Du Bois Lectures* (Cambridge: Harvard University Press, 1998) 20–21.

"within and without the Veil of Color."[74] "Such a double life" as he describes, "with double thoughts, double duties, and double social classes, must give rise to double words and double ideals."[75]

How should we read the phrase "must give rise"? Is it a matter of consequences and results or is it a solution, a way out? I would prefer to see it as both a statement of consequence *and* a statement of solution—in effect, a double word. For Du Bois the solution of the ultimate democratic double—to be both a Negro and an American—cannot be left solely to the ostensive conjunction of "separate but equal" out of which emanates the disjunctive practices of inequality, practices that "tempt" the African American mind "to pretence or to revolt, to hypocrisy or to radicalism" (165). Such disjunctive temptations—Negro *or* American—will be mediated by the strategic use of "double words," or puns, and the "inflection of voice" that, in part, constitute transitivity.

For pragmatists, as Richard Poirier points out in *Poetry and Pragmatism*, "the condition of thinking partakes of a condition of punning." He goes on to say that "[p]uns hold us to a double meaning, each side of which salvages the other at the very instant when one or the other seems about to be lost."[76] The structural relationship between desire and meaning articulates, for Poirier, a pathos of gains and losses: if, for instance, we tease out the pun in "salvage" and turn it to "savage," each side then savages the other when the other is about to be *found*. Likewise Arnold Rampersad, in his influential *Art and Imagination of W. E. B. Du Bois*, underscores this condition of punning

---

[74] Du Bois, *Souls*, 164. Carby discusses Du Bois as "both an exceptional and a representative individual." She shows the site of convergence of these apparently contradictory positions in the body of the "*gendered* intellectual" (*Race Men*, 30–31, emphasis original). In other words—and not necessarily Carby's—Du Bois stakes himself, his "I," as the money form of value. This is reflected in his rhetorical "need" to add the fact of his blackness (his insider's perspective relative to racist social protocols) while at the same time his status as an intellectual seems to require the distance of a perspective that could regulate those experiences from a position outside or above those practices. But the "real" money form, as I imagine Carby to be implying by her stress on gender, is reflected in the appropriation or eclipse of Eve's position relative to Adam when Du Bois claims to be "bone of the bone, and flesh of the flesh." Does this mean he represents women? If so, he doesn't do it very well in *The Souls of Black Folk*, as Carby and others have noted. While my factoring in Du Bois's revision of James makes things more complicated, I don't think it absolves Du Bois of the anxiety of gender.

[75] Du Bois, *Souls*, 165.

[76] Poirier, *Poetry and Pragmatism*, 47; 63.

when he suggests that the "souls" of *Souls of Black Folk* is a "play on words, referring to the twoness of the African American."[77] If punning articulates double-consciousness at the level of individual words, could we not then go in the opposite direction and read Du Bois's "double-consciousness" as the articulation of a self trapped in the solitary confinement of a massive social pun? "One ever feels his twoness," Du Bois writes in the first chapter of *Souls*, "—an American, a Negro; two souls, two thoughts, two unreconciled strivings; two warring ideals in one dark body, whose dogged strength alone keeps it from being torn asunder."[78] *Souls* can then be read as an attempt to overflow that confinement and to apply "dogged strength" in the creative activity that Poirier, in reference to puns, calls "a continuous and generative interaction" with the world.

Du Bois's matrimonial trope—"wed with Truth"—to which I would now like to return can be read as a signally important instance of what the *condition* of punning or doubling of key words might signify for Du Bois, especially in light of the fact that "truth" and "troth" (as in betrothal) are etymologically related. For Du Bois, and certainly also for James, truth *implies* the "I do" of betrothal. In *Pragmatism* James envisions "new truth" as "a go-between, a smoother over of transitions" that "marries old opinion to new fact so as ever to show a minimum of jolt, a maximum of continuity."[79] And, a bit later he writes, "[p]urely objective truth, truth in whose establishment the function of giving human satisfaction in marrying previous parts of experience with newer parts played no role whatever, is nowhere to be found. The reasons why we call things true is the reason why they *are* true, for 'to be true' *means* only to perform this marriage-function."[80] What I take James and Du Bois to be insisting on behind the thin veil of their matrimonial tropes is the performative relation between will and the world as promise, the continuous *I do*, as it were, between subjective agents saturated with old opinions and the contingency that breeds new facts and breathes new hope into a "tramp and vagrant world."

---

[77] Arnold Rampersad, *The Art and Imagination of W. E. B. Du Bois* (Cambridge: Harvard University Press, 1976) 74.

[78] Du Bois, *Souls*, 5.

[79] James, *Pragmatism*, 35.

[80] Ibid., 37, emphasis original.

III.

In the following passage from "Of the Sons of Master and Man," Du Bois reflects back to his readers by way of the cracked mirror of the southern Black Codes against vagrancy and miscegenation, the betrayal of truth. Pitching the scene from the point of view of a "casual observer" of the "Negro problem," Du Bois describes an "awakening."

> Slowly but surely his eyes begin to catch the shadows of the color-line: here he meets crowds of Negroes and whites; then he is suddenly aware that he cannot discover a single dark face; or again at the close of a day's wandering he may find himself in some strange assembly, where all faces are tinged brown or black, and where he has the vague, uncomfortable feeling of the stranger. He realizes at last that silently, resistlessly, the world flows by him in two great streams: they ripple on in the same sunshine, they approach and mingle their waters in seeming carelessness, —then they divide and flow wide apart. It is done quietly; no mistakes are made, or if one occurs, the swift arm of the law and of public opinion swings down for a moment, as when the other day a black man and a white woman were arrested for talking together on Whitehall Street in Atlanta.[81]

As double-consciousness emerges from the "seeming carelessness" of intermingled waters, Du Bois splits the stream of thought into two constitutive tributaries implicitly embodied by "a black man" and "a white woman." The "strong arm" of Southern legal and social codes betrays the necessarily interdependent relationship between the transitive and substantive parts of the stream of American consciousness. Rather than an exemplary instance of un-veiled "truth," the scene becomes instead a grotesque example of the hyper-sexualized fear of all things pertaining to "the Negro."

Once the dynamic relationship between (substantive) "resting places" and (transitive) "places of flight" is racialized by situating it in a local and particular American context (Whitehall Street in Atlanta), we can begin to read Du Bois's historical turn not as the reinstatement of "race" or even vagueness but rather as the reinstatement of the African *American* to his "proper" place. For Du Bois, the "proper," as place, would no longer be a fixed space of service, subjection, or segregation but rather a space of full

---

[81] Du Bois, *Souls*, 148–49.

and fluid participation, of positive *influence* at long last acknowledged in the production of value and significance in the world.

Appropriating the transitive as the historical function of African-Americanness allowed Du Bois to signify on James's trope of "free water" in terms of two related sociopolitical concepts. Simply put, both freedom and mobility were white entitlements, a relation made perfectly clear, as Du Bois well knew, in the post-emancipation incarceration of blacks to forced labor by the Southern Black Codes against vagrancy. In South Carolina, a "vagrant" was defined as any person "without fixed and known places of abode and lawful employment"; and in Georgia, for instance, where much of *Souls* takes place, a black person could not "wander or stroll around in idleness."[82] In fact, as Du Bois writes in "Of the Quest of the Golden Fleece," "[a] black stranger in Baker County, Georgia, ...is liable to be stopped anywhere on the public highway and made to state his business to the satisfaction of any white interrogator."[83] In Mississippi, the legal conception of vagrancy extended even to "lewd" speech.[84] But perhaps the annihilation of freedom-as-motion reached its nadir in Albany, Georgia, where, as Du Bois writes, "it was said a policeman had shot and killed" a "black boy" "for loud talking on the sidewalk."[85] Here, black folk are not even allowed the *inflections of voice* James says characterize aspects of transitivity.

What happens to personhood when such freedoms are curtailed? What happens, in turn, to pragmatism's valorization of homelessness when space and situation are thus codified? A passage from James's "Stream of Thought," while depicting a state of mind, nonetheless constructs the appropriate dramatic narrative:

> Now it is very difficult, introspectively, to see the transitive parts for what they really are. If they are but flights to a conclusion, stopping them to look at them before the conclusion is reached is really annihilating them. Whilst if we wait till the conclusion *be* reached, it so exceeds them

---

[82] W. E. B. Du Bois, *Black Reconstruction in America, 1860–1880* (New York: Meridian Books, New York, 1964) 173, 175.

[83] Du Bois, *Souls*, 125.

[84] Henry Steele Commager and Milton Cantor, *Documents of American History*, v. 1 in two volumes. (Englewood Cliffs NJ: Prentice Hall, 1988) 1:444. I am grateful to Theodore B. Wilson for this citation in his *Black Codes of the South* (Tuscaloosa: University of Alabama Press, 1965) 68.

[85] Du Bois, *Souls*, 106.

in its vigor and stability that it quite eclipses and swallows them up in its glare. Let anyone try to cut a thought across in the middle and get a look at its section, and he will see how difficult the introspective observation of the transitive tracts is. The rush of the thought is so headlong that it almost always brings us up at the conclusion before we can arrest it. Or, if our purpose is nimble enough and we do arrest it, *it ceases forwith to be itself.*[86]

What James describes as an interior psychological narrative Du Bois recognizes as the external, daily drama of the application of the vagrancy laws within the carceral regime of Southern Black Codes. Blacks arrested for vagrancy were generally given the Hobson's choice of prison or "employment" to the highest bidder, the first of which figures "annihilation" by way of extreme social stasis and the second of which figures "eclipse" by way of expropriative white "glare." This is one more manifestation of the social pun of double-consciousness alluded to earlier, and it is a situation, as Du Bois makes emphatically clear, that "yields him no true consciousness."[87] Choosing to reinstate an essential, liberating vagrancy into the flow of African-American life was a way for Du Bois to both point out and overturn the ongoing sanction against "negro" movements, be they geopolitical or aesthetic. One way of circumventing or disrupting such sanctions was to interpose the liquidity of music within the linear complications of his written argument.

While I surely want to keep Jamesean transitivity in mind, we ought also to turn, as does Du Bois, toward Hegel. The turn from James's "individualist" to Hegel's "absolutist modes of consciousness" articulates, for Du Bois, an intellectual dilemma structurally equivalent to double-consciousness.[88] The trick was to find a mutual revision in which James's "esteem for risk, particularity, and residuum," as Posnock phrases it, interacted with Hegel's "insistence on the primacy of mediation, of social bonds, of the contextual" without either one subsuming the other.[89]

Shamoon Zamir has persuasively elaborated the extent to which Du Bois incorporates key concepts from the middle sections of Hegel's *Phenomonology of Mind.* According to Zamir, in "using Hegel as a resource,"

---

[86] James, *Principles*, 243–44, emphasis added to last clause.
[87] Du Bois, *Souls*, 5.
[88] Rath, "Echo and Narcissus," 482.
[89] Posnock, *Color and Culture*, 121, 120.

Du Bois "neither psychologizes history nor reproduces a progressive and optimistic teleology of enlightenment. He moves instead toward a complex historicization of psychology."[90] While clearly one such "psychology" being historicized was the introspective psychology he had learned from James, Du Bois was also attempting, by way of the sorrow songs, to link the psychology of soul in relation to a history of, and the history embodied in, black music. "The chief *task* of music," Hegel writes in his *Aesthetics*, "consists in making resound, not the objective world itself, but, on the contrary, the manner in which the inmost self is moved to the depths of its personality and conscious soul." The "same is true of the *effect* of music," according to Hegel. "What it claims as its own is the depth of a person's inner life as such; it is the art of the soul and is directly addressed to the soul."[91] The "art" and "manner in which the inmost self is moved" speaks to a world of feeling that, as Kevin Thomas Miles surmises, "exceeds the economy of explanation for Du Bois."[92] As we recall from his self-review, Du Bois himself was aware of how "difficult" it had been to "translate the finer feelings of men into words." "The Thing itself," he lamented, as if to acknowledge his failure to abide by the protocols of signification, "seems fearfully uncouth and inchoate." "Nevertheless," he insisted, "as the feeling is deep the greater the impelling force to seek to express it. And here the feeling is deep."

Neatly underscoring the problem of translation, Eric Sundquist suggests that the "musical epigraphs" are "an example of a cultural 'language'...*that cannot be properly interpreted*, or even 'heard' at all, since it fails to correspond to the customary mapping of sounds and signs that make up the languages of the dominant...culture." He goes on to say that "the bars of music posed a pointed challenge to their contemporary audience, for they demanded a familiarity with a cultural language that most whites did not have and that an increasing number of middle-class blacks renounced as an unhealthy reminder of slavery."[93] True enough, the relationship between textual exposition and musical imposition does defy the cartography of custom, and the "mapping of sounds and signs" is one more manifestation of

---

[90] Zamir, *Dark Voices*, 115.

[91] G. W. F. Hegel, *Aesthetics: Lectures on Fine Art*, vol. 2 in two volumes, trans. T. M. Knox (Oxford: Clarendon Press, 1975) 2:891.

[92] Kevin Thomas Miles, "Haunting Music in *The Souls of Black Folk*," *boundary 2* 27/3 (Fall 2000): 201.

[93] Eric Sundquist, *Wake the Nations*, 470, emphasis added.

the protocols that we have been speaking of all along. Given this, what feeling could be so intense that Du Bois would actually risk indifference, bewilderment, or loathing on the part of his readers? By way of narrative repetition, Du Bois, for all his resistance to certain protocols, nonetheless maps a sensory trajectory from the "preemptory" "glance" of the white girl who refuses to exchange greeting cards in chapter 1 to an older, wiser Du Bois in chapter 14, listening, as he says, to the "bursts of wonderful melody, full of the voices of my brothers and sisters, full of the voices of the past."[94] In moving from preemptive oversight to redemptive overhearing, we move from a feeling of contempt to something that Miles suggests might be "similar" to "love."[95] Having been claimed by racism (need we add that?) and by the sorrow songs, Du Bois in turn makes claims upon his readers by way of his synaesthetic attempt to translate the depth of his feeling.

IV.

Du Bois's strategic repetition of the place name "Housatonic" in the first and last chapters of *Souls* links seeing and hearing, contempt and love, beginning and end. The "shadow" of the *feeling* of being a problem "swept across" him, Du Bois says in that first chapter, when he "was a little thing. Away up in the hills of New England, where the dark Housatonic winds between Hoosac and Taghkanic to the sea." Likewise he invokes the Housatonic in chapter 14 as he recalls the image of his grandfather's grandmother, who "was seized by an evil Dutch trader two centuries ago; and coming to the valleys of the Hudson and Housatonic, black, little, and lithe, she shivered and shrank in the harsh north winds, looked longingly at the hills, and often crooned a heathen melody to the child between her knees, thus"[96]: and here, the reader encounters music and a language that has yet to conform to the contours of linguistic mapping.[97]

Once my readers have accessed page 5 of the website http://web.grinnell.edu/cts/dubois/ and clicked the audio prompt, I have no doubt that many are hearing for the first time this "heathen melody" that

---

[94] Du Bois, *Souls*, 4, 251.

[95] Miles, "Haunting Music," 214. On the trajectory from seeing to hearing, see also Zmier, 196.

[96] Du Bois, *Souls*, 207.

[97] According to Lewis, the meaning of "Do Bana" remains uncertain, as "the exact origin and translation…continue to defy linguists" (*Biography of a Race*, 14).

meant so much to Du Bois. And, like me, they will no doubt have been profoundly moved. But to be moved now, as I claim you are, is also to participate in a liquidation of the "soul" trapped in the nexus of visual representations that are unavoidable in the production and consumption of any book, representations with which we are so comfortable. For I dare say many of us who have read and even taught this text have never budged beyond the lazy contours of precisely the kind of "familiarity" with the cultural knowledge that Sundquist discusses: we either know these songs or we don't, and seldom do we ever bother to raise ourselves up out of the protocols of static visual reception to so much as tease out the melody. We move from left to right, top to bottom, our devotion to the two-dimensionality of the page underwritten by the solipsistic comforts of a favorite armchair and the soothing glow of a reading lamp. Under those circumstances, it is a hassle, quite frankly, to hunt up the individual songs, hook up the audio equipment, or make a room change and plunk out a reasonable facsimile of the melody—on what? A piano? A guitar? It's not a given that you even have anything in the house with which to make music other than your own voice—and then only if you know how to read music. And if you think having your own voice handy rather convincingly brings us round to Du Bois's ulterior motive of getting culturally knowledgeable readers to lift up their voices in song as they proceed apace with the reading, then think again, *because nobody knows the song with which he connects the reader to his own African past.* And if nobody knows it, and nobody takes the trouble to play it, then nobody knows the sorrow it knows, which is truly disturbing, as the affect from that song is deep enough to claim us all.

Indeed, when I first heard my colleague Ralph Russell play this on the synthesizer as we were putting together the components of the web page, I realized that in a fundamental way I was "reading" *The Souls of Black Folk* for the first time. Or, to pitch this from a less flattering angle, in never having bothered to liquidate the music frozen into the linear contours of the text, I had been misreading *Souls* for lo these many years. Sure, I could always claim to have *seen* what Du Bois meant—and hadn't he precisely meant for me to *see* the problem of music within the text? But now I could claim to *feel* the argument for the first time, as Ralph Russell, the musicologist, David Berk, the audio specialist, and Munindra Khaund, the web page designer, brought "Do Bana" to life. *I couldn't have done it by myself.* But far from indicating a loss of individual authority for me, such an admission signals victory for Du Bois's notion of the binding energy of *soul*.

As in the trajectory from contempt to love, the interplay between gains, losses, presence, and absence articulated in the song enacts the structural extremes between which Du Bois elaborates his response to the seldom asked but frequently felt question: "how does it feel to be a problem?" Du Bois's response, we should take care to note, is, "I answer seldom a word." Ending almost entirely on a musical note, Du Bois gives white America an answer that is precisely "seldom a word," an answer that graphically articulates the poignancy of how it feels to be designated a constant problem in a sociopolitical context whose primary solution is supposed to be equality. Moving inexorably toward an ever-increasing musicality, Du Bois tropes the feeling of being a problem as a rupture in the lining—the linearity—of the text of race.

Such a rupture, which resists notions of fixed racial identities and other forms of closure,[98] is created and maintained by Du Bois's use of synaesthesia. In a key paragraph of "Criteria of Negro Art" (1926), Du Bois, addressing the notion of "who shall describe beauty," "remember[s]...four beautiful things: The Cathedral at Cologne, a forest in stone, set in light and changing shadow, echoing with sunlight and solemn song; a village of the Veys in West Africa, a little thing of mauve and purple, quiet, lying content and shining in the sun; a black and velvet room where on a throne rests, in old and yellowing marble, the broken curves of the Venus of Milo; a single phrase of music in the Southern South—utter melody, haunting and appealing, suddenly arising out of night and eternity, beneath the moon."[99] Keith Byerman, in his analysis of this passage, identifies each of these four instances as being "synaesthetic in character."[100] In Du Bois's passage, "a forest in stone...*echoing* with sunlight" and a "*black* and *velvet* room" are both examples of perceptual translation from one sense to another. In the former, light resounds, and in the latter, velvet implies the touch of the color black.

---

[98] The resistance to closure—identity, essence, the stolidities of "aboutness"—is a fundamental part of the pragmatist outlook. Such concerns inform Du Bois's Jamesean mediation of Hegel's "absolute construct of the world soul," which Du Bois "disparaged for its resemblance to the working of race relations in the United States" (Rath, "Echo and Narcissus," 473).

[99] Du Bois, *W. E. B. Du Bois, A Reader*, ed. Andrew Paschall, intro. by Arna Bontemps (New York: Collier Books, 1993) 88. This passage is cited in Keith E. Byerman, *Seizing the Word: History, Art, and Self in the Work of W. E. B. Du Bois* (Athens: University of Georgia Press, 1994) 103.

[100] Byerman, *Seizing the Word*, 103.

"Such is beauty," Du Bois continues, "[i]ts variety is infinite, its possibility is endless. In normal life all may have it and have it yet again."[101] What would we have of beauty, then, as Du Bois tropes it, if not a series of synaesthetic experiences, whereby all, black and white, could dislocate themselves from the tyranny of single vision, of generic limitations, and of racial degradation? But ours, he implies, are not *normal* lives. "The mass of human beings are choked away from it, and their lives distorted and made ugly."[102] Du Bois would insist that while the appreciation for beauty can be entertained in the abstract, the practice of beauty cannot be separated from the binding duties of truth and right; therefore "all Art is propaganda."[103] Propaganda, for Du Bois, is the mediation whereby black aesthetic desire or force, as in an Hegelian moment of overcoming, "will compel recognition." Until such recognition is achieved (long overdue, to be sure), black folk, he feared, would "not be rated as human."[104]

With its sly invocation of lynching, I take Du Bois's use of the verb "choked" to be the effect, then, of systematic sensory and political limitation along the color line. It articulates the antithesis of synaesthesia. And in typical Du Boisean fashion, its ugliness turns out to be as much a part of white life as black. Indeed, it was the affective aftermath of one of the ugliest scenes imaginable—the lynching, burning, and butchering of Sam Hose in 1899—that compelled Du Bois to "turn away" from science toward the more ameliorative promise embedded in the "art" of propaganda. If the scandal of Sam Hose brought anything home to Du Bois, it was the hard problem of salvaging beauty, truth, and goodness *in "detached" isolation* from a world in which a man's knuckles could "go on exhibition at a grocery store."[105] Nearly thirty years later, while addressing the members of the NAACP on the "Criteria of Negro Art" (from which I have been citing), Du Bois would liquidate his culture's investment in such restrictive evaluative schemas by recognizing and utilizing what E. H. Gombrich, writing on

---

[101] Du Bois, Du Bois, *Reader,* ed. Paschall, 89.

[102] Ibid., 89.

[103] Ibid., 94.

[104] Ibid., 96.

[105] See Du Bois, *Dusk of Dawn,* 67–68 (emphasis added to "detached"). By "isolation" I mean to imply, as I think Du Bois does, the privileged separation of the ivory tower and the solitary quest for scientific, ethical, and aesthetic ideals, each imagined to be separate, and separable, from the other.

synaesthesia, called "the splashing over of impressions from one sense modality to another," "a fact to which all languages testify."[106]

The turn to synaesthesia would be one more manifestation of Du Bois's commitment to the reinstatement of transitivity. But while synaesthesia as a literary trope has been around for a very long time, the fact of its increasing interest to science at the end of the nineteenth century makes it an attractive vehicle for the kind of aesthetic propaganda Du Bois has in mind.[107] According to John Harrison, in the ten-year period between 1882 to1892, the study of synaesthesia really begins to proliferate as a discursive activity, with no fewer than 27 articles written about it.[108] During this time period, Du Bois entered Fisk (1885), Harvard (1888), the University of Berlin (1892), and, upon returning to the States, had his dissertation approved by Albert Hart at Harvard (1895). Du Bois thus took philosophy and psychology from William James during a time when scientific interest in synaesthesia was at its peak. In fact, James was in frequent correspondence with Theodore Flournoy, the Swiss psychologist who did groundbreaking work on *audition coloree* (colored hearing). In 1894 James reviewed Flournoy's *Des phénomènes de synopsie* (audition colorée) [*On the phenomena of synopsia* (colored hearing)], taking time from a fairly technical discussion of "synaesthesias" and "synopsias" to offer the reader the following aside: "The present writer has no photisms, and almost no visual images, but discovered, in reading [Flournoy's] book, that by a process of exclusion the vowel-sound *ee* (French *i*) seemed to have for him more affinity with emerald-green than with any other tint. It is entirely incongruous with blue, yellow, red, black, white, or brown."[109] He ended his favorable review on a typically Jamesean tone of pragmatic optimism by concluding that Flournoy's observations would

[F]ill the reader with a wondering sense of the complication of our mental workshop, and, by increasing his insight into the extraordinary diversity of inner scenery, so to speak, by which different men's minds

[106] Cited in Carol A. Donnell and William Duigan, "Synaesthesia and Aesthetic Education," *Journal of Aesthetic Education* 11/3 (July1977): 72.

[107] For a comprehensive list of writings on visual-auditory synaesthesia over time, see Lawrence E. Marks, "On Colored-Hearing Synesthesia: Cross-Modal Translations of Sensory Dimensions," *Psychological Bulletin* 82/3 (May 1975): 305–307.

[108] Harrison, *Synaesthesia*, 26.

[109] James, *The Works of William James: Essays, Comments, and Reviews* (Cambridge: Harvard University Press, 1987) 464.

are characterized, it will tone down his hopes, if he ever had any, of a general union of all intelligences on a purely logical and articulable basis. Unformulable sympathies and repugnances amongst our ideas have more to do with our thinking than logicians will ever admit; but (with tolerance once established as the law of the land) probably human life will be much richer so than if this were not the case.[110]

Nearer at hand for Du Bois, however, would have been the *Principles of Psychology*, wherein James cites Francis Galton on mental imagery, pointing his readers (and students, too, no doubt) to pages 83–114 of Galton's *Inquiries into Human Faculty and its Development* (1883).[111] Considered a seminal figure in the early analysis of synaesthesia, Galton has a section on "color associations" in which he discusses "[t]he instantaneous association of colour with sound characteristics."[112] This phenomenon, according to Galton, occurs among a "small percentage of adults," although, as he goes on to say, "it appears to be rather common, though in an ill-developed degree, among children."[113] I'll have a bit more to say about the racial context in which Galton's work is framed, but first I want to suggest one more instance in which the proliferation of synaesthesia that Harrison talks about would have been available to Du Bois.

In 1892, James and Du Bois "made an excursion one day out to Roxbury" and stopped to visit Helen Keller at the Perkins Institute. In writing about it, Du Bois tells us nothing about why they went out there, but he does indicate how deeply moved he was by the encounter.

> We stopped at the Blind Asylum and saw a young girl who was blind and deaf and dumb, and yet who, by infinite pains and loving sympathy, had been made to speak without words and to understand without sound. She was Helen Keller. Perhaps just because she was blind to color differences in this world, I became intensely interested in her, and all through my life I have followed her career. Finally there came the thing which I had somehow sensed would come: Helen Keller was in her own state, Alabama, being feted and made much of by her fellow citizens. And yet courageously and frankly she spoke out on the iniquity and foolishness of the color line. It cost her something to speak. They wanted

---

[110] Ibid., 467.

[111] See James, *Principles,* 2:56.

[112] Francis Galton, *Inquiries into Human Faculty and its Development* (New York: Macmillan and Company, 1883) 145–54.

[113] Ibid., 147.

her to retract, but she sat serene in the consciousness of the truth that she had uttered. And so it was proven, as I knew it would be, that this woman who sits in darkness has a spiritual insight clearer than that of many wide-eyed people who stare uncomprehendingly at this prejudiced world.[114]

The first part of the description seems to lay the groundwork for something in the way of scientific interest. According to Keller herself in a 1929 account, "we talked about my sense perceptions and he [James] wove a magic web into my discourse." After offering her an ostrich feather, James told her "in our problems and processes of thought we do not greatly differ from one another."[115] A review article James wrote in 1904 on the life of *Laura Bridgman*, by Maud Howe and Florence Howe Hall, might perhaps shed further light on why James and Du Bois visited Helen Keller. James begins that review by situating the reader firmly within the contingency or flux of the world: "The world changes, and the minds of men."[116] The main thrust of his review is a comparison of Bridgman and Keller, each unique in herself but representative, too, of her particular historical moment. "Laura," for instance, "was primarily regarded as a phenomenon of conscience, almost a theological phenomenon. Helen is primarily a phenomenon of vital exuberance. Life for her is a series of adventures, rushed at with enthusiasm and fun."[117] Toward the end of the review, James, attending to the question of why Helen Keller is so "superior" to Laura Bridgman, shifts his line of inquiry from context to individual psychology. Here he invokes Galton: "Since Galton first drew attention to the subject, every one knows that in some of us the material of thought is mainly optical, in others auditory, etc., and the classification of human beings into the eye-minded, the ear-minded, and the motor-minded, is familiar."[118] This portion of the review is an

---

[114] Du Bois, *Writings in Non-Periodical Literature Edited by Others*, ed. Herbert Aptheker (Millwood NY: Kraus-Thomson Organization Limited, 1982) 164. The episode to which he refers occurred at "a public meeting in Selma with a "Negro-baiter," to which I shall soon refer.

[115] Helen Keller, *Midstream: My Later Life* (Doubleday, Doran and Company, Inc., 1929) 316–17. James was a favorite writer of Annie Sullivan, Keller's justly celebrated teacher, and this visit seems to have made quite a strong impression on both of them. Alas, Keller does not mention Du Bois in this account.

[116] James, *Essays, Comments, and Reviews*, 545.

[117] Ibid., 546.

[118] Ibid., 549.

elaboration of his mention of Laura Bridgman in his chapter on "Imagination" in the second volume of *Principles of Psychology* published fourteen years earlier (1890). "The imagination of a blind-deaf mute like Laura Bridgman must be confined entirely to tactile and motor material," he writes, 6 pages after his long citation of Galton.[119] He would reiterate this statement in his 1904 review comparison of Laura and Helen: "Their entire thinking goes on in tactile and motor symbols. Of the glories of the world of light and sound they have no inkling."[120]

But James was too savvy an observer of the complex human possibilities imbedded in transitive relations to view this condition as only a limitation:

> Nevertheless, life is full of absorbing interest to each of them, and in Helen's case thought is free and abundant in quite exceptional measure. What clearer proof could we ask of the fact that the relations among things, far more than the things themselves, are what is intellectually interesting, and that it makes little difference what terms we think in, so long as the relations maintain their character. All sorts of terms can transport the mind with equal delight, provided they be woven into equally massive and far-reaching schemes and systems of relationship. They are then equivalent for intellectual purposes, and for yielding intellectual pleasure, for the schemes and systems are what the mind finds interesting.[121]

During that 1892 visit, then, the twelve-year-old Helen Keller must have affirmed for James, the teacher, the individually unique but intellectually equivalent systems of transitivity. *The world changes.*

For Du Bois, the student, Helen Keller's sensory adaptations could test not only the validity of recent work in the psychology of mental imagery; she could also prove or disprove accounts of the "natural operations" of color such as those discussed by Edmund Burke, for instance, in his classic treatise *A Philosophical Inquiry into the Sublime and Beautiful*. In that account Burke recalls Cheselden's "very curious story" of a boy blind from birth, who, at the age of thirteen or so, was "couched for a cataract" and thus regained his sight. Apparently, upon first seeing a "black object, it gave him great uneasiness." Shortly thereafter, "upon accidentally seeing a negro woman," the boy "was struck with great horror at the sight." According to

---

[119] James, *Principles*, 2:62.

[120] James, *Essays, Comments, and Reviews*, 549.

[121] Ibid., 549–50.

Burke, since the boy had no previous habits of association upon which to draw, the idea of blackness or darkness must be "terrible in its own nature."[122] Burke's analysis of this event relies implicitly on synaesthesia. In this case, the color black produces an affect of horror. But it's never as simple as that. Notice how the "black object" seen first only produces a feeling of "uneasiness." However, once blackness is embodied in the form of a "negro woman," uneasiness intensifies into "great horror." Whose symptom might this be?

Now, the case of Helen Keller is certainly not identical; once blinded, she would remain blind all her life.[123] But Du Bois nonetheless uses her sensory anomalies, a virtual embodiment of synaesthetic displacements— color-blindness, speaking without words, understanding without sound—to destabilize the ideology of color prejudice implicit in classic accounts such as Burke's and in newer accounts such as Galton's. Most readers know a little something about Galton's foundational role in the formulation and subsequent ascendancy of eugenics during the same period in which the study of synaesthesia reached its early peak. Indeed, John Harrison begins his review of the "classic literature" of synaesthesia with Galton's *Inquiry*, and he begins that with something like a disclaimer or apology for Galton's "well-intentioned but repugnant views" on the genetic improvement of species.[124] At one point in the *Inquiry*, for instance, while discussing the "Influence of Man upon Race," Galton expresses the hope that the "yellow races of China," well on their way to "becom[ing] one of the most effective of the colonizing nations," might "extrude hereafter the coarse and lazy Negro from at least the metaliferous regions of tropical Africa."[125] The

---

[122] Edmund Burke, *A Philosophical Inquiry into the Sublime and Beautiful and Other Pre-Revolutionary Writings*, ed. David Womersly (London: Penguin Books, Ltd, 1998) 173. In a less pejorative vein, there is a case made famous by John Locke concerning a blind man who, when asked to define *scarlet* insisted that "It was like the sound of a trumpet" (*Essay*, III, iv). John Locke, *An Essay Concerning Human Understanding*, in two volumes, collated and annotated by Alexander Campbell Fraser (New York: Dover, 1959) 2:38.

[123] According to Dorothy Herrmann in *Helen Keller: A Life* (New York: Alfred A. Knopf, 1998), Keller at nineteen months contracted what was at the time diagnosed as "brain fever," thereby losing both sight and hearing. The exact cause of her condition remains "a mystery" (9).

[124] Harrison, *Synaesthesia*, 28.

[125] Galton, *Human Faculty*, 316–17.

Oxford English Dictionary defines extrusion as "the process of pressing metals...into the required shape by extruding them through dies." In this case the die is cast in the rigid formulations of the discourse of *race*, as Galton's metaphor of extrusion, so proximate to the much desired "metaliferous regions" themselves, turns "lazy" black folk into useful metal. Too greedy to wait for the Chinese to catch up, the extrusion process was attempted by European colonial powers, as Du Bois pointedly reminds us in "Criteria of Negro Art." "Have you heard the story of the conquest of German East Africa?" he asks. He then proceeds to tell an "untold tale" of thousands upon thousands of bleached bones and the redistribution of colonial flags, the ugliness of which is recuperated, from Du Bois's perspective, by the thousands of black men from "East, West, and South Africa, from Nigeria and the Valley of the Nile, and from the West Indies" who "struggled, fought and died."[126]

For Du Bois, the postcolonial struggle for liberation would not merely offer a new die with which to recast the story of the consequences of a racial caste system; it would also liquidate the extrusion process itself by reinstating the individual idiosyncrasies and intellectual value of synaesthetic relations. Our access to insight or beauty in the world, as Du Bois implied in "Criteria of Negro Art," is precisely *disabled* by "normative" conventions of race, genre, and creed. In light of that, he would keep Helen Keller in mind, from 1892 on, as a paradigm of the virtue inherent in sensory dislocation. "I have followed her career," he tells us.[127] Thus Du Bois's attempt in *Souls* to achieve spiritual insight in spite of wide-eyed prejudice is analogous to the way Keller achieves human fullness and complexity in spite of what would normally be perceived as disability. When she later stood her ground in Selma, when the "Negro-baiter" asked if she believed in marriage between whites and Negroes, she responded, "no more than they do." When she refused even to shake the man's hand, she explained it was because she "saw at once what he was." Yes, it "cost her," as Du Bois reminds us, for it "shocked" her family and friends, but here was the very "thing" which Du

---

[126] Du Bois, *Reader,* ed. Pachall, 90.

[127] Indeed, in 1916 Du Bois printed in the NAACP newsletter a letter from Keller to Oswald Garrison Villard, who was then vice president of the NAACP, in which she enclosed a check along with a message excoriating "Christians" who espoused racism. See Herrmann, *Helen Keller,* 204.

Bois had "sensed would come" since first he met her.[128] Here was spiritual insight unveiled at last at the wedding of truth. "All sorts of terms," James had written in regard to Helen Keller, "can transport the mind with equal delight, provided they be woven into equally massive and far-reaching schemes and systems of relationship." In a fundamental way, the example of Helen Keller enabled Du Bois to see the value in salvaging synaesthesia from the "massive and far-reaching schemes" of the supremely white science of the Galtons of the world.

The disability induced by racial hysteria had a counterpart in the discourse of psychology as practiced in the late nineteenth century, a discourse that Du Bois, as a student of James, could not have avoided. An 1890 article published by James in *Scribner's* is particularly resonant in terms of the language used to describe the various psychological defects under observation. "The Hidden Self," as it was entitled, was a review of then-current research on the "unconscious mental life" undertaken by French psychologists Pierre Janet and Alfred Binet in which James pointed out that

> [O]ne of the most constant symptoms in persons suffering from hysteric disease in its extreme forms consists in alterations of the natural sensibility of various parts and organs of the body. Usually the alteration is in the direction of defect, or *anaesthesia*. One or both eyes are blind, or blind over one half of the field of vision, or the latter is extremely contracted, so that its margins appear dark, or else the patient has lost all sense for color. Hearing, taste, smell may similarly disappear, in part or in totality.[129]

A bit later in the review, James muses on the "law" postulated by Janet that "anaesthesias carry 'amnesia' with them."[130] Careful in this and later instances to make clear his opinion that the "generalizations" made by Janet

---

[128] Van Wyk Brooks, *Helen Keller, Search for a Portrait* (New York: E. P. Dutton and Co. Inc., 1956) 138. While her family was initially "shocked," as Keller recalls, they eventually "forgot" it.

[129] William James, "The Hidden Self," *Scribner's Magazine* 7/3 (March 1890): 363. For differing takes on the impact of the discourse of psychology on Du Bois, see Schrager, for whom Du Boisean double consciousness is "certainly linked" to a "growing medical discourse" on "dual personality" (p. 569); and, Rath, who, following Lewis, implies a "lack of avowed interest" in such matters on the part of Du Bois (479); Du Bois himself wrote that "the study of psychology under William James" had "prepared" him for the "Freudian era" (*Dusk of Dawn,* 296).

[130] James, "The Hidden Self," 365.

were "based" on "too limited a number of cases to cover the whole ground,"[131] James nevertheless expressed the hope that "these investigations" would have some "possible application to the relief of human misery."[132] The misery to which he referred was embodied, in part, in Janet's notion that "the secondary [or hidden] self is always a symptom of hysteria, and that the essential fact about hysteria is the lack of synthetizing power and consequent disintegration of the field of consciousness into *mutually exclusive parts.*"[133] The language here is compelling, especially from the perspective of what Du Bois is trying to do in *Souls*: if "anaesthesias carry amnesia" and hysterics "lack synthetizing power," might not synaesthesia, then, offer at least a rhetorical antidote to the "disintegration of the field of consciousness into mutually exclusive parts?" Viewed through the prism of Du Boisean double consciousness, the "Negro," whose feelings Du Bois had been trying to articulate and whose contributions he had been trying to make visible, becomes the "hidden self" of the American body politic.[134] And if amnesia was both the cause and the consequence of racial hysteria, then synaesthesia, in "carrying" the memory of a more accurate history, might point to the possibility of a better future.

In "Of the Sorrow Songs," Du Bois reminds his readers that "actively we have woven ourselves with the very warp and woof of this nation,"[135] the very warp and woof, music and words, of which he has woven the pages of *The Souls of Black Folk*. "Would America have been America without her Negro people?" Troping the long history of denial that precedes that question, Du Bois turns negation—after all, to answer "no" is to be historically accurate—into an acknowledgment of the need to turn from a substantive America, with its disjunctive logic of separate but equal that in *essence* denies African Americans their democratic personhood, to a transitive, fluid, consensual America. Such negation is built into and

---

[131] Ibid., 373.

[132] Ibid., 371.

[133] Ibid., 373, emphasis added.

[134] For a now-classic discussion on African-American interventions on racial identity in relation to the psychological discourse of the latter nineteenth century, especially in terms of the influence of James's "The Hidden Self," see Thomas Otten, "Pauline Hopkins and the Hidden Self of Race" *ELH* 59/1 (Spring, 1992). According to Otten, Hopkins viewed "race" as "a pathologically hidden side of the self" that could then "be therapeutically brought to the surface and refigured" (229).

[135] Du Bois, *Souls*, 215.

underscored by the problem of music in the midst of a linear text. Do we, in fact, skip over it? Or, recognizing it as "music," are we instead compelled to enact a response that moves from the realm of sight to the realm of hearing? How else do we negotiate the complex social relations imbedded in the day to day, much less the greater pathos of a history and politics of betrayal if not through the ear? Are we not then being invited to violate, à la Keller, James, and Du Bois, the protocols of precisely the teleology implicit in such betrayals?

Du Bois well knew that the ear had the power to transform perception and evaluation in ways that the eye could not. At the very beginning of "The Sorrow Songs," he reminds his readers of the transformative power of these songs by invoking Jubilee Hall at his alma mater, Fisk University. Turning now to the trope of synaesthesia, he reminds his readers how that building was constructed: "To me Jubilee Hall seemed ever made of the songs themselves, and its bricks were red with the blood and dust of toil. Out of them rose for me morning, noon, and night, bursts of wonderful melody, full of the voices of my brothers and sisters, full of the voices of the past."[136] I have called the figure I just cited "synaesthesia." But when does *figure* itself become hard fact? For surely Du Bois is also literally invoking the very real history of the Jubilee Singers, who, beginning in 1871, sang the sorrow songs to all the world in order to raise funds for Fisk University in general and Jubilee Hall in particular.[137] And just as surely, Du Bois is aware of the *locus classicus* of synaesthetic citation handed down from Goethe to Schelling to Hegel (and even to Emerson by way of Mme. De Stael)—*architecture is frozen music.*[138] Indeed, at Fisk, as Du Bois reminds us, music *is* the very

---

[136] Ibid., 204.

[137] See J. B. T. Marsh, *The Story of the Jubilee Singers; with Their Songs*, rev. ed. (Boston: Houghton, Mifflin and Company, 1881) chapter 3 for first tour, 1871, and chapter 9 on the completion of Jubilee Hall in 1875.

[138] The genesis of this citation is very slippery indeed. Hegel mentions it in his *Aesthetics* (2:662), attributing it to Friedrich von Schlegel. Hegel's translator, T. M. Knox, suggests that "Schlegel" is a mistake for "Schelling," although he does leave room for the possibility that Schlegel may have said this in Jena within earshot of both Hegel and Schelling. F. W. J. Schelling, in *The Philosophy of Art*, ed. and trans. Douglas W. Stott (Minneapolis: University of Minnesota Press, 1989) sec. 107, writes: "*The anorganic art form or the music within the plastic arts is architecture*" (163, emphasis in original); a few paragraphs later, he reflects on "[t]he assertion that architecture = music…" (164). Emerson, in his *Journal*, musing on the "genealogy of thoughts," writes

ground of architectural possibility: "A tract of twenty-five acres, on a commanding site overlooking the city of Nashville, had been purchased for the permanent location of Fisk University.... The students had worked with the laborers to level the earthworks, and the foundations had been laid for a noble building for university purposes, to be called Jubilee Hall."[139] As materialized in the hard fact of Jubilee Hall, aurality, the interplay of soaring voice and receptive ear, had at long last liquidated the commodification of African-American bodies. The Euro-American ear had finally recognized what the eye had resolutely refused to acknowledge.

By way of synaesthesia, then, Du Bois posits the reader of *Souls* as the receptive subject of the Hegelian moment of recognition. This is not recognition on sight, however, but a resoundingly deep aural response to the intricate manipulations of a "co-worker in the kingdom of culture."[140] The double-consciousness Du Bois graphs out between linear text and music is thus a reminder that "America," *as* transitivity, has imbedded in it the hope of providing no firm grounds for an *essential* American identity. One then

---

"And Mme De Stael's {or Goethe's} 'Architecture is frozen music,' borrowed from Goethe's 'Arch[itectur]e is dumb music,' borrowed from Vitruvius, who said, 'the Architect must not only understand drawing but also Music'" (*The Journals and Miscellaneous Notebooks of Ralph Waldo Emerson*, vol. 4 in 16 volumes, ed. Alfred R. Ferguson [Cambridge: Belknap Press, 1964] 4:337). Donnell and Duigan also mention this phrase, but they trace A line attributable to Schelling, De Stael, and Byron by way of Crabbe Robinson" (p. 83, n. 14).

[139] Marsh, *Jubilee Singers*, 46. Marsh's dates are hard to track, but the land was apparently purchased out of the $40,000 the Jubilee Singers made in what I take to be their initial 1871 tour.

[140] Du Bois, *Souls*, 5. While making clear my debt to Zamir on the issue of Hegelian recognition, I want to take this occasion to also remark on Robert Gooding-Williams's critique of Cornel West's analysis of Du Bois's pragmatistic roots in *The American Evasion of Philosophy: A Genealogy of Pragmatism*. According to Gooding-Williams, "*Souls* cannot be read without distortion as the work of a *Jamesian* and thus anti-idealist intellectual, which may be the reason that West, when reading *Souls* as an Emersonian text, keeps silent regarding its relation to James' 'nourishing' influence on DuBois." Later he adds, "West's failure to show that DuBois should be read as a pragmatist has *substantive* as well as methodological implications." I agree that West does not present a convincing case for direct influence in his text, but I stress Gooding-Williams's use of "substantive" in order to underscore the way in which I think Du Bois has, in fact, been "nourished" by Jamesian transitivity. See Gooding-Williams, "Evading Narrative Myth, Evading Prophetic Pragmatism: Cornel West's *The American Evasion of Philosophy*," *Massachusetts Review* 32/4 (Winter 1990–1991): 528, 530.

has nothing to assimilate *to* except the democratic compulsion to honor the relational space between "one" and the "other." We can then all engage our necessary—because *residential*—responsibilities as we sing along with Du Bois, "Let us cheer the weary traveller, cheer the weary traveller, cheer the weary traveller, along the heavenly way."[141] Such transitive cheer will produce its fair share of movement and pathos, but it need not—ought not—in this synaesthetic moment be the pathos of ascripted identities.[142] For we ought all to hold to the promise of "novelties in the world." Thus in moving toward the morning sun, Du Bois moves us toward the possibility of renewal and beginning. But in mapping an eastward teleology rather than the more familiar American westward advance, Du Bois moves us toward a reminder of the constitutive role of our shared American past in any vision of the future that we, the people, might find worthwhile in 1903. Reading him now, will we heed his cry in this, the dawning of the next new century?

Works Cited

Andrews, Stephen. "Salvaging Virginia: Transitivity, Race and the Problem of Consent." Ph.D. dissertation, University of Washington, 1998.

Aptheker, Herbert, editor. *Selections, 1934–1944.* Volume 2 of *The Correspondence of W. E. B. Du Bois.* Amherst: University of Massachusetts Press, 1976.

——, editor. *Book Reviews by W. E. B. Du Bois.* Millwood NY: KTO Press, 1977.

——. *W. E. B. Du Bois, Writings in Non-Periodical Literature Edited by Others.* Millwood NY: Kraus-Thomson Organization Limited, 1982.

Beckson, Karl. *Arthur Symons: A Life.* Oxford: Clarendon Press, 1987.

---

[141] Du Bois, *Souls*, 215–16; see <http://web.grinnell.edu/cts/dubois/>, 15.

[142] David Levering Lewis remarks that Du Bois often claimed a consensual relationship to "Negro" identity: "He was a negro not because he had to be—was born immutably among them—but because he had embraced the qualities of that splendid race and the moral supriority of its cause" (*Biography of a Race*, 72). I borrow the word "pathos" from Walter Benn Michaels, "Race into Culture: A Critical Genealogy of Cultural Identity," *Critical Inquiry* 18/4 (Summer 1992): 685: "It is only the appeal to race that makes culture an object of affect and that gives notions like losing our culture, preserving it, stealing someone else's culture, restoring people's culture to them, and so on, their pathos."

Brooks, Van Wyk. *Helen Keller, Search for a Portrait*. New York: E. P. Dutton and Co., Inc., 1956.

Bruce, Dickson D., Jr. "W. E. B. Du Bois and the Idea of Double Consciousness." *American Literature* 64/2 (June 1992): 299–309.

Burke, Edmund. *A Philosophical Inquiry into the Sublime and Beautiful and Other Pre-Revolutionary Writings*. Edited by David Womersly. London: Penguin Books, Ltd, 1998.

Byerman, Keith E. *Seizing the Word: History, Art, and Self in the Work of W. E. B. Du Bois*. Athens: University of Georgia Press, 1994.

Carby, Hazel. *Race Men: The W. E. B. Du Bois Lectures*. Cambridge: Harvard University Press, 1998.

Chesnutt, Charles. *The Marrow of Tradition*. Ann Arbor: University of Michigan Press, 1990.

Commager, Henry Steele, and Milton Cantor. *Documents of American History*. Volume 1. Englewood Cliffs: Prentice Hall, 1988.

Cook, Nicholas *Analysing Musical Multimedia*. Oxford: Clarendon Press, 1998.

Derrida, Jacque. *Positions*. Translated by Alan Bass. Chicago: University of Chicago Press, 1981.

Donnell, Carol A., and William Duigan, "Synaesthesia and Aesthetic Education." *Journal of Aesthetic Education* 11/3 (July 1977): 69–85.

Du Bois, W. E. B. *Black Reconstruction in America, 1860–1880*. New York: Meridian Books, New York, 1964.

———. *Dusk of Dawn: An Essay Toward an Autobiography of a Race Concept*. New Brunswick: Transaction Publishers, 1984.

———. *The Souls of Black Folk*. New York: Penguin, 1989.

———. See *The Papers of W. E. B. Du Bois* (microfilm, 89 reels, Microfilming Corporation of America, 1980), reel 88, "Philosophy Notes," frames 204–205.

Ferguson, Alfred R., editor. *The Journals and Miscellaneous Notebooks of Ralph Waldo Emerson*. Volume 4. Cambridge: Belknap Press, 1964.

Galton, Francis. *Inquiries into Human Faculty and its Development*. New York: Macmillan and Company, 1883.

Harrison, John E. *Synaesthesia: The Strangest Thing*. Oxford: Oxford University Press.

Hegel, G. W. F. *Aesthetics: Lectures on Fine Art*. Volume 2. Translated by T. M. Knox. Oxford: Clarendon Press, 1975.

————. *Lectures on the Philosophy of History.* Translated by J. Sibree. London: Henry G. Bohn, 1856.

Hoopes, James, editor. *Charles Sanders Peirce.* Durham: University of North Carolina Press, 1991.

http://web.grinnell.edu/cts/dubois.

James, William. "The Hidden Self," *Scribner's Magazine* 7/3 (March 1890): 361–73.

————. *The American Scene.* Edited with an introduction by W. H. Auden. New York: Charles Scribner's Sons, 1946.

————. *Pragmatism and The Meaning of Truth.* Cambridge: Harvard University Press, 1978.

————. *The Principles of Psychology.* Volume 1. New York: Dover Publications, 1950.

————. *The Works of William James: Essays, Comments, and Reviews.* Cambridge: Harvard University Press, 1987.

Lemert, Charles. "A Classic from the Other Side of the Veil: Du Bois's *Souls of Black Folk.*" *Sociological Quarterly* 35/3 (August1994): 383–96.

Lewis, David Levering. *W. E. B. Du Bois: Biography of a Race.* New York: Henry Holt and Company, 1993.

Marsh, J. B. T. *The Story of the Jubilee Singers; With Their Songs.* Revised edition. Boston: Houghton, Mifflin and Company, 1881.

Michaels, Walter Benn. "Race into Culture: A Critical Genealogy of Cultural Identity." *Critical Inquiry* 18/4 (Summer 1992): 655–86.

Miles, Kevin Thomas. "Haunting Music in *The Souls of Black Folk.*" *boundary 2* 27/3 (Fall 2000): 99–214.

Otten, Thomas, "Pauline Hopkins and the Hidden Self of Race." *ELH* 59/1 (Spring, 1992): 227–56.

Paschall, Andrew, editor. *W. E. B. Du Bois, A Reader.* New York: Collier Books, 1993.

Poirier, Richard. *Poetry and Pragmatism.* Cambridge: Harvard University Press, 1992.

Posnock, Ross. "The Distinction of Du Bois: Aesthetics, Pragmatism, Politics." *American Literary History* 7/3 (Fall 1995): 500–24.

————. *Color and Culture: Black Writers and the Making of the Modern Intellectual.* Cambridge: Harvard University Press, 1998.

Rampersad, Arnold. *The Art and Imagination of W. E. B. Du Bois.* Cambridge: Harvard University Press, 1976.

Rath, Richard Cullen. "Echo and Narcissus: The Afrocentric Pragmatism of W. E. B. Du Bois." *Journal of American History* 84/2 (September 1997): 461–95.

Schelling, F. W. J. *The Philosophy of Art*. Edited and translated by Douglas W. Stott. Minneapolis: University of Minnesota Press, 1989.

Schlereth, Thomas J. "Columbia, Columbus, and Columbianism." *Journal of American History* 79/3 (December 1992): 937–68.

Scholes, Robert. *Protocols of Reading*. New Haven: Yale University Press, 1989.

Schrager, Cynthia D. "Both Sides of the Veil: Race, Science, and Mysticism in W. E. B. Du Bois." *American Quarterly* 48/4 (December 1996): 551–86.

Sundquist, Eric. *To Wake the Nations: Race in the Making of American Literature*. Cambridge: Belknap Press, 1993.

Turner, Frederick Jackson. *The Significance of the Frontier in American History*. Edited by Harold Simonson. New York: Frederick Ungar Publishing Co., 1963.

Wald, Priscilla. *Constituting Americans: Cultural Anxiety and Narrative Form*. Durham NC: Duke University Press, 1993.

Washington, Booker T. *Up from Slavery*. New York: Signet, 2000.

Wilson, Theodore B. *The Black Codes of the South*. Tuscaloosa: University of Alabama Press, 1965.

Zamir, Shamoon. *Dark Voices: W. E. B. Du Bois and American Thought: 1888–1903*. Chicago: University of Chicago Press, 1995.

"The Most Hopeless of Deaths... Is the Death of Faith": Messianic Faith in the Racial Politics of W. E. B. Du Bois[1]

Marta Brunner

> "Sing a song full of the faith that the dark past has taught us,
> Sing a song full of the hope that the present has brought us...."
> "Lift Every Voice and Sing" ("The Black National Anthem")
> —James Weldon Johnson and J. Rosemond Johnson

In her preface to Cedric Robinson's *Anthropology of Marxism*, Avery F. Gordon is struck by Robinson's suggestion that a potent catalyst for socialist activism is the belief that men and women are the divine agents of that revolutionary change. She explains, "To conceive of ourselves as *divine agents* is to see ourselves the executors—not the supreme rulers, but the guarantors—of our world and our imaginations. To ground socialist aspirations in a divine agency is to remove the stigma attached to the utopian and to measure our freedom less by what subordinates us and more

---

[1] I am grateful to Angela Davis, Susan Gillman, Gary Lease, Bruce Levine, and members of the History of Consciousness Race and Ethnicity Writing seminar for providing invaluable input at various stages of this project, and to Mary Keller for prompting the finishing touches. Special thanks, as always, to Peter R. Murray for all the conversations and encouragement. A revised and expanded version of this paper appears in my dissertation, " 'Faith' in Social Change: Three Case Studies from American Social Movement History, 1890-1940."

by what we are capable of divining."[2] Gordon, following Robinson's lead, blurs the line between the human and the transcendent by drawing simultaneously on both senses of the word *divine*: the condition of being transcendent or of deity, and the act of foreseeing or making the future intelligible. It seems, then, that knowledge facilitates a sort of human transcendence that can become both the motivator for and the goal of revolutionary struggles.

Gordon's explanation of divine agency raises a key question that seems to have concerned W. E. B. Du Bois in the first half of the twentieth century. During this time, his writing reflects his attempts to discern whether liberatory racial revolution could depend on human action alone or required some kind of transcendent or miraculous source outside human experience for its success. Or perhaps his questions lay not in whether transcendence was necessary but whether *faith* in something or someone transcendent was a necessary motivator for activism. It is clear from his texts during this time that he saw faith as an indispensable part of liberatory racial consciousness. As a leader, then, he needed to decide what kind of faith his rallying cries would invoke—faith in historically bound human action or faith in something transcendent, outside of history, like a messiah or messianic fulfillment of some kind.

Conventional theological definitions of *divine* and *transcendent* refer to God rather than to humans. In my discussion of Du Bois, unless otherwise noted, I will use the two terms to refer to that which operates outside the realm of human control or outside of history. I do so because I believe this is most likely the starting definition held by Du Bois and his contemporary readers, who were influenced by (even if skeptical of) Christianity. However, in the course of my discussion, it should become clear that understanding the implications of Du Bois's messianic writing requires a more expansive definition, one that makes room for human action, knowledge, and experience as transcendent and divine.

Du Bois's writing in the first four decades of the twentieth century prompts me to ask the following questions. What is the role of faith in liberatory social movements? How does faith—in the possibility of achieving a socially just world, for instance—translate into action? Or, to put it another way, what distinguishes faith-based action from other types of

---

[2] Cedric J. Robinson, *An Anthropology of Marxism* (Aldershot UK: Ashgate, 2001) viii, emphasis original.

action? It should be evident by now that I am not equating the term *faith* with the term *religion*. Faith—along with related terms like devotion, hope, confidence, and trust—shows up frequently in the testimonies of social movement participants. Often, the term is used to express what it means to take part in a liberatory social movement, what is involved in giving oneself over to a cause. Paying attention to Du Bois's references to faith thus help us gain a better understanding of what he was calling activists of color to do or to be. One way to clarify the role of faith in Du Bois's racial politics is to examine his reliance on messianic language and thinking. Du Bois made use of messianism in his major texts, including the genre-blurring book *Darkwater* (1920) and the novel *Dark Princess* (1928), as well as to a less overt extent the autobiography *Dusk of Dawn* (1940).[3]

Messianism becomes a useful lens through which to explore the relationship of faith and action because of its galvanizing quality, its ability to mobilize groups of people in a common movement. It entails faith in a coming messiah or something that has taken on a messianic character, as in the case of messianic understandings of time or of a particular race. Messianism therefore participates in an eschatology of some kind. Although it has been most firmly associated with major religions (Judaism, Christianity, Islam), messianism can also be found in ostensibly secular versions in which the object of faith is not necessarily bound to a religious tradition.[4] The key variable is in fact this question of who or what becomes the object of messianic faith. The term *object of faith* could refer to the person or thing that inspires faith and/or the person or thing in which faith

---

[3] Surprisingly little focused attention has been given to Du Bois's use of messianic tropes and messianic thinking. The most concentrated, comprehensive attention to Du Bois's messianism has been on the part of Wilson J. Moses and Eric J. Sundquist, both of whom are writing within the field of American historical and literary studies. Both scholars analyze black messianism in order to understand its place in the history of black nationalism and black political culture. Wilson J. Moses, *Black Messiahs and Uncle Toms: Social and Literary Manipulations of a Religious Myth* (University Park: Pennsylvania State Press, 1993); Eric J. Sundquist, "The Spell of Africa," in *To Wake the Nations: Race in the Making of American Literature* (Cambridge: Belknap Press, 1993) 540–625.

[4] For a useful and far more nuanced genealogy of the messianic or charismatic ideal of leadership, see Cedric J. Robinson, "The Messiah and the Metaphor," in *The Terms of Order: Political Science and the Myth of Leadership* (Albany: SUNY Press, 1980) 110–59. For a genealogy of messianism in the black tradition, see Wilson J. Moses, *Black Messiahs and Uncle Toms*.

is placed. In my discussion, I will be placing emphasis on the latter sense of the term. For his part, Du Bois seems torn between calling for faith in a transcendent source (like a messiah figure or apocalyptic miracle) and faith in a nontranscendent source (like human action or economic strategies). Robinson's concept of men and women as divine agents may help to resolve this tension, but it is instructive to look first at the implications of Du Bois's attempt to negotiate the issue because such analysis can yield a deeper understanding of the role messianism played in his racial politics.

My essay thus attends to shifts in Du Bois's use of messianic language and thinking in order to better understand the nature of the faith undergirding his racial politics. Between 1920 and 1940, the years book-ended by *Darkwater* and *Dusk of Dawn*, what emerges is a shift from overt uses of a black messiah trope and other explicitly messianic language to a more sublimated but nonetheless influential strain of messianic thinking. Although *Dusk of Dawn* seems to leave black messianism behind, I argue that the book continues to participate in a messianic revolutionary framework given the quality of faith that is operating. Du Bois's continuing use of messianic language has less to do with theology—he appears to have been more or less agnostic from early stages of his life—than with his convictions about the nature of racial formation and solutions to racial oppression.[5] Instead, I see Du Bois struggling in the course of this shift with the questions of how soon and in what form blacks should expect revolutionary racial salvation, what role they should take in bringing about this revolution, and what kind of faith would galvanize such activism. It follows then that attending to the different forms of messianism in Du Bois's writing can enrich our understanding of his struggles to find a viable racial politics.

Darkwater is a pastiche of genres, juxtaposing historical, autobiographical, and analytical essays with poems, vignettes, short stories, prayers, and litanies. Though *Darkwater* was published in 1920, many of its component texts had appeared previously in such publications as *Crisis*, the NAACP journal Du Bois had edited. Written during and just after the First World War, the texts reflect concern with US and European imperialism, the intensification of racial violence in the US, the place of women in society, the realities of industrial capitalism, and Du Bois's own devotion to Pan-African organizing, among other things. A common thread often tying

---

[5] David Levering Lewis, *W. E. B. Du Bois: Biography of a Race, 1868–1919* (New York: Holt, 1993) 65–66.

these issues together in the book is black messianism. Messianism appears in the form of a black Christ-figure in numerous stories such as "Jesus Christ in Texas," "The Second Coming," and "The Princess of the Hither Isles." Messianism also operates through a tension between hopeful patience and outraged impatience. In "Credo," the opening piece of the book, Du Bois proclaims prophetically that white oppressors will inevitably be unseated. He writes, "I believe that the wicked conquest of weaker and darker nations by nations whiter and stronger but foreshadows the death of that strength."[6] Salvation will definitely come, although it does not appear immediate, for the credo culminates in Du Bois's assertion, "I believe in Patience—patience with the weakness of the Weak and the strength of the Strong, the prejudice of the Ignorant and the ignorance of the Blind; patience with the tardy triumph of Joy and the mad chastening of Sorrow; —patience with God!"[7] Notably, this patience seems to reference a past period of suffering and does not necessarily place the moment of salvation in the distant future.

Though Du Bois's confession of faith does not specifically reference the transcendent, the concept of patience is certainly not at odds with messianic thinking. Awaiting the return of a messiah or the coming apocalyptic moment is a common theme in both Christian and Jewish thought. Furthermore, Du Bois's phrase "patience with God" suggests the need to have patience alongside God, to share the patience of a transcendent deity who must have patience with the lamentable tendency of humans to perpetuate their own suffering. In this sense, Du Bois is assuming a transcendent role. Still, there is a reversal in that Du Bois also appears to be putting his faith in Patience itself rather than God or a messianic figure. In fact, God—typically the one who is patient—becomes the one with whom Du Bois must have patience. Faith does not necessarily rest in God because God may not be the way out of oppression. Thus Du Bois maintains a tension between the transcendence and the immanence of his own position, and by extension, the position of those he wishes to mobilize. On the one hand, if his position is truly transcendent, he risks undermining an immanent, materially-based critique of the oppressive situation in which he and others of color find themselves. And yet, the fact that there is patience

---

[6] W. E. B. Du Bois, "Darkwater: Voices from within the Veil," in *The Oxford W. E. B. Du Bois Reader*, ed. Eric J. Sundquist (New York: Oxford University Press, 1996) 485.

[7] Ibid.

(in fact, Patience with a capital P) suggests there is something *after*, that there is the possibility of transcending the history of human suffering.[8]

Du Bois addresses patience again in "A Litany at Atlanta." Although this call and response piece appears after "Credo" in *Darkwater*, it was written much earlier, having been penned after a violent 1906 race riot. In "Litany" Du Bois demonstrates that patience is no panacea for blacks. He calls into question the assumption that blacks should place their faith in God; for God may indeed be the cause of their suffering. The leader of this anguished prayer petitions a silent, apparently unresponsive God, urging God to speak and, better yet, to act. The litany thereby reinforces Du Bois's earlier expression of the need for patience with God. What comes to the fore in the litany is the notion of interstitial silence, as suggested by the Hebrew term *selah*. The litany ends,

> But whisper—speak—call, great God, for Thy silence is white terror to our hearts! The way, O God, show us the way and point us the path!
>
> ....
> ....
>
> Whither? To life? But not this life, dear God, not this. Let the cup pass from us, tempt us not beyond our strength, for there is that clamoring and clawing within, to whose voice we would not listen, yet shudder lest we must, —and it is red. Ah! God! It is the red and awful shape.
> *Selah!*
> In yonder East trembles a star.
> *Vengeance is Mine; I will repay, saith the Lord!*
> Thy Will, O Lord, be done!
> *Kyrie Eleison!*
> Lord, we have done these pleading, wavering words.
> *We beseech Thee to hear us, good Lord!*
> We bow our heads and hearken soft to the sobbing of women and little children.
> *We beseech Thee to hear us, good Lord!*
> Our voices sink in silence and in night.

---

[8] Thanks to Alexis Shotwell for helping me clarify the relationship of patience to the issue of transcendence and immanence.

Hear us, good Lord!
In night, O God of a godless land!
Amen!
In silence, O Silent God.
Selah![9]

This litany is an Old Testament form, modeled after the Psalms, with New Testament content. The speaker places blacks in the role of the suffering Christ, begging that the cup pass and temptation ease, but mingles these tropes with the Old Testament call for vengeance.

Because of the urgency expressed in this litany, I am struck by Du Bois's use of the term *selah*. The etymology of *selah* is uncertain, making it difficult to pin down a precise definition for the term. *Selah* appears frequently in the biblical books of Psalms and Habakkuk, and appears to have been a liturgical interjection or instruction of some kind.[10] In current Jewish and Christian usage, *selah* is defined most often as either an interjection akin to "amen" or as a call for a moment of silent contemplation and anticipation between liturgical episodes.[11] However, it is difficult to know whether these interpretations were in circulation when Du Bois was writing.

Then which interpretation did Du Bois intend in "A Litany at Atlanta"? The final lines of the litany indicate a possible answer to this question. The speaker says, "We bow our heads and hearken soft to the sobbing of women and little children," voices "sink[ing] in silence and in night."[12] This suggests that *selah* is meant to invoke an interstitial silence of

---

[9] W. E. B. Du Bois, "Darkwater: Voices from within the Veil," in *The Oxford W. E. B. Du Bois Reader*, ed. Eric J. Sundquist (New York: Oxford University Press, 1996) 485.

[10] A good source for etymological information on *selah* is Francis Brown, S. R. Driver, and Charles A. Briggs, *A Hebrew and English Lexicon of the Old Testament* (Oxford: Clarendon, 1968) 699–700. I thank Gary Lease for pointing me to this source.

[11] Online searches for *selah* provide a glimpse at current popular understandings of the term. See Hal Upchurch, "A Study Guide to Psalms 23," <http://tenderbytes.net/hal/23dpsalm /study11.htm> (10 January 2003); Colin Campbell, "Stepping Stones to Reflection," http://www.messengers-of-truth.org/Articles/stepping_stones.htm (28 February 2002); AISH, "Ask the Rabbi," http://www.aish.com/rabbi/ATR_browse.asp?1=s&offset=6 (28 February 2002).

[12] Du Bois, "Darkwater," 497.

contemplation. The petitioners cease their pleading and wait for an answer, asking only for mercy—"*Kyrie Eleison!*"—and for a generous hearing—"*We beseech Thee to hear us, good Lord!*" Interestingly, this silence is echoed again and ironically doubled in the penultimate line, just prior to the final "*Selah!*" The speaker prays, "In silence, O Silent God," recalling the accusation that God's silence is "white terror."[13] Thus *selah* ends the litany on an ambiguous, somewhat ironic note. As long as God is a white god, as long as God is true to the prevailing white version of Christianity, there will only ever be a damning, racially oppressive silence. Silence becomes a prelude to imminent, dramatic change rather than a final condition; for in Du Bois's messianic framework, both God and Christ are black. In effect, Du Bois is calling into existence an ambiguously transcendent black messiah and black God that consist of black people themselves. It is here, in themselves, that blacks must place their faith. Coupled with the term *selah*, the image of silence as white terror both racializes the messianic promise and transforms the lingering silence into present action. There may be lengthy silence, but it will not linger uselessly; it is an instrumental silence, a period of anticipatory preparation. In the presence of a silent, unresponsive God, blacks must consider taking things into their own hands, becoming their own agents of salvation.

Though Du Bois's critiques of a white God and white versions of Christianity could be seen as calls to secular bases for organizing, his concerns have continued to resonate in black theology as articulated by theologian James Cone. In *A Black Theology of Liberation*, published some thirty years after *Darkwater*, Cone argues for the blackness of Jesus and God in Christian theology. "The black community is an oppressed community primarily because of its blackness; hence the Christological importance of Jesus must be found in his blackness.... Our being with him is dependent on his being with us in the oppressed condition, revealing to us what is necessary for our liberation."[14] What makes Jesus black are the values or qualities being emphasized in representations of him. Jesus reflects the values of a community being systematically oppressed and in need of liberation; in short, a community with little use for lessons on love, mercy, and longsuffering patience.[15] Similarly, Du Bois is emphasizing that if a

---

[13] Ibid., 496.

[14] James Cone, *A Black Theology of Liberation* (Maryknoll NY: Orbis, 1986) 120.

[15] Ibid., 111.

white God can be silent and inactive in the face of atrocities, He (to use the idiom of the time) does not warrant the faith of blacks.

At this point, I want to address the gendered implications of Du Bois's messianism. Although he appears to be calling all blacks into a messianic role, the effect is gendered in particular ways. As Du Bois articulates the prospects for achieving racial consciousness and salvation, he is simultaneously attempting to define an appropriate form of leadership for black people. As Hazel Carby observes in *Race Men*, "Du Bois constructed particular personal, political, and social characteristics of a racialized masculinity to articulate his definition of black leadership."[16] This form of racialized masculinity included intellectual maturity, the ability to educate others, the political *savoir-faire* to be "missionaries of the nation-state"— leadership not by brute force but partly through intellect and partly through charisma.[17] It follows, then, that the black messiah trope or messianic thinking in general was compelling for Du Bois because of its resonance with his model: a wise, servant-*like* leader, to be sure, but only symbolically a servant. The real servant role—an essential role but one that cannot claim any real, power-holding, intellectual leadership capacity—is played by women. Du Bois's reliance on the messianic trope serves to keep the figures in his stories, poems, essays, and prayers within established gender roles, with men as leaders—even if they are suffering, Christ-like men who pass as servants—and women as strong, spiritually-sensitive followers, the faithful who enable black men to lead, either by giving birth to them or otherwise laboring on their behalf.[18]

These roles are played out more explicitly in "The Call," a short parable in which the most marginalized individual, the unmarried black servant woman, drops everything to serve her black God. Du Bois's emphasis here is on the need for present response to racial oppression. Although the call comes from a presumably transcendent god figure, Du Bois implies that the real emancipatory work is done by human revolutionary effort, not miraculous, apocalyptic revolution. The particular work asked of the servant is militant. "Go, smite me mine enemies, that they

---

[16] Hazel Carby, *Race Men* (Cambridge: Harvard University Press, 1998) 11.

[17] Ibid., 35. While I find Carby's description of Du Bois's persona useful for understanding his participation in messianic discourse, I do not necessarily wish to apply all of the negative critique in her analysis in this particular instance.

[18] See Cedric Robinson on the relationship between charisma and messianic leadership in *The Terms of Order*.

cease to do evil in my sight." Alone, and facing an apparently impossible task, the woman goes "forth on the hills of God to do battle for the King."[19] Although the action is immediate, the fruits of her efforts will not come immediately, given the magnitude of the problem she must confront. The woman may be militant but she is still the servant—the follower, not the leader.

Other messianic poems and stories in *Darkwater* lay out gender roles along similar lines. In *To Wake the Nations*, Eric J. Sundquist takes up the role of black women in *Darkwater*'s messianic framework. Sundquist argues that the black messiah-figure functions to redeem black mothers from the stigma of rape and illegitimate births. Often the product of rape, Du Bois's messiah figures have the crucial ability to bring about redemption of violation.[20] Though Sundquist emphasizes that "the theological value of the [black messiah] trope [is] less significant than its ideological value," the trope does point to a transcendence, at least at the level of allegory. While the black/mixed-race son may allegorically represent the African diaspora, he is still a messiah-figure, imbued with the ability to transform "the debauchery and bastardy left in the wake of slavery and colonialism" into a revitalized Pan-African nation.[21]

My reading of *Darkwater* thus far suggests that Du Bois's calls for faith in messianic salvation oscillate between the transcendent and the historical. He depicts activists and leaders who transcend human limitations, as in the woman who battles evil single-handedly at God's behest or the black Christ-figures throughout *Darkwater* who bring promised salvation to the racially oppressed. Alternately—sometimes simultaneously—he calls the transcendent into question, emphasizing the need for present human action in order to bring about salvation. For Du Bois, salvation is a carrot hanging not merely irresistibly but unattainably in the activist's future.

In the last two poems of *Darkwater*, Du Bois makes it clear that he is calling for a faith-based politics of the present. In the penultimate poem "The Prayers of God," a white speaker comes to the painful realization that Christianity has placed the messianic sacrifice in the wrong historical

---

[19] W. E. B. Du Bois, "Darkwater: Voices from within the Veil," in *The Oxford W. E. B. Du Bois Reader*, ed. Eric J. Sundquist (New York: Oxford University Press, 1996) 564.

[20] Sundquist, *Wake the Nations*, 592.

[21] Ibid.

moment, in the past rather than the present. The colonialism and the
imperialist conquest of darker nations, as well as the lynchings perpetrated
stateside in God's name, all constitute the suffering of Christ. The speaker
winces:

> That black and riven thing—was it Thee?
> That gasp—was it Thine?
> This pain—is it Thine?
> Are, then, these bullets piercing Thee?
> Have all the wars of all the world,
> Down all dim time, drawn blood from Thee?
> Have all the lies and thefts and hates—
> Is this Thy Crucifixion, God,
> And not that funny, little cross,
> With vinegar and thorns?
> Is this Thy kingdom here, not there,
> This stone and stucco drift of dreams?[22]

The penitent white speaker subsequently realizes God is praying to
him or her for help—perhaps a resolution of the earlier tension in "A Litany
at Atlanta" between God as agent of patience and God as object or target of
patience. Whites, then, are also called to bring about salvation. This poem
suggests that successful race revolution is predicated on concurrent action of
people on both sides of the color line. Most importantly for the discussion at
hand, the key revelation is that "Thy Kingdom [is] here, not there."
Salvation is not to be sought in some far-off moment; salvation can be found
in the same place and time as the suffering that requires it. Here, faith
requires a revised understanding of the Christian narrative, an
understanding that takes into account the racialized nature of suffering in
the present moment. According to James Cone, "The appearance of Jesus as
the black Christ also means that the revolution is God's kingdom becoming
reality in America."[23] For Cone, failure to confront racial oppression in
America is thus tantamount to not recognizing the messiah.

---

[22] W. E. B. Du Bois, "Darkwater: Voices from within the Veil," in *The Oxford W. E.
B. Du Bois Reader*, ed. Eric J. Sundquist (New York: Oxford University Press, 1996)
610.

[23] Cone, *Black Theology*, 124.

That said, it bears repeating that the messianic rhetoric and thinking throughout *Darkwater* do not necessarily kindle renewed faith in God or religion. Indeed, Du Bois ends the book dispensing with God in favor of deified humanity. At the close of the final poem in *Darkwater*, Du Bois addresses not God but a Hegelian "World-Spirit." He writes:

> Save us, World-Spirit, from our lesser selves!
> Grant us that war and hatred cease,
> Reveal our souls in every race and hue!
> Help us, O Human God, in this Thy Truce,
> To make Humanity divine![24]

In this final, salvific act, humanity merges with, or perhaps even supplants, God. As a result, people of the African diaspora must place their faith in humanity and the paradoxically divine nature of their own actions. This faith may be what saves humans from their "lesser selves." Faith in this case implies a consciousness. This literary call to consciousness coincides with Du Bois's real-life political agenda in the years the material for *Darkwater* was written: his goals of Pan-African coalition-building, education, propaganda, and militant agitation, as is reflected in Du Bois's organization of the Pan-African Congresses, in his work at Atlanta University, in his role as editor of the *Crisis*, and in his founding role in the Niagara Movement and the NAACP. His actions were attempts to foster race-consciousness and instill faith in the possibility of change in the face of brutal lynchings, imperialist expansion, and Jim Crow discrimination.

Despite Du Bois's efforts to articulate or envision racial revolution in historical terms, I see in *Darkwater* a recognition on his part that his readers may need a source of transcendence in which to place their faith—a black messiah or the promise of messianic salvation from racial oppression. Patience becomes not resignation but active preparation for coming salvation. Still, he also seems to be urging readers who are operating within a transcendent faith system (like Christian theology) to place more faith in themselves or at least to reevaluate their faith in a white God or white messiah whose values ill suit the needs of revolutionary action.

Patience and activism are closely tied to messianic faith in Du Bois's second novel, *Dark Princess* (1928). The novel follows the Pan-African

---

[24] Du Bois, *Darkwater*, 623.

revolutionary struggles of a young black American man, Matthew Towns, and his East Indian lover, the princess Kautilya. Throughout the story, Towns struggles to find a viable politics with which to sustain his hope for salvation of the "darker races." Du Bois's novel examines the crisis of racial faith that occurs as people of color try to envision the ways change could occur in their contemporary world. As in *Darkwater*, the struggle against racism requires patience and human effort, but there remains in *Dark Princess* an urgency that only an explicit messiah-figure is able to address. In the novel, faith has temporal and spatial implications for Du Bois's messianism; for the time frame and location within which revolutionary action takes place, in effect, determines the sort of faith that will sustain revolution. The messianic elements of *Dark Princess* also have implications for gender roles in liberatory racial politics.

When the book opens, Matthew Towns is a medical student just being turned away from his obstetrics program because he is black. Dejected, he travels to Berlin where by chance he meets Princess Kautilya. In these passages, Matthew is rather transparently modeled on Du Bois's own experiences at Harvard and in Germany. When Kautilya realizes Matthew is an American Negro, she invites him to a gathering of revolutionary leaders from non-European countries, all people of color. During this meeting, Matthew proclaims his faith in the revolutionary power of the masses rather than the elite. In part 2, Matthew has become a Pullman porter in order to survey the possibilities of racial revolution in the United States and to begin his activist career. Unfortunately, a thwarted sabotage plan and the lynching of a fellow porter lands Matthew in prison for ten years. By the time part 3 opens, Matthew has been "bought" out of prison by Sara Andrews, the power-hungry young black woman who sees Matthew as her ticket to political and financial success. Physically and emotionally, Sara provides a contrast to Kautilya. Unlike the dark Indian princess, Sara can pass for white when she finds it strategically useful, though she makes no overt efforts to hide her mixed-race background. She is not beautiful but is well-groomed and professional with "intelligent, straight gray eyes."[25] Her politics involve improving her own social and financial status rather than improving the world in any meaningful way. Indeed, Sara enthusiastically takes part in the existing power bases of "machine politics," playing individuals, political

---

[25] W. E. B. Du Bois, *Dark Princess* (Jackson: University of Mississippi Press, 1995) 111.

parties, and even diametrically opposed groups like the Ku Klux Klan and black voting blocs off each other in order to achieve her own ends. In the wake of his failed stint as a revolutionary, Matthew has no illusions about his relationship to his "rescuers," Sara and her political boss Sammy Scott: "They had bought and paid for him. All his enthusiasm, all his hope, all his sense of reality was gone…. He gave up all thought of a career, of leadership, of greatly or essentially changing this world."[26] In self-preservation mode, Matthew allows himself to take part in Sara and Sammy Scott's political machine so that he can make something of a living. Sara soon molds Matthew into an effective, if excessively honest, politician, eventually pushing him into the state legislature and ultimately toward a seat in Congress.

Early in part 3, Matthew has been elected to represent a small district of Chicago at Sara's urging. One day he is confronted by a Chinese acquaintance from the Berlin meeting who is startled to find that Matthew no longer believes in the cause of "Freedom, Emancipation, Uplift—union with all the dark and oppressed."[27] When the Chinese man requests Matthew's aid in building coalitions with labor interests in order to quell organized crime, Matthew's sardonic response belies both his loss of faith and his cynicism regarding morality: "I'm not running this [political] district as a Sunday School."[28] In other words, he sees no human goodness worth nurturing and no long-term value in furthering the cause of social justice. The Chinese friend laments, "The most hopeless of deaths…is the death of Faith"[29]—for without faith there can be no hope for revolution.

Matthew allows Sara to pull him deeper into the cogs of the political machine, making it increasingly difficult for him to exercise what shreds of conscience he has left. Though he finds himself withdrawing from her, he is unable to simply walk away. Matthew has no real interest in continuing his political career—he even resigns his seat in the state legislature, a move Sara is able to spin publicly as a commitment to his bid for a seat in Congress—but he has little idea of what he might do instead. On the eve of Matthew's nomination to the congressional election race, Kautilya comes to the formal reception dinner at the Towns's home to save Matthew's soul

---

[26] Ibid., 126.
[27] Ibid., 135.
[28] Ibid., 136.
[29] Du Bois, *Dark Princess*, 136.

from hell in a gender-reversed sort of Orpheus and Eurydice quest. Later, the princess reflects on this moment, telling Matthew that throughout his political career she had been sending representatives to him in order to save him from his "slow and sure descent into hell." To her chagrin, he had been resistant. "You knew, but you would not understand. You sneered at the truth. You would not come at my call," says Kautilya.[30] Matthew defends himself, claiming not to have recognized her "voice." But she admonishes him, "You knew the voice of our cause, Matthew—was that not my voice?" In 1 Samuel 3:1–18, young Samuel repeatedly mistakes the Lord's voice for that of his mentor Eli. Samuel, unlike Matthew Towns, is very willing to accept the call once he recognizes its source. This allusion to an Old Testament story is appropriate because, as readers discover in part 4, the messiah's birth is yet to come. Additionally, in light of Matthew's resistance, Kautilya's admonishment echoes that of Jesus in Matthew 25:34–46. In that passage, Jesus reminds his listeners that representatives of the Lord will come unannounced and in unexpected guises ("I was a stranger and you welcomed me."). For this reason, believers must treat others as extensions of the Lord's being. Matthew should have given Kautilya's emissaries the same attention he would have given her, but he was missing the key ingredient—faith in the cause that bound her to those representatives, and thus bound her to Matthew across time and space.

At their reunion in the Towns's home, the princess pronounces her "benediction," declaring, "I have sought you, man of God, in the depths of hell, to bring your dead faith back to the stars."[31] Matthew consequently experiences a dramatic, if troubled, conversion somewhat reminiscent of Saul on the road to Damascus (although Du Bois reserves the "scales falling from the eyes" trope for Kautilya in a later scene). Matthew hears Kautilya's benediction and "suddenly there was light. And suddenly from Matthew dropped all the little hesitancies and cynicisms. The years of disbelief were not."[32] It seems that this newly regained faith will enable the revolutionary couple to take on the white world, but it is not clear that faith alone can support revolution. Furthermore, it is not easy for Matthew to maintain this faith, particularly when he is separated from Kautilya.

[30] Ibid., 224–25.
[31] Ibid., 210.
[32] Ibid., 210.

In *Dark Princess*, female characters act as foils for Matthew's faith. It is worth noting the role played by Matthew's wife, Sara. Given that Sara embodies a politics devoid of faith, Matthew's loss of faith intensifies while under her influence. Sara willingly participates in the political machine rather than transcending it and, as a result, pulls Matthew into the machine (and down into a faithless hell) with her. Faith would constitute a form of dependence that Sara finds abhorrent. Du Bois's narrator observes,

> Sara was in no sense evil. Her character had been hardened and sharpened by all that she had met and fought. She craved wealth and position. She got pleasure in having people look with envious eyes upon what she had and did. It was her answer to the world's taunts, jibes, and discriminations.... Really, down in her heart, she was sorry for Matthew. He seemed curiously weak and sensitive in the places where he should not have been; she herself was furious if sympathy or sorrow seeped through her armor. She was ashamed of it. All sympathy, all yielding, all softness, filled her with shame. She hardened herself against it.[33]

Above all, she does not want to depend on anyone or be seen as dependent. If she has faith, it is only in herself. The longer Matthew stays with Sara, the more he draws into himself, perhaps learning from her that he must learn to rely on himself alone. Without Kautilya's intervention, he would have continued to see faith as a liability rather than an asset. I will demonstrate Kautilya's role in more detail below.

Du Bois uses part 4 of *Dark Princess* to plumb the relationship between faith and revolution, and to consider the place of the messianic in racial struggle. The written correspondence between Matthew, who is now performing hard labor in Chicago, and Kautilya, who is living in Virginia, grapples with a number of faith-based questions in regard to the "darker races" of the world. First and foremost, is faith enough? Kautilya continually asks for Matthew's patience and perseverance, but in his mind-numbing, back-breaking job as a subway construction laborer and stockyard worker he is unable to see the point in having faith and sees little use for patience. But even if patience alone is not enough to foment real revolution, what form(s) of action ought to be entailed in faith? Local action or global action? Indeed, in what location and within what time frame must faith be enacted?

Matthew becomes increasingly convinced that Chicago is the most effective center for race and labor activism, while Kautilya touts rural

---

[33] Du Bois, *Dark Princess*, 200–201.

Virginia. Each location would require a different sort of revolutionary action. For Kautilya, Virginia is a pastoral, preindustrial home "at the edge of the black world," where Matthew and others would be "free and able to act" in an anticolonial project.[34] Although Virginia has been the site of slavery and lynching, it is also the place where the messianic birth is coming to pass—the birth of their son, the next maharajah and African-American savior. Du Bois places Kautilya in a pastoral setting, perhaps reinforcing the assumption that women are not appropriate leaders for modern revolutionary movements in an industrialized world. Indeed, as strong a character as Kautilya is, she is only as effective as the child she carries. Her leadership role depends on men to both enable her (via impregnation) and take over for her (as her son will take over political responsibility for her people). For Matthew, Chicago is the center of the industrial world—indeed, the epitome of American evil—and is thus the best place to foment a revolution led by the union of "Brain and Brawn."[35] When in his letters Matthew becomes impatient and militant in his calls for violent revolution, Kautilya admonishes him, writing, "For all that [revolutionary work] we need, and need alone, Time; the alembic Time. The slow majestic march of events, unhurried, sure…. Your mother's Bible puts it right: 'A day unto the Lord is as a thousand years, and a thousand years as one day.'"[36] Matthew bitterly mourns the lack of time as he sees time in less messianic terms: "Endless time! He was almost thirty. In a few years he would be forty, and creative life, real life, would be gone; gone forever."[37] Kautilya's messianic faith allows her to see time as both open-ended and compressed, as a progressive refinement of human history. Matthew's nonmessianic conception of time prevents him from seeing time as either open-ended or progressive. To him, time is always in the process of running out. Time is a source of urgency but not a source of hope.[38]

---

[34] Ibid., 286.

[35] Ibid., 282.

[36] Ibid., 286–87.

[37] Du Bois, *Dark Princess*, 287.

[38] Walter Benjamin's "Theses on the Philosophy of History" provides a useful framework for understanding messianic time. His framework suggests the liberatory potential of thinking about time in nonteleological fashion. Walter Benjamin, *Illuminations: Essays and Reflections*, ed. Hannah Arendt (New York: Schoken, 1968) 253–64.

More important to the outcome of this particular story is the question of whether faith alone is enough to carry the revolution by virtue of anticipated miracles, such as a messiah's birth. That is, can a revolution depend on miracles? Du Bois gives a mixed response to this question. The book's messianic ending suggests that a colored messiah is the only way to bridge the dual goals, expressed by Kautilya, of "our own social uplift and our own defense against Europe and America."[39] "Can we accomplish this double end in one movement?" she asks. Yes, suggests Du Bois, as he contrives a black, male messiah to provide both charismatic leadership to the nonwhite populations and serve as maharajah to Kautilya's people in their specific anti-imperial struggle. But the very fact of the messianic ending throws into question the power of secular revolution and of the *human* efforts to organize—without a messiah there is no hope. The birth of Kautilya and Matthew's son can be seen as both miraculous and nontranscendent: on the one hand, if Matthew and Kautilya's child had been a girl, for instance, there would have been no miracle to save the cause, no fulfillment of faith (which begs the question, Is the birth of a boy rather than a girl to be read as lucky or miraculous?). A woman could not become a maharajah—Kautilya herself is only an interim leader until a maharajah can be found—and, in terms of Du Bois's leadership model, she would not likely be an effective leader for black Americans. On the other hand, the key to this messiah's effectiveness is that he will become the impetus for organization, for human rather than miraculous or apocalyptic revolution. Du Bois sees the need for transcendence in the face of terrible odds (the legacy of slavery, the intransigence of white racism, and the problem of imperialism, as well as the alienation of laborers in industrialized society) but wants to resist it as well by making the messiah/maharajah of human birth. Indeed, though his messiah-figures in *Darkwater* are frequently the product of the white rape of black women, the messiah in *Dark Princess* is conceived in the context of healthy black sexuality.

It is important not to define faith too narrowly in *Dark Princess*. The novel incorporates faith in revolution, faith in reason, faith in a messiah, faith in romantic love, faith in machine (politics)/machines (technology)/machinery (social institutions and industry). A full discussion of faith in the novel would address the interplay of all these forms of faith. I will not take the time to discuss that now but for the moment will look at a

---

[39] Du Bois, *Dark Princess*, 257.

single instance where these faiths come together. Kautilya herself embodies multilevel, hybrid faith. First, she freely mixes Christianity and Buddhism in her faith, perhaps because a hybrid faith is most appropriate for a project based on coalitions among the "darker races." Hinting at her messianic pregnancy, she writes to Matthew, "'My soul doth magnify the Lord!' And now my spirit is rejoicing, and the ineffable Buddha, blood of the blood of my fathers, seems bowing down to his low and doubting handmaiden."[40] Drawing on New Testament language of the Virgin Mary, she acknowledges both the blessings from her Indian religion and the fact that those blessings came in spite of her faltering faith. She invokes both her past genealogy and her future role as servant or "handmaiden" in the messianic salvation of the darker races. Kautilya's faith in the messianic salvation is much firmer than Matthew's faith can ever be because of her belief in the power of transcendent blessing and because her physical experience of the pregnancy confirms the messianic promise for her in a way he cannot access. Du Bois seems to deny Matthew access to knowledge of Kautilya's pregnancy in order to put him through the crises and subsequent renewals of faith.

But Kautilya's faith is not only a religious one; she also bases her faith on Matthew's own prophecy in Berlin, something to which he does have direct access. In response to Matthew's later assertion that common people are not fit for democratic self-governance and require oligarchy to live in society, Kautilya writes, "Dearest, in spite of all you say, I believe, I believe in men; I believe in the unlovely masses of men; I believe in that prophetic word which you spoke in Berlin and which perhaps you only half believed yourself. And why should I not believe?"[41] Can a peaceful revolution happen without a certain degree of messianic faith? I think Du Bois is ultimately suggesting in the novel that it cannot, or at least ought not. The challenge is to sustain faith through time, from the moment of prophecy to the moment of revolutionary or messianic fulfillment.

The explicit messianic tropes found in *Darkwater* and *Dark Princess* give way in *Dusk of Dawn* to less overt messianic thinking. Messianism in this book comes through in Du Bois's conception of who or what will save the world from racial self-destruction, with new suggestions regarding in what or whom blacks ought to place their faith. Hope appears to lie in alternative

---

[40] Ibid., 282.
[41] Ibid., 286.

economic models. Though not without reservations, Du Bois has placed his faith more firmly by this time in socialism and black economic cooperatives. *Dusk of Dawn* contains few, if any, explicit uses of the messiah trope; perhaps the only real messianic figure Du Bois presents in this book is John Brown, described as a martyr who died so that blacks would be free. Significantly, that description comes in a quotation from Du Bois's 1906 Niagara Movement resolutions, predating his most explicitly messianic writing.

Du Bois begins *Dusk of Dawn* with an "Apology," in which he explains the trajectory of his own political and intellectual development over the past four decades. This introduction raises the issue of distinguishing between historical evidence of Du Bois's intellectual development and his own hindsight narrativizing of that development. Nevertheless, the "Apology" testifies to Du Bois's understanding of the ways his thinking on revolutionary racial politics has changed over time. He writes, "'The Souls of Black Folk,' written thirty-seven years ago, was a cry at midnight thick within the veil, when none rightly knew the coming day. The second, 'Darkwater,' now twenty years old, was an exposition and militant challenge, defiant with dogged hope. This the third book started to record dimly but consciously that subtle sense of coming day which one feels of early mornings even when mist and murk hang low."[42] Along the way, *Dusk of Dawn* became distinctly autobiographical, he notes, but remained firmly within the realm of racial analysis, the "autobiography of a race concept." Although *Dusk of Dawn* differs from Du Bois's earlier books, in terms of his own sense of purpose and in the sense of being more generically consistent throughout, it reiterates and reconceives ideas from those works.

Du Bois continues contrasting his earlier, perhaps overexuberant political ideas with his current ones in the opening chapter of *Dusk of Dawn*, "The Plot." Rather than anticipating "a series of brilliant assaults" on racial oppression or some other cataclysmic form of revolution, Du Bois now envisions a "long siege" at the level of ideology.[43] Du Bois comes to see that a time of racial salvation lies in the perhaps distant future because oppressive racial ideology is tenacious and will not fall easily. "[T]ime is needed to move the resistance in vast areas of unreason and especially in the minds of men where conscious present motive has been built on false

---

[42] W. E. B. Du Bois, *Dusk of Dawn: An Essay toward an Autobiography of a Race Concept* (New Brunswick NJ: Transaction, 1995) xxix.

[43] Du Bois, *Dusk of Dawn*, 6.

rationalization."[44] Unlike his earlier work, in which change was purportedly imminent and paired with militant revolutionary action, *Dusk of Dawn* prepares readers for a long haul—for, as Du Bois reemphasizes in the final chapter, effecting ideological change of a revolutionary nature is "slow, painfully slow."[45]

Not surprisingly, Du Bois wavers in *Dusk of Dawn* between hope and frustration, perhaps owing to his own struggle to maintain faith in liberatory change. In particular, his chapter "White World" reflects more resignation and less revolutionary fervor than similar essays in either *Souls of Black Folk* or *Darkwater*. The frustration comes with the insight that white racial ideology is imbricated with not only racial attitudes but also nationalist, imperialist, and capitalist ideologies. Consequently, Du Bois calls for a two-pronged approach to revolution. Significant change will only come with long-term efforts at transforming oppressive racial ideology, but "[m]eantime, the immediate problem of the Negro [is] the question of securing existence, of labor and income, of food and home, of spiritual independence and democratic control of the industrial process."[46] In other words, the ideological change should be a long-term goal accompanied by short-term attention to material and social conditions. Thus, Du Bois's emphasis in *Dusk of Dawn* on long-distant salvation remains grounded in present political action.

Since he now sees that change ought to grow out of the working classes rather than just from an educated elite, Du Bois devises a political program accessible to the masses. Specifically in chapter 7, "The Colored World Within," he touts black economic cooperatives so that people of color can together wield economic power in their everyday lives. Cognizant of the damaging effects of contemporary racial segregation in post-Depression America, Du Bois clarifies that his solution based on economic self-segregation is but the means to a later end; that is, economic segregation is not meant to ossify into permanent social segregation but rather to be a way to make life livable for people of color until ideological reform can take root. Economic strategies are thus both "fundamental and prophetic," setting the stage for real salvation at a future moment.[47]

---

[44] Ibid., 6.

[45] Ibid., 311.

[46] Ibid., 6–7.

[47] Du Bois, *Dusk of Dawn*, 280.

Dusk of Dawn's prevalent economic emphasis may make it easier to assume that messianism has slipped from its pages. But messianism continues to manifest itself in at least two ways. First, as in earlier books, Du Bois emphasizes the messianic promise people of color hold for the world's future; faith in human action and specifically faith in "American Negroes" and people of color elsewhere in the world are key to achieving messianic salvation. He explains, "all that I really have been trying to say is that a certain group that I know and to which I belong…bears in its bosom just now the spiritual hope of this land because of the persons who compose it and not by divine command."[48] There is messianic promise in people of color but this promise comes from the people themselves at this particular moment in time. In making this distinction, Du Bois emphasizes that his politics is not dependent on other-than-human transcendence. People of color are messianic not because they are a "chosen people" in whose lives God will benevolently intervene. But neither are they messianic due to common phenotype; they work together for mutual salvation because of the common bond of oppression. Du Bois explains in an oft-quoted moment, "the black man is a person who must ride 'Jim Crow' in Georgia"; race is "a cultural, sometimes an historical fact" defined in the present moment by distinctly material circumstances that have been shaped by white-supremacist ideology.[49] He spells out his message in no uncertain terms—"[W]e black folk are the salvation of mankind"[50]—but he warns readers that salvation will only be achieved if there is "faith in the ability of American Negroes to extricate themselves from their present plight," to be their own divine agents.[51] Salvation is to be achieved through human action that enables people to transcend the moment or circumstances of oppression. In this way, messianism provides a way to conceive of the transcendent in the material. Messianic thinking enables its participants to apply an agency to transcendence; typically the agent has been a divine (and male) messiah but the important contribution of thinkers like Du Bois or Cedric Robinson is to place messianic agency squarely in the hands of those who seek salvation. And *Dusk of Dawn*, especially, emphasizes that such human messianic agency is best utilized in collective efforts. The messiah is

---

[48] Ibid., 153.

[49] Ibid., 153.

[50] Ibid., 141.

[51] Du Bois, *Dusk of Dawn*, 206.

no longer a single deified individual but a decidedly human people whose transcendence is derived from the collectivity of the group itself. Du Bois's repeated emphasis on faith in the black race(s) does not necessarily preclude the participation of white allies. As in *Darkwater*'s "Prayers of God," Du Bois emphasizes in *Dusk of Dawn* the need for whites to work actively toward black salvation, if only by coming to terms with their own oppressive ideological assumptions about race. I should note that Du Bois's discussions of the messianic promise held by people of color does not address the question of what place women of color might hold in black activism, whether they can extricate themselves from their plight as women in a male-dominated and racially oppressive society.

Second, there is still a messianic temporality at work in Du Bois's thinking. Where does Du Bois derive his hope for salvation, now so far in the future? His reflections on the trajectory his own writing has taken over time act as reminders to his readers that the larger political struggle or movement will need to reflect similar changes. Change will be incremental rather than immediate. Nevertheless, change will come if its advocates remain committed to the cause. Reminiscent of *Darkwater*'s "Credo," *Dusk of Dawn*'s message is that hope lies in the *inevitability* of racial justice. Du Bois explains that the ideological revolution he has laid out in the pages of *Dusk of Dawn*

> works with the vast deliberation or perhaps that lack of rational thought which is characteristic of the human mind; but its ultimate triumph is inevitable and complete, so long as the ideas are kept clear and before the minds of men. I shall not live to see entirely the triumph of this, my new emphasis; but it will triumph just as much and just as completely as did my advocacy of agitation and self-assertion. It is indeed a part of that same original program; it is its natural and inevitable fulfillment.[52]

Past, present, and future come together in this passage. Du Bois positions himself prophetically in the past of later generations. He prophesies both a present for those subsequent generations that will have been the scene of active efforts to bring about ideological change and a future (beyond his lifetime and perhaps even the lifetimes of his readers) of inevitable, triumphant fulfillment. Du Bois's assertion of the complete triumph of his earlier projects may strike some readers as hyperbolic, but such a claim serves to reinforce his prophecy. Furthermore, in making this

---

[52] Ibid., 311.

claim, he is modeling faith in his achievements just as he has been calling blacks to have faith in their own achievements. Most significantly, inevitability is itself dependent on human action. So long as future intellectuals take up Du Bois's role—perhaps as subsequent autobiographers of the race concept—keeping the ideas clear and before the minds of potential activists, the inevitability of racial salvation is ensured. Thus faith in human action is reinforced in his emphasis on inevitability. In any event, the notion of inevitability seems to have been a conscious way of sustaining hope, fostering productive patience, and offsetting the crises of faith experienced by blacks and sympathetic whites in the difficult years of the early twentieth century.

Coupled with inevitability, the human action Du Bois envisions does take on a transcendent quality, although his emphasis on the painful slowness of such revolution seems to keep him teetering on the edge of an outright claim to transcendence. While the above passage in *Dusk of Dawn* does not directly call on transcendence, it does hold out the suggestion of transcendence. In fact, I would like to suggest that Du Bois's thinking in this passage supports and perhaps gives rise to calls by Cedric Robinson and others to rethink the meaning of transcendence.

This new definition of transcendence must admit the potential for humans to be divine agents or guarantors, to use Avery Gordon's language, of their own salvation. The mechanisms by which humans enact transcendence may remain in question, but Du Bois seems to be suggesting that we must recognize knowledge as a key component of this transcendent agency. Without knowledge production and the passing on of this knowledge, people of color will not be able to achieve racial salvation. Further, this knowledge production and dissemination must be accompanied by agitation and self-assertion, by participation in economic cooperatives and other social interventions in order for people of color to truly transcend existing structures of oppression.

This definition of transcendence must also take into account issues of temporality. In the above passage from *Dusk of Dawn*, there is the tension between historical inevitability (such as the inevitability of progress) or the inevitable passage of time and the inevitability of transcendent intervention (such as the coming of a redemptive messiah). This is the tension between historic time and messianic time. A revised definition of transcendence must attempt to grapple with this tension, perhaps finding a way to bring the two modes of temporality together. Walter Benjamin's efforts to combine theology with materialist critique provide a way for current scholars and activists to conceive of a historicism that allows for transcendence. According to Benjamin, redemption is not inevitable in the current trajectory of human history. In order to bring about redemption, activists must attempt to discern messianic possibility, moments in which to transcend history or "make the continuum of history explode."[53] In this way, transcendence involves necessary temporal or historical rupture facilitated by direct human action.

Finally, a new definition of transcendence must take into account the pace with which transcendence comes about. The "painful slowness" of social revolution that Du Bois foresees calls into question the assumption that transcendence would be immediate, that it would not require hard work on the part of those who would be redeemed. This is different model of messianism than that which expects change to come "in the twinkling of an eye," in the apocalyptic moment of a messiah's arrival.[54] Sustaining a social movement in the face of painful slowness requires faith of the sorts Du Bois calls for in *Darkwater*, *Dark Princess*, and *Dusk of Dawn*.

What would Du Bois's inevitable world beyond racial oppression look like? I read the Du Bois of *Dusk of Dawn* telling us that people of color must continue to reconceive their future prophetically, that the future can only be defined in the faith-filled present. Such people must become immanent guarantors of transcendent realities in order to bring the better world into being. If we recognize that such power to reconceive the future is divine or transcendent in some way, then Du Bois's reliance on a messianic idiom becomes all the more potent, though, of course, the gendered implication of his messianism is that women are given less room in which to have their own imaginations heard and their own leads followed. The power of Du Bois's evolving messianic racial politics lies in his later recognition of the time it takes to attain salvation. His is not a failed messianism—it is a politics that has continued to resonate with struggles against racial oppression because it is a continuing call to action. As we turn toward a future still marked by the

---

[53] Benjamin, *Illuminations*, 261. It is important to note that, while Benjamin speaks in terms of redemption, Du Bois speaks instead in terms of salvation. While the two terms are often used synonymously today, the term *redemption* held much different connotations for post-Reconstruction blacks, given the use of the term by white anti-Reconstructionists whose program was to "redeem" the American South from the "oppression" of slave emancipation by establishing and enforcing Jim Crow segregation.

[54] 1Cor 15:52. New Revised Standard Version.

color line, we are faced with instantiations of that line such as preemptive global war, intensified racial profiling and incarceration, and systemic political repression of liberatory voices. Du Bois's call to patiently and relentlessly lift the veil reminds us as we venture into the twenty-first century that transcendent racial salvation lies in immanent struggle.

Works Cited

AISH. "Ask the Rabbi." <http://www.aish.com/rabbi/ATR_browse.asp?l=s&offset=6> (28 February 2002).

Benjamin, Walter. *Illuminations: Essays and Reflections*. Edited by Hannah Arendt. Translated by Harry Zohn. New York: Schoken, 1968.

Carby, Hazel V. *Race Men*. Cambridge: Harvard University Press, 1998.

Cone, James. *A Black Theology of Liberation*. Second edition. Maryknoll NY: Orbis, 1986.

Du Bois, W. E. B. *Dark Princess*. Jackson: University of Mississippi Press, 1995.

———. *The Oxford W. E. B. Du Bois Reader*. Edited by Eric J. Sundquist. New York: Oxford University Press, 1996.

———. *Dusk of Dawn: An Essay toward an Autobiography of a Race Concept*. New Brunswick NJ: Transaction, 1995.

Lewis, David Levering. *W. E. B. Du Bois: Biography of a Race, 1868–1919*. New York: Holt, 1993.

Moses, Wilson Jeremiah. *Black Messiahs and Uncle Toms: Social and Literary Manipulations of a Religious Myth*. Revised edition. University Park: Pennsylvania State Press, 1993.

Robinson, Cedric J. *The Terms of Order: Political Science and the Myth of Leadership*. Albany: SUNY Press, 1980.

Robinson, Cedric J. *An Anthropology of Marxism*. Aldershot UK: Ashgate, 2001.

Sundquist, Eric J. *To Wake the Nations: Race in the Making of American Literature*. Cambridge: Belknap Press, 1993.

Upchurch, Hal. "A Study Guide to Psalms 23."
    <http://tenderbytes.net/hal/23dpsalm/ study11.htm> (28 February
    2002).

Rapporteur's Commentary

Charles H. Long

The French term *rapporteur* carries the following connotations: talebearer, taleteller, reporter, recorder. It is clear that the term is closely related to the other French word *rapporter*, which carries a wider range of meanings; these include: to restore or restitute, to relate, to retrieve, to yield, to tell tales. In addition, there is the African-American colloquialism, rapping. Rapping describes storytelling in an existential situation where the mode of telling carries the meaning of truth and authenticity. During the Civil Rights movement, one famous activist was known as "Rap" Brown; Malcolm X was also called a great rapper. My commentary combines elements of all these meanings.

I. Introduction

W. E. B. Du Bois was born 23 February 1868 in Great Barrington, Massachusetts; he died 27 August 1963 in Accra, Ghana. He was born during the Reconstruction era in the South. His death was reported at the March on Washington, 28 August 1963, where Martin Luther King, Jr. gave his "I Have a Dream" speech. My life and that of Du Bois's overlapped. When I graduated in 1947 from Dunbar Junior College in Little Rock, Arkansas, Du Bois served as the commencement speaker. As class president I had the honor of escorting him two blocks from the bed and breakfast where he resided during his stay in Little Rock to the junior college. I walked with him in admiring awe, both of us attempting to make small talk.

His address to these African-American working-class parents and their friends was entitled "The Principle of Extra-Territoriality in the Charter of the League of Nations." For some reason, the title is all I remember of this address; I don't remember a single other word. This incident needs a bit more deciphering. For example, why would a person of Du Bois's preeminence address a small junior college in Little Rock, Arkansas? And why would he stay in a bed and breakfast instead of a downtown hotel? Finally, why would he speak to this audience in such a highly sophisticated way? In the first instance, it should be made clear that among African-American communities and schools during this era, Du Bois was a household name. We, the members of the senior class, chose him unanimously as our speaker. We knew a great deal about his thought and we knew that our high school and junior college had a liberal arts curriculum because our parents were armed with Du Bois's philosophy when the first high school for African Americans was founded in Little Rock.

Obviously, Du Bois was staying in a black home because he was not permitted to stay in any hotel in the city. Why the particular lecture? This was typical of Du Bois; he did not abide fools easily and he never talked down to an audience. He felt that the content of his address was knowledge black folk needed to know. At this time he was engaged in petitioning the United Nations on behalf of human rights for African Americans. In a very short time, his colleague, Ralph Bunche, an African-American official of the United Nations, would draw upon elements of this charter in negotiations that would lead to the creation of the state of Israel.

II. Du Bois as Public Intellectual: Context, Polemics, and Characterizations

I mention this personal incident for two reasons. I should like for us to recall the important and tremendous public role Du Bois played in the life of African-American communities from the end of World War I until his death; none of the papers touch upon this aspect of his career. The body of his written texts is considerable; he was the intellectual par excellence and probably the exemplar of all African-American intellectuals. He was not, however, the kind of scholar who simply sat in his university study and wrote books. He served for varying periods of time on the faculties of Fisk and Wilberforce Universities, the University of Pennsylvania, and Atlanta University. Correlative with his academic responsibilities he was a major participant in all of the movements related to the situation of African Americans in the United States, extending from the Niagara Movement through the NAACP to the Civil Rights Movement of the 1960s. He lived during a turbulent period of American history that was especially arduous for African Americans. This period covered, among other events, the resurgence of the Ku Klux Klan, the Elaine Arkansas Share Croppers Riot of 1919, the Great Depression, the First and Second World Wars, the struggle over the League of Nations, and the creation of the United Nations. He lived for almost a century and there was hardly a significant event that had to do with peoples of color, the situation of workers, or the problematics of imperialism or colonialism that he did not reflect upon in writing and/or participate in personally. He was, indeed, an authentic public intellectual!

One can not deny the influence of Du Bois's Harvard teachers or his German professors on the formation of his thought but neither should one forget that he also had brilliant interlocutors and adversaries in the African-American community—not only Booker T. Washington but also Alexander Crummel, George Schulyer, Chandler Owen, A. Philip Randolph, and the editors of the *Messenger*. Du Bois was best known among the masses through his editorship of the *Crisis*, but even this highly influential role was marked by tension and strife with the board of the NAACP. In addition, the wide correspondence Du Bois carried on throughout his life shows that he was in touch with ordinary people, world leaders, poets, scholars, and a wide range of persons from every background and persuasion.[1] Through his organization of the several Pan-African conferences as well as his many trips to Europe and other parts of the world, he met an array of scholars, heads of state, leaders, and intellectuals from almost every part of the globe.

None of the papers in this volume address these dimensions of his life and thought. In my comments I shall bring the atmosphere and overtones of this context to bear on my remarks about the papers. In other words, Du Bois was not just another African-American intellectual. While he presents to the academic community much food for thought, we should not forget that the major academic institutions of this country paid little or no attention to him during his very long career.

Mary Keller, in her introduction, gives us a general survey of the papers contained in this volume. For my part, I shall, on the basis of these same papers, set forth another general interpretation of Du Bois's work.

III. The Dual Styles of Du Bois's Intellectual Orientation

---

[1] See the *Correspondence of W. E. B. Du Bois 1877–1963*, ed. Herbert Aptheker, 3 vols. (Amherst: University of Massachusetts Press, 1973), and the archival guide to his papers, at the University of Massachusetts, *The Papers of W. E. B. Du Bois*, ed. Robert W. McDonnell, Microfilming Corporation of America, 1981.

It is clear to anyone who has minimal knowledge of Du Bois that all of his work—his scholarly monographs, articles, correspondence, speeches, novels, novellas, and pageants—all of his productions express a distinctive style. This style was equally a characteristic of his life as a totality. Dwight W. Blight raises the issue of style as it relates to historical methodology in Du Bois's work.[2] Following Arnold Rampersad, Blight argues that Du Bois changed his historical methodology from one of scientific empiricism to that of poetic sensibility. Blight makes the case that this can be seen in his classic work *The Souls of Black Folk*, which was published in 1903 and expressed in a full-blown manner in 1935 in *Black Reconstruction in America*. In the final chapter of his later work, "The Propaganda of History," Du Bois reveals in an explicit manner his historical methodology. I think that more is involved in Blight's commentary than the issue of historical methodology. The notion of poetic sensibility is revelatory not only of much of his work but the very style of Du Bois's career and vocation. While we may point to certain persons and ideas that influenced him—which I will discuss later on—the poetic sensibility was probably a given predilection. Blight notes this in Du Bois's commencement address at Harvard in 1890. The address, "Jefferson Davis as a Representative of Civilization," already expressed a poetic, discerning, critical, and ironic style that can be recognized in most of his work.

It will be my contention that we might be able to understand the meaning of Du Bois's life and work by seeing how he carried through a kind of hermeneutical methodology that he applied throughout his career to create another meaning of the modern world. This alternative meaning was not simply a polemic against reigning interpretations; it was equally and most profoundly the creation of a new foundation and context for the meaning of the modern. From this perspective, I should like to mention two sources that might have enhanced this orientation to his work; both of them emerged from his experience as a student in Germany. I am not dismissing nor ignoring Du Bois's education at Fisk and Harvard nor the influence of

---

[2] David W. Blight, "W. E. B. Du Bois and the Struggle for American Historical Memory," in *History & Memory in African American Culture*, ed. Genevieve Fabre and Robert O'Malley (New York/Oxford: Oxford University Press, 1994) 45–71.

his many friends and associates; I am rather suggesting that all these influences began to form a structure out of his experience in Germany.[3]

In the first instance I point to the influence of the German economist Gustav von Schmoller. At the time of Du Bois's stay in Germany, Schmoller was Germany's leading economist. He was Du Bois's major professor, under whom he prepared a thesis, *"Die Gross und Klein Betrieb des Ackerbach, in der Sudstaaten der Vereinigsten Staaten,* 1840–90" ("The Large and Small-Scale Management of Agriculture in the Southern United States, 1840–1890"). Had he been allowed another year in Germany, he would have extended this thesis, with Professor Schmoller's approval, into a doctoral dissertation under his directorship. In addition, Schmoller wrote letters on Du Bois's behalf requesting that the directors of the Slater Fund extend his stay in Germany to complete the doctoral. Schmoller even went so far as to request from the administration of the University of Berlin that they waive the residency requirements so that Du Bois might receive the doctorate.[4]

Gustav von Schmoller was not only a leading economist and intellectual benefactor to Du Bois; he was at that time the most prominent anti-mercantilist economist in Europe. Known as the leader of the "Younger Historical School," he believed in the production and cultural impact of local industries on the total economic system. It is clear that his influence had an effect upon Du Bois. This can be seen in the thesis and planned doctoral dissertation Du Bois wanted to complete with him.[5] Insights from this orientation in economics can be seen in the *Philadelphia Negro* and the studies Du Bois undertook at Atlanta University. So, it was not so much an abandonment of a certain scientific empiricism but rather whether the studies dealt with specific concrete data of communities or the more abstract data of the market. Mercantile economics tended to understand certain empirical forms of data in terms of the 'logic' of trade and the market rather

---

[3] See Francis L. Broderick, "The Academic Training of W. E. B. Du Bois," *Journal of Negro Education*, 27/1 (Winter 1958): 10–16, and, by the same author, "German Influence on the Scholarship of W. E. B. Du Bois," *Phylon*, First Quarter/2 (Spring 1958): 367–71.

[4] See *Correspondence*, ed. Aptheker, 1:23–28.

[5] It is interesting to note that Fernand Braudel also derived interesting insights from Gustav Schmoller's method; see especially his discussions of demographies, regional industries, and everyday life in *Civilization and Capitalism*, 3 vols., trans. Sian Reynolds (New York: Harper & Row, 1979).

than taking the local and empirical economics as a basis for economic theory.

The impact of Wilhelm Dilthey is more difficult to assess since Du Bois's correspondence makes no prominent mention of Dilthey. We are thus dealing with a great deal of conjecture and speculation but with a more than likely probability of Dilthey's influence. We do know that Du Bois sat in Dilthey's lectures during the second semester in 1893. Dilthey was a pivotal figure in the development of a general hermeneutics for understanding the distinctively human in life. Epistemology from this point of view made a fundamental distinction between the natural and the human sciences. In other words, Dilthey specified the "human" as a distinct and irreducible phenomenon. The human sciences should not be understood in terms of categories extrinsic to it but from intrinsic and inherent categories derived from human life itself.[6] In addition, Dilthey was the philosopher of poetic sensibility par excellence.[7] For Dilthey, poetry and the poetic imagination are essential epistemological tools for the decipherment of human experience as well as its primary forms of expression.

Du Bois's life and work thus expresses two fundamental orientations. It took an intellectual, aesthetic as well as practical feat to hold these two modes together in a single interpretive unity. I shall discuss the papers in this volume from this perspective.

I see two major foci in these papers. In the first instance, there is an emphasis on the experience, expressions, and situation of African Americans in the United States. This concern is interrelated with the second concern: Africa, past and present. It is by means of Africa that Du Bois related to the international order of the world through people of color who have had to undergo oppression, colonialism, and imperialism—the terrors of modernity.

---

[6] Princeton University Press has undertaken the translation of the *Selected Works* of Wilhelm Dilthey. The following have been published: *Introduction to the Human Sciences, Problems of the Human Sciences, Foundations of the Human Sciences, Hermeneutics and the Rise of Historical Consciousness, Poetry and Experience,* and *Philosophy and Life.*

[7] Note that vol. 5 of the translated collected works published by Princeton University Press is entitled *Poetry and Experience.*

IV. Du Bois and the African-American Situation

For purposes of this commentary I shall define the two major orientations of African Americans and Africa by two essays: Carole Stewart's "Challenging Liberal Justice: The Talented Tenth Revisited" to frame the former orientation and for the latter David Chidester's "Religious Animals, Refuge of the Gods, and the Spirit of Revolt: W. E. B. Du Bois's Representations of Indigenous African Religion." These essays establish foci, specifying two broad kinds of data but not poles or extremes. Both sources of data demonstrate Du Bois's employment of poetic sensibility on the one hand and historical social scientific methodology on the other. The remaining essays provide a deciphering mode, mediating between the two broad sources of data and methods.

Carole Stewart's essay, in undertaking a critical examination of Du Bois's notion of the "talented tenth," provides us at the same time with new and original understandings of his most well known text, *Souls of Black Folk*. It is not so much that she makes this notion understandable and plausible but the fact that her analysis of *Souls* enables a more complete view of Du Bois's poetic and pragmatic senses of interpretation, especially as applied to the situation of African Americans. In the first instance, the notion of the "talented tenth" enables us to understand Du Bois's own role in the struggle of the masses of African Americans recently emancipated from enslavement. I think that this is important, for too often intellectual leaders arise espousing various ideologies for the masses but never explain their own role or the legitimacy of their knowledge as it relates to the masses. In too many cases, these leaders' authority was not gained from those they have chosen to lead but from outside authorities, whether malevolent or benign. Du Bois makes it clear that he is not of the masses; he is, in fact and indeed, an intellectual with poetic sensibilities but he has thrown his lot with the masses *as a person and an intellectual!* The sources of his thought and inspiration emerge from serious contemplation of their common situation in life.

This view is directly related to the familiar sentence that begins chapter 2 of *Souls*: "The problem of the twentieth century is the problem of the color line—the relation of the darker to the lighter races of men in Asia and Africa, in America and the islands of the sea." While in chapter one Du Bois gives us a poetic rendering of the situation of African Americans, in chapter two he shows how this issue entails international ramifications. Stewart's essay makes clear that Du Bois did not wish for African Americans to diminish their meaning in the world by succumbing to either the temptation of the American version of the Protestant work ethic on the one hand, as represented by Booker T. Washington, or on the other hand to the civilizing mission of Christianity, as seen in Alexander Crummel. Stewart's critical discussions of Washington and especially Crummel are central to her understanding of Du Bois's meaning of the "talented tenth." It is not the case that Du Bois is simply in opposition either to the Protestant work ethic or to Christianity and civilization per se. Du Bois himself makes use of Christian rhetoric and symbolism throughout his works and recognizes the importance of the work ethic as a discipline for those who have so recently been freed from slavery. In setting forth the notion of the talented tenth and defining a role for himself, Du Bois already anticipated the important study published some twenty years later by Florain Znaniecki, *The Social Role of the Man of Knowledge*.

Stewart shows how Du Bois's *Souls* in its critical reflections is designed to engage and enhance the meaning of African Americans in the United States as a basis for action. Yet at the same time Du Bois redefines the field or arena of action. Stewart states, "Du Bois...redefines the 'meaning of progress' throughout his work; ...for Du Bois, the slaves manifested the negative truth of the 'meaning of progress,' and, to be sure, invoked fear in the hearts of those who had so deeply imbibed theories of racial hierarchies that coincided with a white exceptionalist work ethic.". The situation of the African Americans in the United States is one of the consequences of slavery; as Stewart would have it, "The cross-cultural meetings that occurred during the slave trade and the 'discovery' of different worlds promise a form of religion, a form of Christianity 'that would undergo characteristic change[s] when [it] entered the mouth of the slave.'"

In making her argument against an elitism in Du Bois's notion of the talented tenth, Stewart has recourse to the notion of "the public" as a necessary and essential meaning for any notion of a democratic participatory society. She speaks of "public forums," "public worlds," and "public spheres," and lastly she refers to the Spirituals as "a specific example of public space, the aesthetic and performative space he has in mind as the 'truth' of American Democracy." This is an important argument, for it defines an operative and material modality for the meaning of a political polity. In other words, the meaning of power of any kind must also define a locus. As a matter of fact, the meaning and effect of any power is due to a great extent to its locus, its form of manifestation.

The issues of power, faith, and messianism are brought to the fore in Marta Brunner's essay "The Most Hopeless of Deaths...Is the Death of Faith: Messianic Faith in the Racial Politics of W. E. B. Du Bois." Brunner begins with a query concerning human beings as divine agents. This query presupposes a binary with the human on one side and the divine as the not-human on the other. While the statement of the issue often appears in this form, even this binary rests upon the fact that any recognition of the divine must be in the human realm. From the Greek thinker Euhemerus (third century BCE), who put forth the notion that the gods of Greek mythology were in fact deified humans; through the early Christian councils' affirmation that Jesus of Nazereth was totally human yet equally and simultaneously totally divine; and the veneration of the prophet Muhammad, who is only human yet receives special status and veneration; to Carlyle's *Heroes and Hero Worship*, various traditions in the Western world have pondered the relationship of some kind of *otherness* of the powers manifested in the world. Of course, this seems to be an issue in all cultures but I have limited my attention to the Western tradition. In other words, the issue Brunner raises is not so new or so recent. I feel that this essay might have worked itself out in a different manner had a more precise distinction been made between belief on the one hand and faith on the other. In no religious tradition where the term "faith" looms large has it ever been simply identical with belief, though at times faith might be understood as belief while still maintaining its own unique meaning. There is a meaning of faith which, though it happens to be stated in one religious tradition, would cover its meaning in the religious traditions of Judaism, Islam, and Buddhism. This meaning might equally be used in secular contexts. I refer to the definition of faith given in Hebrews 11:1 of the Christian Bible: "Faith is the assurance of things hoped for, the conviction of things not seen." This is a succinct, precise, and elegant definition. It is comforting , critical, and anticipatory. Hope is not simply a futuristic desire for things to get better but a critical stance that allows one to live in an uncaring world without succumbing to its temptations, blandishments, or terrors. The full manifestation of profound change in the present world is carried in the notion of living in terms of "things not seen." Now this meaning of faith is not a belief but a lived experience, the very manner in which one carries on his or her life.

The notion of faith as belief can be one aspect of the meaning of faith as a "credo," which as a part of worshiping community makes a statement that specifies the power or gods to which a community commits itself. The notion of faith as synonymous with belief became popular during the Enlightenment. The Enlightenment in championing its new critical reason subjected all religion to rational criticism and thus religious belief, from the point of view of the Enlightenment, was non-rational or irrational. What is interesting about Marta Brunner's essay is that she is asking the question of faith from the side of one of history's non-religious modes of thought. She imputes the implication of this kind of issue to Du Bois when she states, "For his part, Du Bois seems torn between calling for faith in a transcendent source (like a messiah figure or apocalyptic miracle) and faith in a non-transcendent source (like human action or economic strategies)." She then suggests that Cedric Robinson's idea of men and women as divine agents might resolve this tension. First of all, this task is not as simple as one might think. If men and women are to be truly and efficaciously divine, we are opening up the same issue that arose in the early councils of the Christian Church where every permutation of that kind of equation was explored. More seriously, if one looks at the modern world, a world that defined Du Bois's point of view, it revealed that most colored people on the globe had and were being exploited, dehumanized, and oppressed; it was a world that could be too neatly divided into the realm of the oppressed and that of the oppressors. Given this enormous fact, the real issue might have to do with the viability of the notion of the human mode of being itself as capable of any benevolent or ameliorative actions—a variation of the problem of theodicy.

What must be understood is that since the creation of the Atlantic World countless millions of people have had to undergo new forms of oppression. To be sure, tragedy and evil did not originate with the commencement of the Atlantic World. It was, however, the Atlantic World that symbolized and emphasized the sufficiency of human agency, the triumph of reason, and the age of democracy, freedom, and human rights. This is the same world Du Bois addressed in his first book on the Atlantic slave trade, and he continued to address the evils that were perpetually obscured through the rhetorical styles of human agency. From the point of view of those who have undergone the terror brought about in history, the issue of human agency is at least as ambiguous as that of transcendent orientations. It is for this reason that I do not think the issue posed by Du Bois is as clear-cut as that stated by Brunner. One must take into account that the oppressed of the world do not experience their time and space in the

same modes as those who dominate. They have other qualities and
ingredients in their traditions that have enabled them to survive and
withstand the onslaught upon their lives' meaning. Du Bois does not dismiss
these elements out of hand. Indeed, he attempts to retrieve, refocus, and
reinterpret these traditions to keep the *otherness* of *an-other* world open for
them. This is precisely the point Stewart makes in examining Du Bois's
admonition of succumbing to either the Protestant work ethic or a
triumphant civilizing Christianity. Du Bois respected those elements that
allowed the enslaved to endure and survive and he praises them as possible
openings to a new meaning of a human world. The significance and
understanding of patience should be seen in this context.

As an aside, it should be noted that messianic and apocalyptic modes
have not been limited to the dominated oppressed in the modern period.
These forms may have been interpolated into the modernizing process itself.
It is difficult to deny the kind of apocalyptic hope that feeds revolutionary
action or that some essential meanings of the "American Dream" thrive on
certain paradisal symbols and rhetoric. By and large the notions of
messianism, apocalypticism, and eschatology have been translated into the
secular language of utopia and utopianisms.[8] "Utopia" can literally be
translated as "no place" or a place that does not yet exist.

Let me now turn to Rodney C. Roberts's essay, "Rectificatory Justice
and the Philosophy of W. E. B. Du Bois." Roberts places the issue of
"reparations" within the philosophical/legal structure of rectificatory justice.
There is some truth to the fact that scholars have not been engaged with the
issue of reparations/rectification but this may be changing. In 2002 I
attended a three-day conference, "Legacy of Slavery: Unequal Exchange,"
sponsored by the Center for Black Studies at the University of California,
Santa Barbara. This was a very serious conference, attracting scholars of the
caliber of Joseph Inikori, Howard Dodson, Gerald Horne, Leon Litwack,
and Robert Hill among others. A quite stellar group of scholars dealt with
the issue of reparations from a variety of theoretical and practical points of
view. To partially confirm Roberts, however, no one among this
distinguished array of scholars presented a philosophical/legal analysis of the
issue.

---

[8] For a discussion of the range of utopias and utopian thought, see Frank E. Manuel,
ed., *Utopia and Utopian Thought: A Timely Appraisal* (Beacon Press: Boston, 1966).

Roberts clarifies the proverbial "40 acres and a mule" mantra that has become the refrain of many reparations discussions. Indeed, he makes it clear that the United States government has never made any promises to former slaves or their progeny in recognition of their former enslavement. Roberts admits that Du Bois did not in his long career make a specific emphasis on rectification or reparations. He then, nevertheless, involves Du Bois in the issue through other statements that relate to reparations. I think Roberts's argument at this point is highly tendentious. Obviously, colonialism and imperialism imply an unjust order that should be rectified, but this does not mean that Roberts's theory—or, for that matter, any particular theory of rectification—is the proper way to address the issues. There are many cases involving the need for justice as reparations; the oppressed parties have been voided of their labor and their land and subjected to forced migrations. While all may fall under a general theory of rectification, I would think that the emendations to any general philosophical/legal theory should be informed by the specific historical context of the injustice and the modes for its relief. This would speak in a direct manner about the location and tradition of oppression and would enable a general theory to take empirical specificities into account.

What is most intriguing in Roberts's theory is the emphasis he makes on the need for apology in any theory of rectification. He says, "...rectification calls for an apology. Since restoration and compensation can only address unjust losses, an apology is necessary in order to effect rectification because it is the apology that addresses the matter of righting the wrong of an injustice. *What makes an injustice* wrong *is the lack of respect shown when one's rights are violated. Hence the righting of the wrong is accomplished by way of an apology, i.e., an acknowledgment of wrongdoing that includes the reaffirmation that those who suffered the injustice have moral standing*" (emphasis added). I think that this is immensely important, for while not denying or rejecting compensation of a monetary or material kind, it moves the issue beyond that of a simple contractual compensation to an ethical and moral situation, to the recognition of rights and wrongs and ultimately to the definition and meaning of human persons.

From my perspective, I feel that our present government, given the choice, would rather expend billions of dollars in compensation than make an apology. To make an apology would mean that this country would be forced to come to terms with its past—with slavery and all its ramifications. The primary fact of slavery is the enslavement of African persons in the

United States; this enslavement was an institution made legal by a democratic constitution. The implications of this institution loom large even in areas not so directly related to slavery, for example, the electoral college that came to the fore in the last presidential election or the use of the Fourteenth Amendment to the Constitution by the United States Supreme Court to decide the case of whether a state has the right to regulate slaughterhouses. The Slaughterhouse Case then turned in a rather weird and eerie manner to deny the rights of the very freed slaves it was promulgated to enhance.[9]

I now turn to Stephen Andrews's "Toward a Synaesthetics of Soul: W. E. B. Du Bois and the Teleology of Race." This essay takes as its point of departure the musicals epigraphs that begin each chapter of *Souls*. Andrews sees this format as a peculiar way in which Du Bois interrupts and reclaims the typographical style of the written word through the interpolation of music into the text. He traces this manner of formatting back to William James's notion of "transitivity"; transitivity, he says, appears in the text of *Souls* as the fluid nexus of felt relations evoked by the text. In *Souls*, Du Bois introduces a novel way of dealing with the protocols and codes of "reading race" that were dominant at the beginning of the twentieth century. Andrews states, "Du Bois claims for black music the privileged typographical space usually reserved for the teleological finesses of the written word." Andrews spends a good deal of time showing the influence and revision of Jamesian principles in this work of Du Bois. He draws heavily on the work of Ross Posnock, Shamoon Zamir, and Eric Sundquist, the most prominent *en vogue* interpreters of Du Bois. No one can deny the feasibility and plausibility of his interpretations of Du Bois in these terms. I do think, however, that an overemphasis along these lines could lead to a serious case of misplaced concreteness.

What is in danger of being lost in the kind of emphasis put forth by Andrews is the fact that the text of *Souls* exudes meanings of black culture that are hardly mentioned in Andrews's essay. One must ask, "Who kept this text alive for almost a century?" Surely it was not read as an addendum to

---

[9] For a discussion of slavery in the forming of the Constitution, see Paul Finkelman, *An Imperfect Union: Slavery, Federalism, and Comity* (Chapel Hill: University of North Carolina Press, 1981). Rayford W. Logan, in *The Betrayal of the Negro from Rutherford B. Hayes to Woodrow Wilson* (New York: Collier Books, encl. ed., 1965) 106ff, gives a precis of the Slaughterhouse Cases.

James's or G. W. F. Hegel's philosophical works. Indeed, probably the name "Du Bois" itself was not known in respectable academic circles in the United States, apart from all black universities, before, let us say, 1975, and I am being a bit generous here. In other words, this was a text written for all Americans but understood, appreciated, and kept alive by black communities. I would furthermore insist that the form and style of the text, while peculiar in the manner Andrews describes, is not completely due to the influence of William James. This mode of stylization and formatting may have been suggested by the rhythms, styles, and manners of the black communities with which Du Bois was familiar. As a matter of fact, while William James may be credited with inventing the philosophical orientation termed Pragmatism, the experimental, improvisational style began among African people in this country almost from the very beginning of their enslavement.

Would not it be closer to home, for example, to attribute the meaning and style of fluidity to the felt and lived memories in the black communities of the Atlantic slave trade and the deep and traumatic impression of "those waters" in the cultures of black people? "The watery passage of the Atlantic, that fearsome journey, that cataclysm of modernity, has served as mnemonic structure evoking a memory that forms the disjunctive and involuntary presence of these Africans in the Atlantic world...One hears the refrain in Negro Spirituals such as "Wade in the Water," "Deep River," or "Roll, Jordan Roll" and in Langston Hughes poem, "The Negro Speaks of Rivers."[10] Andrews finds the sources for Du Bois's use of the "veil" in the Jamesian notion of "penumbra." This may be the case, though the meaning of the caul and the veil are well documented in African-American folklore and colloquial language. Yvonne Chireau, in discussing the topic of anomalous births, has this to say: "Many supernatural specialists were 'born' with the 'gift'—marked, or chosen, at the start of their lives...Being born with a caul, the amniotic veil covering the face of the newly delivered infant, was interpreted as evidence that one was gifted with enhanced insight into the invisible realm. Another well-known belief held that the seventh child of a seventh son or daughter would enjoy an auspicious spiritual heritage. 'If

---

[10] See Charles H. Long, "Passage and Prayer," in *The Courage to Hope*, ed. Quinton H. Dixon and Cornel West (Boston: Beacon Press, 1999). For a comprehensive historical and analytical study of the spirituals, see John Lovell, Jr., *Black Song: The Forge and the Flame* (New York: MacMillan Company, 1972).

you are a double-sighted person and can see ghosts, if you happen to have been born on Christmas Day, or are a seventh son, you are born for magic,' claimed one folklorist."[11] One should also look to the black tradition of preaching and sermons. We know that Du Bois heard more than his share of black sermons and preaching. This tradition portrays a great deal of what Andrews calls synaesthesia, often combining prose, poetry, song, movement, and dance in the performative art of preaching.[12]

I am not, of course, suggesting that the only valid interpretation of Du Bois is from within the African-American cultural experience. Such an interpretation would not be authentic to Du Bois's life nor work; I have already mentioned the influence of Gustav von Schmoller and Wilhelm Dilthey and I shall later continue the discussion regarding Dilthey. I am saying, however, that this same authenticity requires that we not neglect the importance of African Americans and the African-American experience as powerful and determining influences in his life and work. While one can point to the fact that Du Bois might have enjoyed some privileges that the masses of other black persons in the country did not, he still shared and was subjected to those daily discriminations and humiliations that were the common lot of all African Americans in the United States. It is a mark of his genius that he not only lived through these experiences but critically appropriated his experience within the context of the American experience and its history into novel recombinations of meanings and orientations. With intellect and imagination he made use of all of his resources, those derived from being an African American in America as well as his academic experiences at Fisk, Wilberforce, Atlanta University, Harvard, and the University of Berlin; Du Bois was never ashamed of intellectual meaning and rigor but the resources of his life should not be limited to the influences of the history of ideas.

It is clear that Du Bois did not trust those traditions and institutions that demeaned African persons in the creation of the Atlantic world. As long as those institutions and traditions reigned, there was slim hope that a world of democratic freedom would emerge where human beings would be treated

---

[11] Yvonne Chireau, *Black Magic, Religion and the African American Conjuring Tradition* (Los Angeles: University of California Press, 2003) 23.

[12] For African American preaching and sermons, see Dolan Hubbard, *The Sermon and the African American Literary Imagination* (Columbia: University of Missouri Press, 1994), and Bruce Rosenburg, *The Art of the American Folk Preacher* (New York: Oxford University Press, 1971). Hubbard's text carries a comprehensive bibliography.

with justice and fairness. Any notion of progress coming from these traditions would be synonymous with the deprivation of others. Having rejected the meaning of work under the sign of the Protestant work ethic and the civilizing mission under the aegis of a moralizing and triumphal Christianity, Du Bois turned to a reinterpretation of the modern world as the basis for a new orientation and alternative that might form the cultural structures of a viable future. Taking his stance within the tradition of enslaved Africans in the United States, Du Bois undertook a critical and creative reappraisal of the range of alternative human options. It is at this juncture that we see the confluence of his concern with the continent of Africa and Pan-Africanism.

V. Du Bois's Pan-Africanism

Three essays take up the subject of Africanism and Pan-Africanism. They are Robin Law's "Du Bois as Pioneer of African History: A Reassessment of the Negro"; Jemima Pierre and Jesse Weaver Shipley's "The Intellectual and Pragmatic Legacy of Du Bois's Pan-Africanism in Contemporary Ghana"; and David Chidester's "Religious Animals, Refuge of the Gods, and the Spirit of Revolt: W. E. B. Du Bois's Representations of Indigenous African Religion." Robin Law concentrates on Du Bois's early study of 1915, *The Negro*; this text was revised and appeared under the title *The World and Africa* in 1947. The other two essays examine all of the major works on Africa by Du Bois, including *The Negro* (1915); *Africa, Its Geography, People, and Products* (1930); *Africa—Its Place in Modern History*, (1930); *Black Folk Then and Now*, (1939); *The World and Africa*, (1947); and finally the statement prepared for his *Encyclopedia of Africa*, "Africa: An Essay Toward a History of the Continent of Africa and Its Inhabitants" (1963).

In looking back on Du Bois's text of 1915, Robin Law is surprised that later scholars who created the discipline of African history, himself included, paid so little attention to the work of Du Bois. Du Bois was known by his activities devoted to Pan-Africanism and to the issue of the race problem in the United States. Given that the discipline of African history was not established until the 1950s, Law finds Du Bois's ordering of history along the lines of a cultural geography to be remarkably cogent. Now, to be sure, Du Bois's interest in African history had to do with his larger vision; it is clear that through the introduction of the internal history of Africa he is beginning a new kind of world history.

This initial foray into African history is quite remarkable, for though there were not many general texts dealing with this subject matter and Du Bois did not carry on original research himself, he was able to pick out William Winwood Reade's *Martyrdom of Man* and Leo Frobenius's *Und Afrika Sprach*, translated into English in 1913 as *The Voice of Africa*.

A great deal of the meaning of Africa within a universal history has followed Hegel's pronouncement in his *Philosophy of History*, where Hegel set forth his derogatory statements concerning Africa. Among other things Hegel said, 'For it [Africa] is no historical part of World; it has no movement or development to exhibit...What we properly understand by Africa, is the Unhistorical, Undeveloped Spirit, still involved in the conditions of mere nature, and which had to be presented here only as on the threshold of World's History.'[13] While many in the United States would deny Hegel's explicit statement, they were willing to accept the implications of his derogatory statements about Africa and its need for "civilization" either from the point of view of a missionizing Christianity or some notion of evolutionary progress. Hegel's statement seems dictated by the normative value accorded "the West" in most formulations of world history. Du Bois sensed that a new kind of temporality might allow another structure of world history.

Shipley and Pierre show in their essay how Du Bois's interest in Africa took on practical forms; this was accomplished through the several Pan-African Conferences held in Europe between 1919 and 1945. I found two points very important in this paper: first of all, through a series of descriptions the authors enable us to understand the ranges of meaning connoted by the term "Pan-Africanism" and secondly, the authors discuss the significance of the political role Pan-Africanism played in the establishment and history of the state of Ghana. They demonstrate how the several meanings of Pan-Africanism are cumulative. Following J. L. Matory's description of Pan-Africanism as a "live Afro-Atlantic dialogue...that has continued long beyond the end of slavery," they add that "such Pan-African connections and practices ultimately have ramifications that extend beyond intellectual dialogue and explicit political movements; they have produced significant transformations of daily life, symbols, and practices on *both* sides of the Atlantic." Second, the authors present their

---

[13] G.W.F. Hegel, *The Philosophy of History*, (Dover Publishing Co., New York, 1956) 93,99.

own understanding of Du Bois's meaning of the term: "As Du Bois made clear, both in his scholarship and through his political and practical activities, Pan-Africanism is a broadly conceived set of intellectual, political, economic, cultural, and spiritual meanings and practices. It is a movement that is structured by the history of global racial inequality—beginning with the slave trade, the development of global commerce, colonialism, and capitalist expansion—but is certainly not reducible to it."

Pierre and Shipley demonstrate the plausibility of seeing the five Pan-African Conferences between 1919 and 1945, the various African cultural conferences, and Du Bois's movement to Ghana and his collaboration with the Ghanaian government as all part of the same movement. Thus we are able to trace a kind of morphology from Pan-Africanism as an intellectual-cultural orienation to its institutionalization in a state formation symbolized by Du Bois's residence in Ghana and the projected *Encyclopedia of Africa* that was to be published there under his aegis. Robin Law and other African historians had overlooked Du Bois's early interest in African history because they had classified him and his work as concerned only with African Americans in the United States. Du Bois, almost from the very beginning, never separated the situation of African Americans in the United States from the issues and problems of Africa and never considered Africa marginal to world history.

The authors address the fortunes of Pan-Africanism once it became part and parcel of a newly independent African state. In the early days of independence under the influence of president Kwame Nkrumah, Ghana pursued a Pan-African policy aiding and abetting independence from colonialism in other African territories as well as encouraging African Americans to settle and aid in the formation of the Ghanaian state. Nkrumah thus became the practical and symbolic embodiment of Pan-Africanism during this time. Nkrumah's government was overthrown in a military coup in 1966. Since that time a series of military dictatorships have governed the country. Flight lieutenant Rawling came to power in a military coup in 1981, attempting to revive the older Pan-African policies. Given the economic situation of Ghana, any return to these policies had to come to terms with the policies and politics of the International Monetary Fund and other international agencies of global capitalism. Ghana thus raises the practical meaning of Pan-Africanism within the orders of a nation-state.

The end of David Chidester's article raises a similar note. Now, what is surprising here is that Chidester deals explicitly with Du Bois's understanding of African religion and through this discussion implicitly suggests insights into the meaning of Du Bois's own religious propensities. Let me say something about Du Bois's assessment of African religion as reported by Chidester. While Shipley and Pierre bring up organizations such as the International Monetary Fund in relationship to Pan-Africanism, Chidester cites the same organization in relationship to the present expressions of African indigenous religions. Is there some kind of relationship here? Before discussing this possibility, let me turn to Chidester's interesting appraisal of African indigenous religion by Du Bois. Chidester's discussion revolves around three main topics: humanity, divinity, and transatlantic continuity. There is, of course, some ambiguity in this discussion; as Law makes clear in his essay, though Du Bois depended upon secondary sources, his 1915 text *The Negro* was a serious work, a kind of precursor for later works on African history. This does not deny the ideological intent of the work, however; Du Bois wanted to make it clear that Africans had a cultural integrity prior to the advent of colonialism. In other words, they were fully human before becoming enmeshed within the Western world.

One documentation of this humanity is found in Africans' religious expressions, which Du Bois, following the theories of his time, was willing to admit as being fetishism. Instead of seeing fetishism in derogatory terms, however, he viewed it as, to use Chidester's words, a "coherent material philosophy of the spiritual dynamics of life." Now, though he borrowed the notion of fetishism from the literature of his day, in 1915 no prominent interpreter of religion came close to a positive interpretation of fetishism. It is here that Du Bois showed radical independence from the meaning of fetishism by historians of religion and Marxists alike. Since the publication of *Souls*, Du Bois had emphasized the continuity of African religions in the Americas through the forms of obi, voodoo, and Christianity. From this perspective the Negro Church in America is in direct continuity with African religions. Both Law and Chidester mark Du Bois's interpretation of African history and African religion, respectively, in *The Negro* as exemplary. Chidester shows how this portrayal of African religion as fetishism avoided the evolutionary model of the historians of this time as well as the Christian missiologists. Du Bois thus placed African religion within a different kind of history, "Neither a speculative evolutionary history nor a missionary faith history...."

In the revision of *The Negro* published IN 1939 as *Black Folk: Then and Now*, Du Bois drops references to the explorer Kingsley and the missionary Nassau and introduces the Yoruba god, Shango. Shango is a High God, a Supreme Being, and is not the result of the influence of Christian missionaries but an indigenous god of the Yoruba people.[14] Though this new theoretical interest might have been stimulated by the notion of High Gods, it is clear that Du Bois has not followed this up with an interest in new sources of African history in Western languages. By this time several sophisticated works on the precolonial history of Africa were being produced. The interest in Shango is more suited to Du Bois's own project of providing a basis for a Pan-African source of religious and political power. He finds it necessary, therefore, to proclaim Shango not only as this Yoruba god of power but as a god "who soars above the legend of Thor and Jahweh,' thereby transcending the power of the European and Semitic thunder-gods." In his next rendition of African religion, *The World and Africa* (1947), Du Bois's excision of references to fetishism continue; as a matter of fact, Chidester says that he gave limited scope to religion, expanding the role of Shango as the "supreme source of political power, authority, and sovereignty, father of royal rulers, whose 'posterity still have the right to give the country its kings.'" Chidester does not wish to relate Du Bois's changing conceptions of African religion to his biography; I will not follow him in this regard. By 1947, World War II was over and international and domestic maneuvers that would lead to the "Cold War" were being rehearsed. Du Bois, a member of the Cultural and Scientific Conference for World Peace, was involved in various anti-Cold War movements and in groups petitioning the United Nations to make the situation of blacks in the United States an international rather than an internal nation-state policy. In a conference of this organization held in New

---

[14] From the perspective of the history of religions, this discussion of Shango is part of the theory of "primitive High Gods." This phenomenon undercut the evolutionary model in religion that saw a movement from the many to the one, from polytheism to monotheism. In the English-speaking world this notion first attracted attention in Andrew Lang's *The Making of Religion* (London: Longmans, Green and Company, Ltd., 1898). A comprehensive study of this phenomenon is found in Wilhelm Schmidt, *Der Ursprung der Gottesidee* (The Origin of the Idea of God) (Munster: W. Aschendorf, 1926). For a full discussion of High Gods, see chap. 2 of Mircea Eliade, *Patterns in Comparative Religion*, trans. Rosemary Sheed (London and New York: Sheed & Ward, 1958).

York on 27 March 1949, Du Bois made an address that ended with these words:

> I tell you people of America, the dark world is on the move! It wants and will have Freedom, Autonomy, and Equality. It will not be diverted in these fundamental rights by dialectical hair-splitting of political hairs…. Whites may, if they will, arm themselves for suicide, but the vast majority will march over them to freedom!…Race war was not the answer. What we all want is a decent world, where a man does not have to have a white skin to be recognized as a man…where sickness and death are linked to our industrial system…. Peace is not an end. It is the gateway to full and abundant life.[15]

Among his colleagues in this organization were the distinguished Harvard astronomer Harlow Shapley, literary critic F. O. Matthiesen, and acclaimed novelist Norman Mailer. So, even in this post World War II period, where his activity seems to be taken up with exploring the potential of the United Nations and making alliances with intellectuals who were neither African nor African Americans, echoes of the power of the oppressed come through; here I am able to hear echoes of the god Shango, whom Du Bois had evoked a decade earlier.

Following Chidester's outline I would say that Du Bois was, during this phase of his career, concentrating on the translatability of the meanings of Pan-Africanism through the structures of the peace movement and the United Nations. This was not simply a functional or instrumental use of these resources; for Du Bois, peace was not only a precondition for redress, but also called for a radical reassessment of the policies and *raison d'etre* for a democratic society.

VI. Orientation and Beginnings: Interpretations of Religion and the "Religion" of Du Bois

The titles of David Levering Lewis's magisterial two-volume biography are as follows: *W. E. B. Du Bois: Biography of a Race, 1868–1919* and *W. E. B. Du Bois: The Fight for Equality and the American Century, 1919–1963*. The subtitles imply both an identity and a parallelism. To be sure, the meaning and practice of race has gone on for some time before Du Bois's birth but

---

[15] David Levering Lewis, *W. E. B. Du Bois: The Fight for Equality and the American Century, 1919–1963*, vol. 2 (New York: Henry Holt and Company, 2000) 543.

the notion of race as a definition of free persons of African descent begins with the Reconstruction in the South following the Civil War. Du Bois was born in 1868. From his very early years until his death he was a part of every major discussion concerning the nature and destiny of black folk in the United States. One must, therefore, as Lewis's biography suggests, ponder the meaning of his life in relationship to the fortunes of free persons of African descent in the American world. How and where does one begin? The Americans proclaimed their freedom and independence just a century before his birth and the Civil War has just ended. It is the case that neither the Declaration of Independence, the Constitution, nor the Reconstruction seriously undertook a viable political or discursive meaning of freedom for persons of African descent in this land.

American ideology is replete with phrases of freedom and rights but from the beginning, with the Declaration of Independence and the Constitution, "slavery" has been hidden in the patterns of American rhetoric while all the time being practiced and defended. This is highlighted in Rodney Roberts's essay when he speaks of an apology as a basic necessity for any consideration of reparations for the enslavement of African persons in the United States. When I attended the Conference on Reparations in Santa Barbara, California, a new meaning of American history was being enunciated. I thought that even if no material or monetary exchanges were ever made, the discussion of the nature and history of the American Republic that would ensue from the demand for reparations would be invaluable. Strangely enough, very few white persons attended the conference. Reparations were seen as an issue of black people rather than an issue that lay at the very heart of the American Republic. I was afraid that the only way white persons would become interested in the discussion would be to emphasize monetary and material exchanges. Yet I feel that Roberts touched something fundamental when he spoke about an apology. Apology establishes the basis for mutual respect and lays the groundwork for serious public exchange and debate. Even with all the civil rights bills and programs designed for the "uplift of black people," there has been no inclination for the apology that would open the door for serious reassessment.

There are, nevertheless, millions of African people in this land, united by the common past of the legal enslavement of their ancestors under the benign protection of the American Constitution. How does one begin the "biography of a race" out of the negation of freedom and justice and the humiliation of a people? Certain options were presented and the debates, arguments, and tensions associated with Booker T. Washington, Alexander Crummel, and the Niagara movement pointed to certain possible points of departure. Rejecting, as Carole Stewart would have it, the "progressivism" of the Protestant work ethic on the one hand and a Christian civilizing mission on the other, Du Bois opted for a beginning in the very heart of slavery and even earlier in the continent of Africa itself.

Let me turn now to the issue of influence and sources of style and method. In the first instance we must admit that Du Bois's work confronts us with a superior intellect, possessing enormous creative and imaginative capacities. Du Bois's first journey to the South had an impact that remained with him all of his life. I think that this was probably the greatest influence upon his life. It is clear that William James was his favorite professor at Harvard and it is possible to trace specific instances of this influence. One might even say that we can hear echoes of James's "will to believe" in *Souls*, when Du Bois speaks of the double-consciousness of black folk as "two warring ideals in one dark body, *whose dogged strength* keeps it from being torn asunder."[16] There is probably something of the will here but it is not of the type of Jamesian individual will, for the very formulation of Du Bois's double-consciousness expresses the way in which the public nature of slavery and freedom has been internalized within the souls of black folk. Again, we must remember that James defined religion as "...the feelings, acts, and experiences of *individual men in their solitude....*"[17] While Du Bois would share with James the propensity to speak about religion in terms of religious experience rather than the religious institution, they would part company regarding the meaning of the individual and the public as the loci of ultimacy. So while I can see the Jamesian influence in particular insights, I don't think James was ever close to Du Bois's poetic sensibilities.

I feel that it was Du Bois's German experience that enhanced his own personal style and predilections and enabled him to release his intellectual imagination and creativity. Let me return to the influence of Gustav von Schmoller. Schmoller and his school saw economics as historical. As Joseph Schumpeter put it, "He did not call it historical simply, but historico-ethical.

[16] W. E. B. Du Bois, *Souls of Black Folk* (Chicago: A. C. McClurg, 1903; Johnson reprint, New York: Basic Afro-American Reprint Library, 1968) chap. 1, emphasis added.

[17] William James, *The Varieties of Religious Experience*, reprint of original edition published in 1902, Modern Library edition, (Random House, N.Y., n.d.)

The label also carried a different meaning—it was to express protest against the whole imaginary advocacy of the hunt for private profit of which the English 'classics' were supposed to have been guilty."[18] It was from Schmoller that Du Bois probably got a sense that there was a theoretical position for economic analysis that did not lead one to profit-making mercantilist economics and that the specific situation of the modes of production were important in any economic analysis.

Though Du Bois mentions that he sat in Wilhelm Dilthey's seminar, I can find no other reference to their relationship. The reason I believe Dilthey had an influence is because the two men exhibit too many parallels between certain styles. To make this case plausible I shall take the liberty of quoting liberally from Dilthey and sources concerning him.

> For Dilthey, history like philosophy, had to serve the cause of practical reform and regeneration, not merely contemplation…. Dilthey's training and reflection led him to the conviction that neither philosophy nor history, as generally practiced, offered the resources or knowledge which leads to action in the present and the formation of personal social life-values. This negative judgment of prevalent philosophy and history was determinant in his positive conception of a critique of historical reason…. His conviction that "man is not on earth simply to be but to 'act'" disposed him toward a practical activism at odds with the contemplative spirit which dominated the fields of history and philosophy.[19]

In addition to his duties and research as a university professor, Dilthey carried on a crusading journalism contributing to several of the liberal journals, writing reviews and essays on philosophy, literature, historical studies, etc. "His efforts in other areas are so numerous that it must suffice to say simply that Dilthey was anything but a cloistered academic tied down to a narrow specialty."[20] Does this in any way remind you of Du Bois? Allow me to point out another dimension of Dilthey that I think was attractive to

---

[18] Joseph A. Schumpeter, *History of Economic Analysis* (New York/Oxford: Oxford University Press, 1986) 812. Schumpeter carries on quite an extensive discussion of von Schmoller and his theories. A more one-sided and derogatory estimate of von Schmoller can be found in Lionel Robbins, *A History of Economic Thought*, ed. Steven G. Medema and Warren J. Samuels (Princeton: Princeton University Press, 1998).

[19] Michael Ermarth, *The Critique of Historical Reason* (Chicago: University of Chicago Press, 1978) 26–27.

[20] Ibid., 28.

Du Bois—Dilthey's notions of the poet and poetic sensibility as an epistemological probe and orientation:

> A poetics based upon psychology makes possible, above all, the recognition of the *social function of literature*; the feeling of the dignity of the poetic vocation rests upon this recognition.... None of man's historical attitudes can be completely expressed in concepts. The urge to communicate the inexpressible is the source of symbols. Myths grasp the most important relationships of reality from a religious point of view.... In such symbols, the external, distant, and transcendent is always made visible on the level of the lived experience of one's own inner life.... As if by an elemental power, lived experiences are elevated to poetic significance through speech, religion, and mythical thought....[21]

In speaking of the relationship between history, community, and poetry, Dilthey says, "In reality, a *historical situation* contains *a multiplicity of particular facts*.... Their coordination within a given period first constitutes the historical situation.... But the unity of a period and a people that we characterize as the *historical spirit* of an age can only arise from these elements through the *creative power* and self-assurance of a genius.[22]

Allow me to add another link to this chain of plausibility. James and Dilthey read each other's works and James met Dilthey on one of his trips to Germany. Dilthey had on several occasions made use of James's work in psychology though he was at times critical of some of James's formulations. Thus, Du Bois would have been prepared for the kind of psychological epistemology Dilthey employed. What was new was the stylization of the poetic sensibility and its relationship to literature, music, and historical forms, elements missing in James's work.[23]

While I am making the case that there were definite influences from this German sojourn, I am not here speaking of particular ideas or concepts but of a stylization of sensibilities and intellect. David Levering Lewis tells us that during the time of Du Bois's visit, Germany was a "culture in search

---

[21] Wilhelm Dilthey, *Poetry and Experience*, trans. Rudolf A. Makkreel and Frithjof Rodi, vol. 5 of *Selected Works* (Princeton: Princeton University Press, 1985) 168–9, emphasis added.

[22] Dilthey, 162, emphasis added.

[23] See Ermarth, *Critique*, 176, 213–14; Ermarth says that in some circles Dilthey was called the "German William James" (3).

of a nation."[24] This was a very formative period in the young Du Bois and it is my contention that he was able during this "age of miracles" to conceive of an intellectual orientation that combined an empirical historical bent with a poetic and deciphering sensibility. Moreover, this was taking place in the relative freedom far from his land of birth and citizenship; it was here that the vision and vocation of the scholar-intellectual-activist was born in him. It is well for us to note that for a young African-American intellectual, freedom of person and intellect was found away from American shores. Lewis ends chapter 6 ("Lehrjahre") of volume 1 of his biography with this quote: "As the *Wanderjahre* of his Age of Miracles ended with the *Chester's* hawsers being yoked to the pier, Du Bois wrote: 'I dropped suddenly back into "nigger"-hating America.'"[25]

This orientation allowed Du Bois to bring together seemingly contradictory positions into a unity; his poetic sensibility enabled him to deal equally with the empirical and the visionary. This same sensibility operated in a deciphering manner; he turned his attention to heretofore unexamined areas for new forms of knowledge. While he may have been impressed with certain aspects of Hegel's philosophy of history, it is clear that throughout his life he was attempting to give a new structure to the historical record. This entailed bringing Africa into the meaning of a global history, hence his interest in African history. It was not African history simply as a record of the past but as the active meaning of Africans and their descendants throughout the world. In the modern world, Africans in the New World were enslaved and those on the continent were subjected to imperialism and colonialism. The day of Du Bois's death in Ghana completes this symbolism—Martin Luther King, Jr.'s civil rights march for African Americans in the United States, on the one hand, and Du Bois's death in Ghana preparing an *Encyclopedia of Africa*.

It remains for us finally to make an assessment of the understanding of religion and the nature and meaning of religion in the life and work of Du Bois himself. It should be made clear in the first instance that in the main, religion for Du Bois should be seen from the point of view of religious experience rather than religion as the religious institution. This would conform to a tradition of interpretation represented by both James and

---

[24] David Levering Lewis, *W. E. B. Du Bois: Biography of a Race, 1868–1919*, vol. 1 (New York: Henry Holt & Company, 1993) 136.

[25] Ibid., 149, emphasis added.

Dilthey. It should be made clear furthermore that religious experience is not synonymous with "belief in God." As the phenomenologist of religion Gerardus van der Leeuw put it, "Religious experience, in other terms, is concerned with a 'Somewhat.' But this assertion often means no more than that this 'Somewhat' is a vague 'something'; and in order that man may be able to make more significant statements about this 'Somewhat,' it must force itself upon him, must oppose itself to him as being Something *Other*. Thus, the first affirmation we can make about the Object of Religion is that it is a *highly exceptional* and *extremely impressive* '*Other*.'" He continues, "As yet, it must further be observed, we are in no way concerned with the supernatural or the transcendent...but there arises and persists an experience which connects or unites itself to the "Other" that thus obtrudes."[26]

I contend that this is the kind of experience described by Du Bois in *Souls* when he witnesses a black Southern church revival. "I was a country school-teacher then, fresh from the East, and had never seen a Negro revival.... And so most striking to me as I approached the village and the little plain church perched aloft, was the air of intense excitement that possessed that mass of black folk. *A sort of suppressed terror hung in the air and seemed to seize us,—a pythian madness, a demonic possession, that lent terrible reality to song and word. The black and massive form of the preacher swayed and quivered as the words crowded to his lips and flew at us in singular eloquence.*"[27]

For Du Bois this was the experience of the extraordinary, the vague "Somewhat" of van der Leeuw or the "firstness" or "phaneron" of Charles Saunders Peirce.[28] Du Bois's poetic sensibility perceived this experience as a symbolic orientation of ultimate concern. The strange, non-rational reality of the very existence of people of color in a land other than their own, caused to labor and to suffer under the rhetoric and discourses of freedom and self-determination, were in fact inexpressible except in the style of a poesis of history. A line from Countee Cullen's poem captures this ironic mood: "Yet do I marvel at this curious thing/ to make a poet black and bid

[26] Gerardus van der Leeuw, *Religion in Essence and manifestation*, trans. J. E. Turner (London: George Allen & Unwin Ltd., 1938) 23, emphasis added.

[27] Du Bois, *Souls*, 17, emphasis added. See also my discussion of the religious experiences of James and Du Bois in Charles H. Long, "Oppression in Religion and the Religions of the Oppressed," in *Significations, Signs, Symbols, and Images in the Interpretation of Religion*, 2d ed., (Aurora CO: Davies Group, Publishers, 1995).

[28] For a discussion of Peirce's logic see Richard J. Bernstein, ed., *Perspectives on Peirce* (New Haven: Yale University Press, 1965), especially chapter 3.

him sing." We are able to see the ultimacy of the vision stemming from this when he says also in *Souls*, "the problem of the twentieth century is the problem of the color-line."[29] This experience symbolized a primordium of modernity that presented the possibility of an alternative interpretation of the modern. The meaning of African peoples in America would extend to the continent of Africa and its inhabitants and from there to all colored peoples in the world who had become dominated and subjugated through imperialism and colonialism. The primordial meaning of African peoples should be distinguished from any essentialist notion of Africa or African peoples; this fact marks the great divide between Du Bois and Marcus Garvey. As primordium, this structure should be seen epistemologically, allowing Du Bois to make fundamental critiques of the reigning ideologies of those in the modern world who dominated in the name of human freedom.

By employing a hermeneutical epistemology, all of Du Bois's investigations reflected his own formation and the changing standpoints of his situation. This was probably a difficult task for Du Bois; as an intelligent, somewhat arrogant polymath, finding the proper creative role for his ego might have been difficult. Instead of making this simply a problem of the will, I think he made it an issue of method. Limits were built into the structure of his method. While he knew the familiar binaries that characterized most ideologies and methods—e.g., black/white, poetic/scientific, conjunction/disjunction—most of his work could be located on the slash (/) that became the space for new creativity in the modern period. Thus all of his varying interpretations of Africa as specified by Chidester's essay can be related to meanings and movements with which he was engaged in the United States and on the international scene. In the midst of all his work and relationships he returned again and again to the primordial symbolism of the anomaly of African peoples in America. In *Black Reconstruction*, published in 1935, Du Bois characterized the African slave trade as "the most magnificent drama in the last thousand years...the Africans "descended into Hell," and in the Reconstruction they attempted to "achieve democracy for the working millions...." He went on to tell us that this country and the modern period itself act as if none of this ever took

---

[29] Du Bois, *Souls of Black Folk*, 13.

place.[30] It is this story, this drama, that carries the flavor of transcendence through its sense of importance for the whole world. In his notion of fetishism, a notion he abandoned in his later interpretations of African religion, he came very close to anticipating the latest and most brilliant researches on this topic by William Pietz.[31] Had Du Bois combined his earlier research on the African slave trade with his discussion of fetishism, he would have much earlier produced a theory of modern "secular" religion that involved the exchanges of matter and, in the case of the African slave trade, that most exemplary form of matter and materiality—human beings themselves.

David Levering Lewis reports a telling incidence that took place in Ghana as an enfeebled Du Bois approached death; his source for the incident was Vice Chancellor O'Brien of the University of Ghana. At one of O'Brien meetings with students, one student had criticized Moise Tshombe, who in the midst of the independence of the Belgian Congo had led the province of Katanga out of the Congo and formed an independent entity. The student likened Tshombe to Du Bois's old nemesis, Booker T. Washington. O'Brien said, "The old man stirred like a tortoise putting his head out of it shell. 'Don't say that. I used to talk like that.' Du Bois then recalled the chastening words of an aunt to such sentiments. 'Don't you forget that that man, unlike you bear the mark of the lash on his back. He has come out of slavery.... You are fighting for rights here in the North. It's tough, but it's nothing like as tough as what he had to face in his time and in his place.'"[32]

This may be the case of a dying man making peace and reconciling himself with his enemies, but I think it showed that even at this point of his long life, now having immigrated to Ghana and become a citizen of an African state, Du Bois still remembered the primordium of Africa and African slavery as that magnificent, terrifying, and tragic resource that could become the basis for a new humane world order. Similar musing were

---

[30] W. E. B. Du Bois, *Black Reconstruction in America* (New York: Russell & Russell, 1935) 727.

[31] Chidester made reference to the work of William Pietz. Pietz's work on the topic of fetish can be found as follows: "The Problem of the Fetish," *Res* 9 (Spring 1985) 5–17; "The Problem of the Fetish II: The Origin of the Fetish," *Res* 13 (Spring 1987) 23–45; "The Problem of the Fetish, IIIa: Bosman's Guinea and the Enlightenment," *Res* 16 (Autumn 1988) 106–23.

[32] Lewis, *The Fight for Equality*, 569.

expressed by David Brion Davis when he said "...that we can expect nothing from the mercy of God or from the mercy of those who exercise lordship in His or other names; that man's true emancipation, whether physical or spiritual, must always depend on those who have endured and overcome some form of slavery."[33]

Works Cited

Aptheker, Herbert, editor. *The Correspondence of W. E. B. Du Bois, 1877–1963*. 3 volumes. Amherst: University of Massachusetts Press, 1973.

Braudel, Ferdinand. *Civilization and Capitalism*. 3 volumes. Translated by Sian Reynolds. New York: Harper & Row, 1979.

Broderick, Francis L. "The Academic Training of W. E. B. Du Bois." *Journal of Negro Education* 27 (Winter 1958): 10-16.

Broderick, Francis L. "German Influence on the Scholarship of W. E. B. Du Bois." *Phylon* First Quarter, 19/4 (Spring 1958): 367-71.

Chireau, Yvonne. *Black Magic, Religion and the African American Conjuring Tradition*. Los Angeles: University of California Press, 2003.

Davis, David Brion. *The Problem of Slavery in the Age of Revolution, 1770–1823*. Ithaca NY: Cornell University Press, 1975.

Dilthey, Wilhelm. *Poetry and Experience*. Volume 5 of *Selected Works*. Translated by Rudolf A. Makkreel and Frithjof Rodi. Princeton: Princeton University Press, 1985.

Dixon, Quinton H., and Cornel West, editors. *The Courage To Hope*. Boston: Beacon Press, 1999.

Du Bois, W.E.B., *Souls of Black Folk* (New York: Johnson Reprint Co., 1968).

Eliade, Mircea. *Patterns in Comparative Religion*. Translated by Rosemary Sheed. London and New York: Sheed & Ward, 1958.

Ermarth, Michael. *The Critique of Historical Reason*. Chicago: University of Chicago Press, 1978.

---

[33] David Brion Davis, *The Problem of Slavery in the Age of Revolution, 1770–1823* (Ithaca NY: Cornell University Press, 1975) 564.

Fabre, Genevieve, and Robert O'Malley, editors. *History & Memory in African American Culture*. New York/Oxford: Oxford University Press, 1994.

Finkelman, Paul. *An Imperfect Union: Slavery, Federalism, and Comity*. Chapel Hill: University of North Carolina Press, 1981.

Hubbard, Dolan. *The Sermon and the African American Literary Imagination*. Columbia: University of Missouri Press, 1994.

Lang, Andrew. *The Making of Religion*. London: Longmans, Green and Company, Ltd., 1898.

Lewis, David Levering. *W. E. B. Du Bois: Biography of a Race, 1868–1919*. Volume 1. New York: Henry Holt and Company, 1993.

———. *W. E. B. Du Bois: The Fight for Equality and the American Century, 1919–1963*. Volume 2. New York: Henry Holt and Company, 2000.

Logan, Rayford W. *The Betrayal of the Negro from Rutherford B. Hayes to Woodrow Wilson*. New York: Collier Books, 1965.

Long, Charles H. *Significations, Signs, Symbols, and Images in the Interpretation of Religion*. Second edition. Aurora CO: Davies Group, Publishers, 1995.

Lovell, John, Jr. *Black Song: The Forge and the Flame*. New York: MacMillan Company, 1972.

Manuel, Frank E., editor. *Utopia and Utopian Thought: A Timely Appraisal*. Boston: Beacon Press, 1966.

McDonnell, Robert W., editor. *The Papers of W. E. B. Du Bois*. Microfilming Corporation of America, 1981.

Pietz, William. "The Problem of the Fetish, I." *Res* 9 (spring 1985): 5–17.

———. "The Problem of the Fetish, II." *Res* 13 (spring 1987): 23–45.

———. "The Problem of the Fetish, IIIa. *Res* 16 (autumn 1988): 105–23.

Rosenburg, Bruce. *The Art of the American Folk Preacher*. New York: Oxford University Press, 1971.

Schumpeter, Joseph A. *History of Economic Analysis*. New York: Oxford University Press, 1986.

van der Leeuw, Gerardus. *Religion in Essence and Manifestation*. Translated by J. E. Turner. London: George Allen & Unwin Ltd., 1938.

Contributor's Notes

Steve Andrews is an Associate Professor of English at Grinnell College, where he specializes in eighteenth- and nineteenth-century American literature. His poetry appears in a variety of journals, and chapters on civil rights and wilderness and baseball and race are forthcoming in edited volumes. He is currently working on a book-length manuscript on Emerson and landscape.

David Chidester is professor of Religious Studies and director of the Institute for Comparative Religion in Southern Africa at the University of Cape Town. Chidester is the author or editor of over twenty books in American studies, South African studies, and comparative religion, including *Salvation and Suicide: Jim Jones, the Peoples Temple, and Jonestown* (Indiana University Press, 1988; revised edition, 2003), *Savage Systems: Colonialism and Comparative Religion in Southern Africa* (University of Virginia Press, 1996), *Christianity: A Global History* (Harper Collins, 2000), *Nelson Mandela, In His Own Words* (Little, Brown, 2004), and *Authentic Fakes: Religion and American Popular Culture* (University of California Press, 2005).

Mary L. Keller is adjunct professor of Religious Studies at the University of Wyoming and teaches classes for the African American Studies Program and the Religious Studies Program. Previously she was a lecturer in Women and Religion at the University of Stirling, Scotland, from whence she organized the Du Bois and Fanon conference that inspired this collection. She has written *The Hammer and the Flute: Women, Power and Spirit Possession* (Johns Hopkins University Press, 2001), winner of the 2002 Best First Book in the History of Religions. Her articles cover race, gender, sexuality, and religiousness and violence in the postcolonial context.

Robin Law is professor of African History at the University of Stirling in Scotland. Before joining Stirling in 1972, he held positions at the University of Lagos, Nigeria, and the Centre of West African Studies,

University of Birmingham. He has also held visiting positions at the University of Ilorin, Nigeria; Centre of African Studies, Leiden, Netherlands; York University, Toronto, Canada; and the Hebrew University of Jerusalem, Israel. He authored *The Oyo Empire c.1600–c.1836* (1977), *The Horse in West African History* (1980), *The Slave Coast of West Africa 1550–1750* (1991), *The Kingdom of Allada* (1997), *Ouidah: The social history of a West African slaving 'port' 1727–1892* (2004). Formerly editor of the *Journal of African History*, he is also a fellow of the British Academy (2000) and the Royal Society of Edinburgh (2002).

Rodney C. Roberts is a descendant of the African peoples who were enslaved at the Somerset Place plantation in Creswell, North Carolina. He received his Ph.D. in social and political philosophy from the University of Wisconsin-Madison and is currently assistant professor of philosophy at East Carolina University. He was a 2005/2006 Fulbright Lecture and Research Scholar in the Department of Philosophy at the University of Cape Town, South Africa. Professor Roberts's primary research interest is in the conceptual analysis of injustice and related ideas, as well as the development and application of normative injustice theory. He is the editor of *Injustice and Rectification* (2002).

Carole Lynn Stewart specializes in American and African American literature and culture. She has taught in the English Department at the University of Calgary in Canada, and will be Assistant Professor of English at UMBC in the fall, 2007. Parts of this essay appeared in her dissertation, "Conversion, Revolution and Freedom: The Religious Formation of an American Soul in Edwards, Melville and Du Bois." She is in the process of writing a book-length project on civil religion and civil society derived from that work. Stewart has also published in *The Encyclopedia of Religion* (2005) on "Civil Religion" and in *ARIEL: A Review of International English Literature*. She has written forthcoming, accepted papers on Du Bois and Civil Religion, and on Herman Melville.

Marta Brunner received her Ph.D. degree from the History of Consciousness Department at the University of California, Santa Cruz in 2005, and is currently a Council on Library and Information Resources postdoctoral fellow at UCLA's Charles E. Young Research Library. Another version of the essay presented in this volume appears in her dissertation,

"'Faith' in Social Change: Three Case Studies from American Social Movement History, 1890-1940." Her doctoral research explored the question of what is involved when social movement participants give themselves over to their cause. At UCLA, she is working on a variety of projects designed to improve access to primary source materials and secondary scholarship in the field of American studies.

Jemima Pierre is assistant professor of Anthropology at The University of Texas at Austin. Her research ethnographically explores processes of racialization in Africa and the Africa diaspora by comparing and contrasting ideologies and practices of "race" in urban Ghana and for African immigrants in Washington, D. C. Dr. Pierre is currently completing a book tentatively entitled *Race Across the Atlantic: Postcolonial Africa and the Predicaments of Racialization*.

Jesse Weaver Shipley is assistant professor of Anthropology and Africana Studies and director of the Africana Studies Program at Bard College. He received his Ph.D. in sociocultural anthropology from the University of Chicago in 2003. Areas of research include Ghana and the African diaspora; race; British colonialism, postcolonial states, and national citizenship; popular culture and performance; and electronic media, film, hip hop, and television. Publications include "'The Best Tradition Goes On': Popular Theater and Televised Soap in Neoliberal Ghana" (in *Producing African Futures*, edited by Brad Weiss, 2004). He is currently completing a documentary film on hip hop music in Ghana titled *Living the Hiplife* and a book manuscript titled *National Citizens, Consuming Subjects: A Political Genealogy of Performance in Ghana*.

Charles H. Long is professor emeritus of History of Religion at the University of California, Santa Barbara. Prior to his retirement in 1996 he was professor of History of Religions at the University of Chicago and William Rand Kenan, Jr. professor of History of Religions at the University of North Carolina at Chapel Hill and the Jeannette K. Watson professor of History of Religions at Syracuse University. The second edition of his *Significations: Signs, Symbols, and Images in the Study of Religion* was published in 1995. He served on the Board of Editors of the revised edition of the *Encyclopedia of Religion*, edited by Lindsay Jones.

Index

Aesthetics (Hegel), 167
Africa: An Essay Toward a History of the Continent of Africa (Du Bois), 35
Africa: Its Place in Modern History (Du Bois), 35
African Ideas of God (Smith), 53
African Renaissance, 56–57
African Sketchbook (Reade), 24
Agbeyebiawo, Daniel, 67–68
Albanese, Catherine, 7
al-Rahman al-Sadi, Abd, 22
Althusser, Louis, 145
American Negro Academy, 130, 131
American Scene, The (James, H.), 150
Andrews, Stephen, 245; "Toward a Synaesthetics of Soul," 12, 225–229
Appiah, Kwame Anthony, 66
Arendt, Hannah, 122
Art and Imagination of W. E. B. Du Bois (Rampersand), 162–163

baptism, 5–6
Barth, Heinrich: *Travels and Discoveries in Central Africa*, 23
Battuta, Ibn, 22
Benjamin, Walter, 209–210
Berk, David, 169
Bernal, Martin, 26
Black Folk Then and Now (Du Bois), 35, 42, 68; the Black Church, 46–47; divinity, 53–54; fetishism, 51–53; *The Negro* and, 45–47; religion, African, 43; Shango, 44–45, 47; slavery impacts, 45–47; transatlantic continuity, 45–47
Black Reconstruction in America (Du Bois), 122, 216, 240–241; human nature, 134–135; spirituals and, 137–139
"Black Sudan" (Boas), 23
Black Theology of Liberation, A (Cone), 193–194
Blight, Dwight W., 216
Blyden, Edward Wilmot, 20–21; "The Negro in Ancient History," 21
Boas, Franz, 21; "Black Sudan," 23
borders and boundaries, 7–8
Boxill, Bernard, 108
Bridgman, Laura, 174–175
Brunner, Marta, 246–247; "The Most Hopeless of Deaths," 10, 12–13, 221–223
Burke, Edmund: *A Philosophical Inquiry into the Sublime and Beautiful*, 175–176
Burton, Richard, 40
Byerman, Keith, 170

Caillié, René, 40
Campbell, Horace, 65
Campbell, Sue, 101
Carby, Hazel, 161; *Race Men*, 194
Césaire, Aimé: *Discourse on Colonialism*, 50–51
"Challenging Liberal Justice" (Stewart), 11–12, 219–220, 235
Chesnutt, Charles: *The Marrow of Tradition*, 144–147
Chidester, David, 245; "Religious Animals," 9–10, 13, 230–233, 240
Chireau, Yvonne, 226–227
Clodd, Edward, 52
Comte, Auguste, 37

Concepts of God in Africa (Mbiti), 53
Cone, James, 196; *A Black Theology of Liberation*, 193–194
contact and exchange, 6
Conyers, John, 91
Cooley, W. D.: *The Negroland of the Arabs Examined*, 23
cosmology, 7
"Criteria of Negro Art" (Du Bois), 171–172, 177
Crummell, Alexander, 113, 130–139, 220; on civilization, 131
Cullen, Countee, 239–240
Curtin, Philip, 16

Dalzel, Archibald: *The History of Dahomy*, 23
Dark Princess (Du Bois), 12, 156, 188; messianism, 201–204; overview of, 197–204
Darkwater (Du Bois), 12, 116, 188, 189–197; messianism, 190, 194–197; patience, 190–191; promise of novelty, 152–153
Davidson, Basil, 19–20, 25
Derrida, Jacques, 145
Die Gross und Klein Betrieb des Ackerbach in der Sudstaaten (Du Bois), 217
"Dilemma of Determinism, The" (James, W.), 151–152
Dilthey, Wilhelm, 217, 236–237
Discourse on Colonialism (Césaire), 50–51
Douglass, Frederick, 108
Drake, St. Clair, 65, 74
Du Bois, Shirley Graham, 74
Du Bois, W. E. B.: Africa, African-Americans and, 83–85; African history and, 14–17; on African theology, 9–10; biography of, 88–89, 213–215, 232–233; on the Black Church, 41–42; on black work ethic, 126–129; on B. T. Washington, 124; on civilization, 124, 131–132, 135; on cross-cultural exchanges, 136–137;

decolonization and, 67–68; on democracy, 121–123, 129, 137, 220; divinity and, 36–37, 53–54; double-consciousness and, 99–104, 150, 161–163, 164–165; dual styles of, 215–218; exceptionalism and, 114–116, 119–120; faith and, 187, 222–223; Fanon and, 1–8; on fetishism, 51–53, 231; Fourth Pan-African Congress and, 106–107; Frobenius and, 30–31; in Ghana, 73; on humanity, 36–37; on ideal of progress, 128–129; influences on, 217–218, 235–238; messianism and, 12–13, 187–189; methodologies of, 216; music and, 137–139; Nkrumah and, 70–71; North America and, 11–12; Pan-Africanism and, 10, 14, 35–36, 65, 70–74, 83–85; as public intellectual, 214–215; on raced subjectivity, 2–3; rectificatory justice and, 93, 95–96, 104, 106–108; religion and, 2–5, 7–8, 238–241; secularization and, 115–123; self-review, 155–156; on slavery, 41–42, 45, 84, 93, 115–117, 116–117; synaesthesia and, 149–150; "talented tenth" concept and, 113–115, 117–118, 120, 219–220; on temptation of doubt, 133–134; on transatlantic continuity, 54–56, 68–69; transitivity and, 157–158; "vagueness" and, 155–157. *See also under titles of published works*
"Du Bois as a Pioneer of African History" (Law), 9, 228–229
Dunbar, Edward, 16
Dusk of Dawn (Du Bois), 12, 121, 139, 188, 204–211; black work ethic, 126; James, William and, 153; messianism, 204–205, 207–209; political ideas, 205–207; transcendence, 208–211

elitism, 11–12, 112, 117, 121, 220
Emancipation Day, Ghana, 80–83
Encyclopedia Africana, 68, 73, 230, 238
Esedebe, P. Olisanwuche, 64
Euhemerus, 221

Fage, John, 15, 19–20
faith, 221–223
Fanon, Frantz, 1–8; religion, 2–5,
    7–8; *Wretched of the Earth*, 56
Ferguson, Adam, 23
Festival of Black and African Arts and
    Culture (FESTAC), 75
Festival of Negro Arts, 75
Fetichism of West Africa (Nassau), 38
Flournoy, Theodore, 172–173
Fontenot, Chester, 1
Frobenius, Leo, 9, 28–31, 48, 50;
    diffusionism and, 29–30; divine
    kingship and, 29; Ife and, 28; *Und
    Afrika Sprach*, 28–29, 30, 229;
    Yorubaland and, 29, 30–31
"Future for Pan-Africa, A" (Du Bois),
    61

Galton, Francis, 173–174, 176–177
Ghana, 11, 61–85; International
    Monetary Fund and, 78, 230. *See
    also* Nkrumah, Kwame; Rawlings,
    Jerry John
Gift, The (Mauss), 6
Gift of Black Folk, The (DuBois), 126
God in Africa (McVeigh), 53
Gold Coast Native Institutions
    (Hayford), 22
Gombrich, E. H., 171–172
Gooding-Williams, Robert, 133–134
Gordon, Avery F., 186–187
Grant, James, 40
Gregg, Robert, 19, 31

Haddon, A. C., 52
Harlan, John Marshall, 146
Harris, Joseph, 75
Harrison, John, 143, 172
Hayford, James Caseley: *Gold Coast*

Native Institutions, 22
Hegel, G. W. F., 142–143; *Aesthetics*,
    167; Africa, Africans and,
    147–148; *Phenomenology of Mind*,
    166–167; "The Philosophy of
    History," 23–24
Henningsen, Manfred, 105
"Hidden Self, The" (James, W.), 178
History of Dahomy (Dalzel), 23
*History of the Colonization of Africa by
    Alien Races* (Johnston), 22–23
Horton, Robin, 53

"Intellectual and Pragmatic Legacy of
    Bu Bois's Pan-Africanism, The"
    (Pierre, Shipley), 10–11, 229–230
Islam, 20

James, Henry: *The American Scene*,
    150
James, Joy: *Transcending the Talented
    Tenth*, 112
James, William, 142–143, 172, 175,
    225–226, 235; *Dusk of Dawn* and,
    153; *Pragmatism*, 159, 163,
    165–166; *Principles of Psychology*,
    153–155; "The Dilemma of
    Determinism," 151–152; "The
    Hidden Self," 178; transitivity
    and, 12, 143, 150–151, 154, 225
Japanese Americans, rectificatory
    justice and, 97–98
Johnston, Harry, 22–23; *A History of
    the Colonization of Africa by Alien
    Races*, 22–23; *The Opening Up of
    Africa*, 22–23
justice, sense of, 101–104

Keller, Helen, 173–176, 178
Keller, Mary, 245; "On Re-
    Cognizing W. E. B. Du Bois and
    Frantz Fanon.," 215
Khaund, Munindra, 169
King, Martin Luther, Jr., 73, 238
Kingsley, Mary, 39–41, 44, 53
Kisra, 29

Lagos, John O., 22
Law, Robin, 230, 245–246; "Du Bois
    as a Pioneer of African History,"
    9, 228–229
Levering, David: *W. E. B. Du Bois*,
    233–234
Lewis, David Levering, 17–18, 73,
    155, 237–238, 241–242
Livingstone, David, 21
Long, Charles, 5–6, 8, 247;
    "Rapporteur's Commentary," 1
Loria, Achille, 148
Lovejoy, Paul, 16
Lubbock, John, 52

Magubane, Bernard, 66
Mann, Kristin, 16–17
Marrow of Tradition, The (Chesnutt),
    144–147
Martyrdom of Man, The (Reade),
    25–27, 229
Marx, Karl, 52
Matory, J. L., 63, 229
Mauss, Marcel: *The Gift*, 6
Mayfield, Julian, 72–73
Mbembe, Achille, 56–57
Mbiti, John S.: *Concepts of God in
    Africa*, 53
McVeigh, Malcolm J.: *God in Africa*,
    53
Miles, Kevin Thomas, 167–168
Millet, Jules, 143
Moore, Philip, 82
Moore, Queen Mother Audley, 95
Moses, Wilson, 117, 132
"Most Hopeless of Deaths, The"
    (Brunner), 10, 12–13, 221–223

Nassau, Robert Hamill, 37, 39–41,
    44; *Fetichism of West Africa*, 38
Negro, The (Du Bois), 9, 14–31, 40;
    African history, 16–17; African
    religion, 34–36; animism,
    fetishism, 37–39; the Black
    Church, 41–42; *Black Folk* and,
    45–47; divinity, 39–41; divity,
    53–54; fetishism, 51–53, 118;

framework of, 18–20; historical
    conceptualization and, 22–23;
    importance of, 17–18; racist
    stereotypes, 17–18; Reade and,
    28; regional studies and, 23;
    sources, 21–23, 40; theology and
    polity, 40, 54–56; transatlantic
    continuity, 36–37, 41–42
Negro Church (Du Bois), 42
"Negro in Ancient History, The"
    (Blyden), 21
Negroland of the Arabs Examined, The
    (Cooley), 23
Nkrumah, Kwame, 62, 66, 70–71,
    74–75, 230; Pan-Africanism and,
    70–74; United States and, 72–73

"Of the Sorrow Songs" (Du Bois),
    179–180
"Of the Training of Black Men" (Du
    Bois), 160–161
Ogren, Kathy, 69
"On Re-Cognizing W. E. B. Du Bois
    and Frantz Fanon." (Keller), 215
Opening Up of Africa (Johnston),
    22–23
orientation, 5–8, 9

Padmore, George, 62, 72
PANAFEST, 79–80
Pan-Africanism, 70, 229–230;
    Congresses, 65; definitions of,
    64–67; Du Bois and, 10, 14,
    35–36, 65, 70–74, 83–85
Pan-Africanism, contemporary
    recuperation of, 62–63, 77–85;
    post World War II, 65–66;
    tourism and, 78–79
Park, Mungo, 21
Peirce, Charles Saunders, 239
Phenomenology of Mind (Hegel),
    166–167
*Philosophical Inquiry into the Sublime
    and Beautiful, A* (Burke), 175–176
"Philosophy of History" (Hegel),
    23–24
Pierre, Jemima, 247; "The

Intellectual and Pragmatic Legacy of Du Bois's Pan-Africanism," 10–11, 229–230

Pietz, William, 52, 241

Plessy v. Ferguson, 123, 146

Poetry and Pragmatism (Poirer), 162

Poirer, Richard, 148; *Poetry and Pragmatism*, 162

Posnock, Ross, 142–143, 153, 155

Pragmatism (James, W.), 159, 163, 165–166

Présence Africaine, 75

Principles of Psychology (James, W.), 153–155

"Propaganda of History, The" (Du Bois), 216

Provisional National Defense Council (PNDC), Ghana, 76–79

punning, 162–163

Quest of the Silver Fleece, The (Du Bois), 156

Rampersand, Arnold, 216; *Art and Imagination of W. E. B. Du Bois*, 162–163

Rawlings, Jerry John, 76–79, 230

Rawls, John, 103

Reade, Winwood, 9, 24–28; African history and, 26–28; *African Sketchbook*, 24; imperialism and, 25–26; *London Times* and, 24; *The Martyrdom of Man*, 25–27, 229; *Savage Africa*, 24; *The Story of the Ashanti Campaign*, 24–25

Reconstruction, 128; rectificatory justice and, 96

rectificatory justice: "Act to Establish a Bureau for the Relief of Freedmen and Refugees," 91–92, 94; Commission to Study Reparation Proposals for African-Americans Act, 91–92; definitions of, 90–91; Du Bois and, 93, 95–96, 104, 106–108; "forty acres and a mule" and, 91–96, 224; Germans and, 105–106; Hawai'i

and, 103; Japanese Americans and, 97–98, 103–104; Native Americans and, 107–108; objections, 104–108; philosophy and, 88–90; Rectificatory Status Thesis (RST) and, 98–99

"Rectificatory Justice" (Roberts), 11, 223–225, 234

Reindorf, C. C., 22

religion, 4–8, 238–241; borders and boundaries and, 7–8; definition of, 5–6; relevance of, 4–5

"Religious Animals" (Chidester), 9–10, 13, 230–233, 240

Roberts, Rodney C., 246; "Rectificatory Justice," 11, 223–225, 234

Robinson, Cedric, 209, 222; *Anthropology of Marxism*, 186–187, 189

Rumble in the Jungle, 75

Russell, Ralph, 169

Savage Africa (Reade), 24

Schmoller, Gustav von, 217–218, 235–236

secularization, 115–123

selah, 191–193

Shango, 35–36, 43–45, 53, 56–57, 231; in *Black Folk*, 44–45, 47, 232; in *World and Africa*, 48

Shaw, Flora: *A Tropical Dependency*, 23

Shepperson, George, 15, 26, 64

Sherman, William Tecumseh, 92–93

Shipley, Jesse Weaver, 247; "The Intellectual and Pragmatic Legacy of Du Bois's Pan-Africanism," 10–11, 229–230

"Significance of the Frontier in American History, The" (Turner), 148

slavery, 224–225, 233–235. *See also under* Du Bois, W. E. B.

Smith, Edwin: *African Ideas of God*, 53

Smith, William, 48

Sobel, Mechal, 136

Social Role of the Man of Knowledge
    (Znaniecki), 220
Société Africaine de Culture, 75
Souls of Black Folk, The (Du Bois), 4,
    12, 35, 42, 117, 216; black
    culture, 225–226; black work
    ethic, 126; civilization, 131–132;
    contact and exchange, 119;
    Crummell and, 131, 132–133;
    democracy, 112–113; double-
    consciousness, 99–101; ideal of
    progress, 128–129; music,
    142–143, 169–170, 180–181;
    synaesthesia, 143–144, 149–150,
    169–171, 181–182; "talented
    tenth" concept, 219–220;
    transitivity, 157; website, 144,
    168–169
Soul to Soul, 75
Stevens, Thaddeus, 94
Stewart, Carole, 246; "Challenging
    Liberal Justice," 11–12, 219–220,
    235
Story of the Ashanti Campaign, The
    (Reade), 24–25
Sumner, Charles, 91–92, 94
Sundquist, Eric, 130, 167–168, 169;
    To Wake the Nations, 195
*Suppression of the African Slave-Trade
    to the USA, The* (Du Bois), 15
Sutherland, Efua, 79

Tempel, Placide, 52
To Wake the Nations (Sundquist), 195
"Toward a Synaesthetics of Soul"
    (Andrews), 12, 225–229
Transcending the Talented Tenth
    (James, J.), 112
*Travels and Discoveries in Central
    Africa* (Barth), 23
Tropical Dependency (Shaw), 23
Turner, Frederick Jackson: "The
    Significance of the Frontier in
    American History," 148
Tylor, E. B., 37

Und Afrika Sprach (Frobenius),

28–29, 30, 229
Up From Slavery (Washington), 124

Washington, Booker T., 123–129,
    220, 241–242; Atlanta
    Compromise address, 123–124,
    159–160; civilization, 124; ideal
    of progress and, 128–129; *Up
    From Slavery*, 124, 160
W. E. B. Du Bois (Levering), 233–234
"W. E. B. Du Bois and Frantz
    Fanon" conference, 1
W. E. B. Du Bois Memorial Centre
    for Pan-African Culture, 61–62
West, Cornel, 112, 117
Williams, Henry Sylvester, 70
works cited, 13, 31–33, 57–60, 85–87,
    109–111, 182–185, 211–212,
    242–243
World and Africa, The (Du Bois), 14,
    19, 28, 30, 35, 68; fetishism,
    47–50; *The Negro* and, 19–20;
    Pan-Africanism, 50; religion,
    African indigenous, 50; Shango,
    48
Wretched of the Earth (Fanon), 56

Zamir, Shamoon, 142–143, 166–167
Znaniecki, Florain: *The Social Role of
    the Man of Knowledge*, 220